HIDING *in* PLAIN SIGHT

HIDING *in* PLAIN SIGHT

BLACK WOMEN, THE LAW,
AND THE MAKING OF A
WHITE ARGENTINE REPUBLIC

ERIKA DENISE EDWARDS

THE UNIVERSITY OF ALABAMA PRESS
TUSCALOOSA

The University of Alabama Press
Tuscaloosa, Alabama 35487-0380
uapress.ua.edu

Hardcover edition published 2020.
Paperback edition published 2021.
eBook edition published 2020.

Inquiries about reproducing material from this work should
be addressed to the University of Alabama Press.

Typeface: Scala Pro

Cover image: *Porteña, Costume di Eglise,* by Arsène Isabell, lithograph,
1835; courtesy of the John Carter Brown Library at Brown University
Cover design: Michele Myatt Quinn

Paperback ISBN: 978-0-8173-6031-3

A previous edition of this book has been cataloged by the Library of Congress.
ISBN: 978-0-8173-2036-2 (cloth)
E-ISBN: 978-0-8173-9265-9

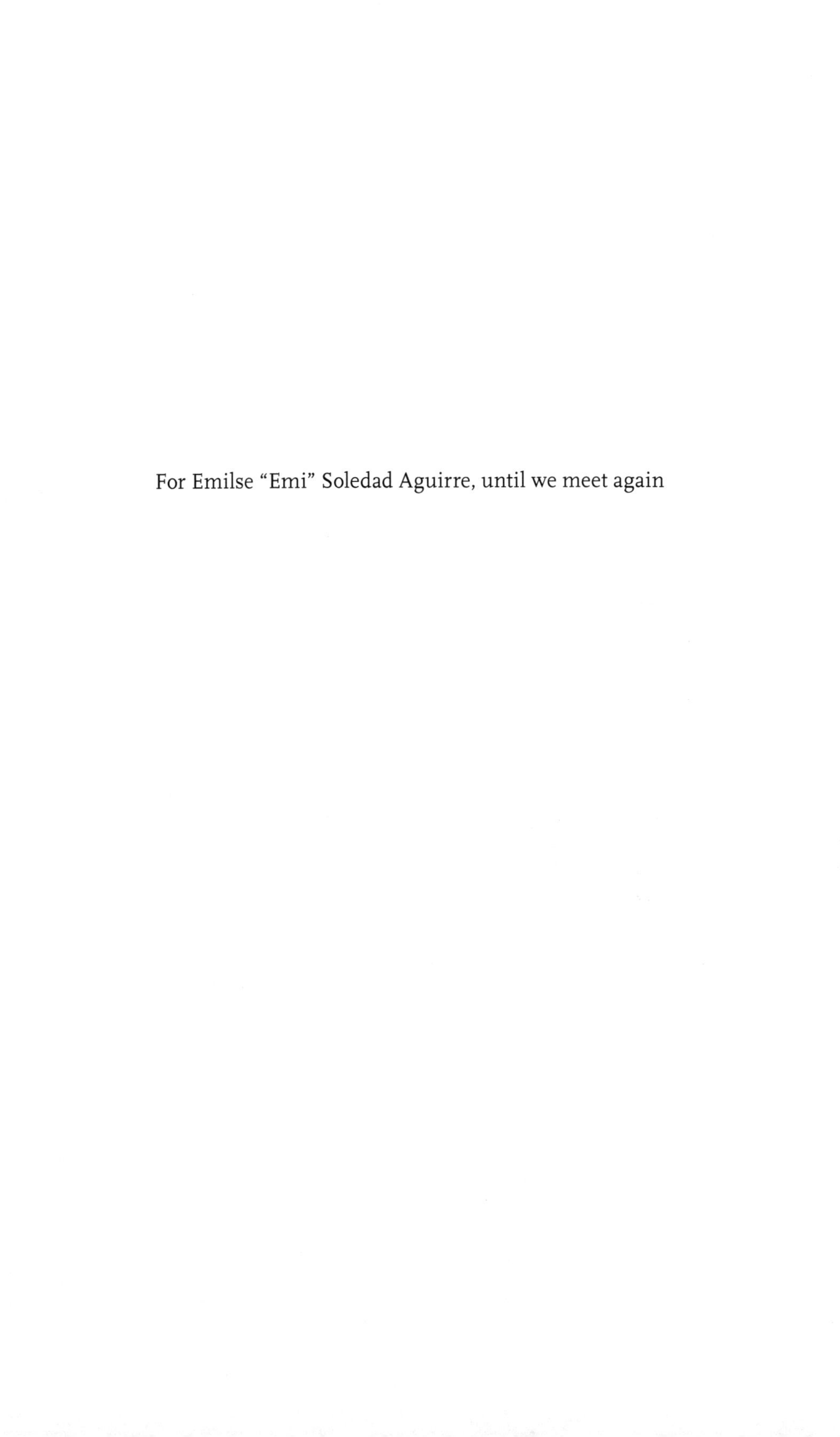

For Emilse "Emi" Soledad Aguirre, until we meet again

Contents

Illustrations

Figures

Tables

Acknowledgments

During a brief trip to Argentina in 2002, I began a love affair with its history, culture, and people that resulted in a journey dedicated to Argentina's black history. Fifteen years of study and research has culminated in a project that could only have been done with the assistance of archivists, colleagues, fellowships, friends, and family who span hemispheres, countries, provinces, states, cities, and towns.

I would like to thank the staff members of the Arzobispado de la Catedral, Archivo Histórico de la Provincia, the Archivo de la Universidad de Córdoba, and the Instituto de Estudios Americanistas. First, I must thank the directors of the archives, María Celina Audisio, Gabriela Parra Garzón, Jacqueline Vassallo, and Silvia Graciela Fois, who granted me access to the archives at times when it was closed for repair, made copies, or helped solve mysteries about the various people and institutions in the book. I must also acknowledge the following archivists who went beyond the call of duty: Dora "Dorita" Bustamante, Marcela Alejandra Varela, Héctor Daniel Ríos, Marcia Nelles Garzón, Mariano Passarelli, and María Luisa González Cabrera. Eduardo Gould's patience will always be appreciated, as he would often sit with me for hours answering my inquiries about the history of Córdoba. Raquel Maggi must be credited for giving me a random *legajo* (file) full of criminal cases that ultimately shifted my focus from Buenos Aires to Córdoba in 2006. She also made sure that I was taken care of, inviting me to her home on numerous occasions. Finally, I must thank Silvia Graciela Fois, again, and María Luz Chavez from the Instituto de Estudios Americanistas. Long after I left Córdoba, they continued to send me primary source material from the Instituto, which allowed me to complete my final chapter. Intellectual discussions with historians Mónica Ghirardi, Federico Sartori, Clarisa Pedrotti, Marcos Javier Carrizo, Florencia Guzmán, Valentina Ayrolo, Sonia Colantonio, Cecilia Moreyra, María Carmen "ChiChina" Ferreyra, and Claudia Garcia assisted in the project's development. Mónica Ghirardi's invitation to provide lectures at the National University of Córdoba and the Junta Histórico de Córdoba and publish with her research team is greatly appreciated. I am also in debt to Chichina's wealth of knowledge about the city and cannot thank her enough for inviting me to her home to share her personal library and emailing me primary source material when I could not make it to Córdoba.

Travel to Argentina was made possible by various grants and fellowships that include Grand Valley State University's McNair Scholars Program and Barbara Padnos Scholarship, which supported my first trip in 2002, the Tinker Field Research Grant, the Fulbright Fellowship, Florida International University's Doctoral Evidence Acquisition Fellowship, University of North Carolina at Charlotte's Faculty Research Grants, and the University of North Carolina at Charlotte's College of Liberal Arts and Sciences Frances Lumsden Gwynn Research Grant, which funded subsequent trips over the past fifteen years. I am also grateful to the following fellowships and grants that gave me the time to process the collected data and to write: the Ford Foundation, Florida International University, the University of North Carolina at Charlotte's College of Liberal Arts and Sciences Junior Faculty Development Award, and the American Association of University Women's Fellowship.

Throughout my travels, I met so many wonderful Argentines who have since become close friends. I will forever be indebted to the Alaniz family (Coco, Gabby, Uli, Santi, Ale), Mariana Kliszczewski, and María "Ceci" Barrios, who welcomed me with open arms during my first and subsequent trips to Buenos Aires and became my family. In addition, I must thank Alejandro Bienaimé, who helped me fall in love with Argentina during my first trip sixteen years ago. Having had the unique opportunity to travel and live in Argentina for extended periods, I also want to acknowledge the importance of living in Belgrano and Lanus in Buenos Aires, which are two very distinct but equally important barrios that make Argentina special. They taught me more about the country than I will ever read in a book. Being in a foreign country can be lonely at times, especially after the archives close at 6:00 p.m. Thank you, Natalia "Ná" and Giuseppe González, Daniel "Dani" Paez, Gaspar Arroñade, Clarisa Pedrotti, Carlos Prieto Lamas, and the Aguirre family (Nidia, Patricia, Raquel, Emilse, Flavia, Mildred), who helped me fall in love with the city of Córdoba. Emilse "Emi" Aguirre became a dear friend who was taken too soon. I dedicate this book to her memory.

As the project developed, I asked various people to read drafts of my manuscript and I am forever grateful for their feedback. They include Lyman Johnson, Carol Higham, and Peter Blanchard, who read the entire manuscript, and Karen "Kym" Morrison, Michelle McKinley, Herman Bennett, George Reid Andrews, Jurgen Buchenau, Carmen Soliz, Peter Ferdinando, Devyn Benson, Chris Cameron, Steven Hyland, Julio Cesar Capó, John David Smith, and various participants of the Río de la Plata Workshop who read chapters and provided valuable comments. Lyman Johnson, my mentor, has been there for me since I started at UNCC. I am forever grateful for his friendship and our conversations about the Río de la Plata over coffee.

I also must highlight Carol Higham, who has become a trusted friend and mentor. If academic angels exist, she is one. I thank Peter Blanchard, for his critical feedback, which made this a better book. To Carmen Soliz, I cannot stress enough that her encouragement at times was all I had to keep me putting finger to keyboard. I must also thank the peer reviewers and acquiring editor Wendi Schnaufer at the University of Alabama Press.

Collecting and analyzing the data is half the battle; the other half is having the strength and stamina to get it written. I could not have finished the book without emotional support and encouragement during the writing process. Sonya Ramsey, Cheryl D. Hicks, Janaka Lewis, Brenda Mitchner, Brenda Tindal, Shanice Cameron, Altanese Phenelus, Diane Ghogomu, and Tiffany Joseph: I thank you for being beautiful black mentors and phenomenal women! Other friendships and words of wisdom came from Gabi Kuenzli, Jane Landers, Rachel Sarah O'Toole, Tatiana Sejas, Oscar de la Torre, Yvette Huet, Gregory Mixon, Maren Elhers, Steven Sabol, Benny Andres, Robert McEachnie, Kate Borick, Leigh Robbins, Aaron Toscano, Beth Whitaker, William "Bill" McCarthy, David "Tio" Stark, Louise Clark, John Cox, Miriam Jorge, Monica Díaz, Yanna Yanakakis, and Bianca Premo.

Friendships beyond the academic world that reminded me to look up from the computer were also crucial to the completion of this book. Aman Muqeet, Donovan Dawson, Darren Shilingford, Sara Conklin, Joseph Holbrook, Phillip Rincón, Lisa Sevilla, Briana Baker, and Dawn Holmes, thank you for being there during the good times and the not-so-good times and thank you for being you! Melissa Nerone, Kendria Bruce, Kristy Bell, Claudia Arce, Amy Gurske, Carolina "Caro" Zumaglini, and Loraine "Lori" de la Fe are my sisters and have been with me throughout the stages of my life and I adore you.

I must thank my hometown, Gwinn, Michigan, and most specifically the Lions Club for financing my first trip to Washington, DC, where I would learn about Argentina for the first time. Finally, I could not have done this without my family's unconditional support. They laughed, cried, and celebrated the completion of this book. My father, Claude Edwards, always encouraged me to keep moving forward. I am my mother's daughter and could not ask for more. Thank you, Bridgett Edwards, for everything. Lydia Edwards, my twin sister (otherwise known as my wombmate), is my hero. Jax, my beautiful Lab and Pitbull mix, listened patiently about my book during our walks and curled up next to me during late nights of writing, revising, and editing. Lastly, I thank my husband, Michael Jackson, whose love, encouragement, and strength constantly inspire me and whose smile brightens my day.

1573 Jerónimo Luis de Cabera, Spanish conquistador, establishes Córdoba City.

1588 First slaves from Buenos Aires arrive in Córdoba.

1613 First university in Argentina is established by Jesuits in Córdoba.

1767 Spain expels Jesuits from the Spanish Indies.

1776 Creation of the viceroyalty of the Río de la Plata (River Plate), a governing jurisdiction that makes Buenos Aires the capital. The Río de la Plata consisted of modern-day countries Argentina, Bolivia, Paraguay, and Uruguay.

1776 Royal Pragmatic, a decree that regulates "unequal marriages" in Spain. Two years later, the Spanish Crown implemented this decree with some revisions throughout the Spanish Indies.

1782 Bishop Joseph Antonio San Alberto establishes the Orphanage and School for Girls in Córdoba.

1783 Intendancy of Córdoba: The city becomes the capital of the intendancy, a smaller governing jurisdiction that included Córdoba, Mendoza, San Juan, and San Luis and La Rioja provinces.

1783–1797 Rafael de Sobremonte (Marqués de Sobremonte) is appointed governor intendant of Córdoba.

1785 Governor Intendant Marqués de Sobremonte institutes Edicts of Good Governance.

1805 Royal decree that specifically racialized the Royal Pragmatic of 1776.

1808 Napoleon Bonaparte invades Spain and replaces King Ferdinand IV with his brother Joseph Bonaparte. This sets into motion the question of legitimacy and right to rule throughout the Spanish Indies.

1810 May 25 Revolution, led by Buenos Aires leadership, removes the viceroy and claims sovereignty.

1810 United Provinces of the Río de la Plata, a sovereign governance, is created through the removal of the viceroy and the creation of a governing junta in Buenos Aires.

1810 July Counterrevolution led by Córdoba is defeated quickly but marks a regional divide between Buenos Aires and the interior of the country.

1810–1819 Wars of Independence begin with the counterrevolution.

1811–1813 United Provinces of the Río de la Plata abolishes Indian labor and tribute in the Río de la Plata.

1811 Orphanage for the School for Girls creates a segregated class for parda girls in Córdoba.

1812 United Provinces of the Río de la Plata abolishes the slave trade.

1813 United Provinces of the Río de

la Plata enacts the Free Womb Act, the gradual abolition of slavery.

1816 July 9, Congress of Tucumán, an assembly of delegates from various provinces in the Río de la Plata, declares independence from Spain.

1819 Constitution of 1819 is implemented that declares Buenos Aires the capital of the United Provinces of the Río de la Plata, which interior provinces reject.

1819 Interior provinces declare themselves independent republics.

1820 Battle of Cepeda, a disagreement between Buenos Aires and the provinces about the constitution and future leadership of the country erupts and results in the defeat of Buenos Aires. It also signifies the end of the United Provinces of the Río de la Plata, and a national government will not arise in the Río de la Plata until 1861.

1820 Córdoba, an independent republic, declares independence from Spain.

1820–1829 Juan Bautista Bustos, a Federalist advocating provincial and decentralized rule, becomes the first governor of Córdoba.

1821 Córdoba creates its first constitution, the Reglamento Provisorio.

1825 Bustos creates the Junta Protectora de Escuelas, the school board that oversees primary education in Córdoba.

1829–1831 José María Paz becomes the second governor of Córdoba. His political affiliation, the Unitarians, promotes centralized rule, in opposition to the Federalists.

1829 José María Paz desegregates public schools.

1831–1835 Various Fedealists rule Córdoba.

1835–1840 Manuel López becomes the seventh governor of Córdoba. He is a Federalist and a close ally of Juan Manual de Rosas, who ruled Buenos Aires from 1829 to 1832 and from 1835 to 1852.

1840 October–December, Unitarians defeat Governor Manuel López and regain power in Córdoba.

1840–1852 Governor Manuel López reestablishes Fedealist rule in Córdoba.

1853 Abolition of slavery in all provinces except Buenos Aires. Buenos Aires abolished slavery after it joined the Argentine Confederation in 1861.

1858 Orphanage in Córdoba closes the parda class.

Introduction

The research for this book began unexpectedly in 2002 while I was studying abroad in Argentina. As a young black woman in a very white country, I stood out. I epitomized the "other." At first, I felt uncomfortable, but then I realized that my blackness did not mean the same thing in Argentina as it did in the United States. My blackness, which defines my identity in the United States, became invisible in Argentina. Despite encouraging Argentines to call me *negra* (black), they found other terms such as *morocha* (an inoffensive term referring to people who have darker skin) or *mulata* (a mixture between African and European descent) to describe me.

Although most Argentines refused to call me negra, that did not mean they did not use the term. Instead, I heard Argentines unhesitatingly use the label "negro" to refer to others who by US standards did not look phenotypically black! "Negro" affectionally described loved ones or negatively referenced the poor. Whether used as a term of endearment or of offense, "negro" applied to anyone who physically did not fit Argentina's definition of whiteness.[1] Yet, I, an African descendant, remained invisible despite phenotypically looking black.

The ironic inclusive yet exclusive use of "negro" piqued my interest, and I began exploring Argentina's black history by asking Argentines the following question: "What happened to the black population?" The most common response I received from Argentines was, "There are no blacks. They disappeared."[2] I continued to ask this question on subsequent trips as my research developed. I received various answers, such as the Argentine government used black soldiers as cannon fodder during the wars of independence (1810–1819), ensuing civil wars (1820–1861), and Paraguayan War (1864–1870); blacks contracted yellow fever and died; or blacks migrated to Uruguay.[3] But the most common phrase uttered in Argentina was, "There are no blacks. They disappeared."

Over time, I made two observations from this short and popular response. First, the phrase "there are no blacks" perpetuated the national narrative of Argentine exceptionalism. Many Latin American countries acknowledge their ethnic diversity, often touting a national narrative of *mestizaje* (mixed identity). Argentina did not fit that model. Instead the image of Argentina remains an exception because of European immigration, which made it a white rather than a mixed country. Second, the answer "they disappeared" suggested that what happened to the black population remained a mystery.[4] If blacks disappeared, then they had previously existed. Based on these observations, a black population does not fit Argentina's national image.

Acknowledging this conundrum, I shifted my research. While previously I had a narrow approach that could not pinpoint a specific cause for black disappearance, I began to examine the origins of black invisibility, eventually producing a comprehensive study of identity in Argentina.[5] Black invisibility is the process of "editing out" or the erasure of African descendants' contributions to the national narrative. As George Reid Andrews has noted, "most countries can acknowledge slavery," but after abolition African descendants "peacefully and successfully integrated into a national society, ceasing to exist as a separate, identifiable, and 'visible' group."[6] Delving into the characteristics that define identity within Argentina revealed that the issue of black invisibility marked Argentina's ongoing construction of racial categories. Race is not a fixed characteristic in Argentina; instead political, economic, and social conditions constantly shape it and create an identity that remains in flux. For instance, the notion of whiteness equates to privilege, wealth, freedom, and education and has its roots in the colonial period (between the sixteenth and nineteenth centuries). Conversely, the notion of blackness equates to disadvantage, poverty, slavery, and ignorance and also began in the colonial period. As a result, the ideal choice for many African descendants throughout Argentina's history has been, when possible, whiteness.[7]

Hiding in Plain Sight traces African descendants' ascent to whiteness, both as a series of choices made by themselves and as an institutionalized project constructed by governing and ecclesiastical authorities. I argue that black invisibility is rooted in the intimate relationships formed between African descendants, on the one hand, and slaveholders and their families, ecclesiastical authorities, and/or political elites, on the other. To examine these intimate relationships, I focus on African-descended women because of the role they played in the household, a key space of intimacy.[8]

My focus on African-descended women accomplishes two objectives. First, examining African-descended women reveals that late-eighteenth- and early-nineteenth-century politics, social policies, and economic activities enhanced black invisibility, which African-descended women used in their quest for whiteness. Second, it makes women of African descent the protagonists rather than the victims.[9] These women freed themselves of the "stain" of their color; thus, they negotiated their own invisibility.[10] Moreover, women of African descent learned the rules of whiteness and, when and *if* possible, improved their lives and the lives of their children. Their decision to acquire whiteness reveals how some African-descended women survived enslavement and freedom. This decision cannot be underestimated; whiteness meant a better life for African-descended women who could attain whiteness, and for some that was the only choice. I focus on how African-descended concubines, wives, mothers, and daughters navigated and learned the contours of whiteness and forged their own experiences.[11] However, I acknowledge and the book details that whiteness was not available to all women of African descent. Some women of African descent did not adhere to the rules of patriarchy and whiteness, and others lacked the relationships necessary to achieve whiteness. Nonetheless, by tracing African-descended women's adoption of whiteness, this book examines the origins of black invisibility in Argentina and engages the existing literature about invisibility in two areas: periodization and gender.

PERIODIZATION AND BLACK INVISIBILITY

African descendants' pursuit of whiteness has led to black invisibility in other Spanish American countries besides Argentina.[12] Their decision to abandon their blackness coupled with governing authorities' willingness to reject their nation's black and African history create two different scenarios of national identity: those nations that claim a *mestizo* (mixture of Indian and European ancestry) identity rather than a black identity in the Andean region, Central America, and Mexico, and those that claim a white rather than a black identity in the Southern Cone (Chile, Argentina, Uruguay). The erasure of blackness can be traced to the late eighteenth century, a period characterized by *calidad* (an individual's reputed public persona that often indicates racial background), political flux, and social unrest, and to the early nineteenth century with the passage of the Free Womb Act (i.e., gradual abolition) in 1813.[13]

Labels such as *español* (Spaniard, white, and referring to people born in Spain or the Americas), *indio* (Indian), and *negro* (black; often synonymous with slave status) formed the nexus of calidad along with a person's occupation, wealth, place of origin, and honor.[14] The later appearance of other calidad labels, such as mestizo, *mulato* (a mixture of African and European ancestry), *zambo* (a mixture of African and Indian ancestry), and *pardo* (brown, synonymous with mulato in the colonial period and referring to those formerly labeled *casta:* African or mixed-race descent, in the republican period) marked centuries of miscegenation and attempts by governing officials to incorporate people identified by these labels into a complex social hierarchy known as the *sistema de castas* (racial classification system). Calidad depended on various social, economic, and political factors, which meant that an individual's identity remained in flux and dependent on the perception of others.

Nonetheless, labels such as *mulatos blancos* or *mulatos claros* found in notarial and probate records or sayings found in judicial proceedings that described individuals as "the color of [a] Spaniard" revealed, according to historian Verónica Undurraga Schuler, a marked "social reality and understanding that white colored castas existed," and these individuals represented an "absolute subversion" of social hierarchy.[15] These "white colored castas" disrupted social order and complicated identity because of the confusion they caused. This became more of a problem as the eighteenth century unfolded, because color increasingly defined calidad. Those who could pass did, and according to governing authorities, African descendants' achieved whiteness contributed to the growth of social unrest in the eighteenth century.

Social unrest marked an ongoing tension between an ancien régime and enlightened ideals that circulated throughout the Atlantic World.[16] These tensions came to the forefront during the Age of Revolution, a period of rebellions and wars of independence throughout the Americas. To confront what authorities considered an increasing affront to their privileged Spanish status, the Spanish Crown enacted the Bourbon Reforms, a series of policies that reinforced social hierarchies to increase the Crown's revenue from the mid-eighteenth through the early nineteenth centuries.[17] Exploring these policies, such as the Edicts of Good Governance, that targeted African descendants' social ascent localizes and individualizes political discourse and social resistance during the late eighteenth and early nineteenth centuries.

Coupled with African descendants' reputed whiteness, the Free Womb Act (i.e., gradual abolition) freed all babies born to slave mothers and marked a formative escape from blackness.[18] In Spanish America, Chile was the first republic to enact the Free Womb Act during the Age of Revolution, in 1811, followed by the United Provinces of the Río de la Plata in 1813, Gran Colombia in 1824, and Peru in 1825, signifying slavery's slow demise.[19] Burgeoning republics granted slaves an avenue to freedom because republics unlocked the chains that bound African descendants to their blackness. But before they could be completely free, authorities put in place institutional social grooming or public education to achieve a desired whiteness that prepared these children for freedom. Socially groomed and no longer enslaved, freed African descendants achieved a measure of whiteness that late-nineteenth-century intellectuals extoled as the ideal.

Most scholars who examine black invisibility focus on this latter period of exemplar whitening known as *blanqueamiento,* a whitening process throughout Latin America that lasted from 1860 to 1914 and claimed that a white nation was a modern nation and advanced economic and political polices to increase European immigration.[20] Like Argentina, many other Latin American countries looked to European immigrants as the way to bring modernization and progress to their shores.[21] Late nineteenth-century intellectuals justified policies that encouraged European immigration using pseudoscientific theories that purported to prove the biological superiority of "whites" over "nonwhites." Instead of enforcing segregation policies to sanction white superiority, Argentine authorities sought to eliminate blackness through European immigration and miscegenation. The constant arrival of European men through immigration made this goal attainable. Intellectuals, such as Domingo Faustino Sarmiento (1811–1888), often touted mulatos as proof of progress because they "retain the fiery blood of the African . . . [and] at the same time the organization of his skull links him to the European family." Sarmiento argued, "Dumas, Placido, Barcala [are] . . . noble mulatos . . . [known] for the arts, music, poetry, and medical sciences. . . . [The] brilliant moral qualities of this race intermediates between white, which enervates the equatorial climates, and the incapability of the black to rise to the high regions of civilization."[22] In effect, Sarmiento and similar intellectuals joined other Latin American countries that espoused blanqueamiento.[23]

However, a focus on the end of the nineteenth century does not explain the origins and everyday decisions that African descendants made to acquire whiteness or the transition to institutionalized whitening, which occurred before the consolidation of the nation-state at the end of the nineteenth century. To understand how and why intellectuals and politicians subscribed to modern notions of blanqueamiento, it is imperative that the scholarship delves into the prior period. My time frame, the late eighteenth and early nineteenth centuries, covers an important transformation of African descendants' adoption of whiteness—the shift from individual choice to institutionalized whitening—and joins scholarship that provides a more complex and cohesive story of black invisibility.[24]

GENDER AND BLACK INVISIBILITY

Beginning with the late-eighteenth-century context of the Bourbon Reforms, I examine how the roles of women of African descent in the household (cohabitation, marriage, motherhood, and education) aided their social ascent. Concubines chose to engage in illicit relationships with elite Spanish men and to subvert sumptuary laws, which came about in 1785 to prevent Spanish emulation. Similarly, fiancées gained social mobility by marrying elite Spanish men despite restrictions on unequal marriages via the enactment of the Royal Pragmatic in 1776. Mothers fought for their freedom and their children's freedom in contested freedom cases that continued into the nineteenth century. Daughters learned desired behaviors through formal education, which the Church enacted in 1811. Together, these women of African descent figuratively gave birth to a whitened nation.

Concubines' decisions to cohabitate with elite Spanish men granted them access to privilege and protections, provided they remained in that relationship.[25] Defined by governing and ecclesiastical authorities as "illicit friendships," cohabitation and other intimate relationships between African-descended women and Spanish men flourished despite their illegality and unequal power relations. This intimacy could manifest as loving relationships, and some slaveholders freed their enslaved concubines and their children.[26] Despite the illegality, these intimate relationships not only provided freedom but also allowed women of African descent to emulate Spanish women. Having lighter skin, which documents often describe as "the color of [a] Spanish woman," and dressing the part of a Spanish woman facilitated the pursuit of whiteness by some women of African descent.[27]

Similarly, fiancées accused of having *mala sangre* (tainted blood), which referenced their African ancestry, married Spanish men for the legal protections and privileges that afforded.[28] In response to the growth of "unequal marriages," the Spanish Crown enacted the Royal Pragmatic of 1776, which was enacted two years later throughout the Spanish Indies and was often referred to as the 1778 decree.[29] To marry their fiancés, women accused of mala sangre claimed to be Spanish or Indian, because both identities erased affiliations with slavery, which encompassed blackness. Fiancées who argued that they were Spanish proved their whiteness by affiliations with Spanish familial and social networks. Women accused of having mala sangre also took advantage of the 1778 decree that declared that Indian caciques (chieftains) belonged in the same class as "distinguished Spaniards" and were subject to the same conditions as Spaniards under the law. Claims of Indian identity by fiancées stemmed from differences in legal definitions of Indians and African descendants.[30] The law excluded most African descendants because they lacked the honor that warranted the same protections.[31] Women accused of having mala sangre worked within the court system, arguing that accusations of mala sangre were untrue and declaring themselves Spanish or Indian and thereby equal to their fiancés based on the 1778 decree, which led the civil court to grant them permission to marry.

Accusations of mistaken identity also led mothers who, along with their children, were regarded as slaves to challenge that legal condition in contested freedom cases. In court, women and their children relied on an Indian identity, which meant they inherited free status, to gain their freedom. In defense of the mother's or her children's Indian status, *defensor de los pobres* (court-appointed lawyer who represented slaves, women, and other castas in court) tasked with protecting the rights of slaves and other marginalized groups employed *partus sequitur ventrem*, a Roman law from the thirteenth century and continued by the Spanish Crown that decreed that a child inherited the mother's status regardless of the father's status.[32] This code continued to define status in the Americas. Moreover, partus sequitur ventrem emphasized maternity's vital role in deciding the freedom or enslavement of children. Thus, a child inherited freedom or enslavement based on the mother's status, which could perpetuate slave or free status for generations. By conforming to legal meanings of what constituted an Indian, fiancées accused of having mala sangre married Spanish men, and women and children accused of being slaves won their freedom in contested court cases.

To uplift the children freed via the Free Womb Act of 1813, ecclesiastical and governing officials established schools that targeted African descendants and instituted whitening. First implemented by the Church and later by governors, public education taught free girls of African descent morality, virtue, and civility, characteristics that epitomized whiteness and distanced them from their blackness, which was equated with immorality, dishonor, and ignorance.[33] These school lessons provided a way for free women of African descent to contribute to the nation as "republican mothers" who uplifted their children from their blackness and taught them the lessons of whiteness, giving them an integral role in the republic.[34]

My gendered analysis of black invisibility moves beyond the more masculine notions of citizenship. Scholars have preferred to concentrate on the individual and collective efforts of African-descended men on the battlefield to trace the fight for freedom.[35] At the time, the link between military service and national identity defined citizenship as a masculine endeavor.[36] The masculine nature of citizenship on the battlefield transferred to the ballot box shortly after the foundation of various republics. Women, and especially African-descended women, did not fit this definition of citizenship, and governing officials prohibited them from voting. Scholarship must look beyond masculine definitions of citizenship to fully grasp how women, and especially women of African descent, continued to play an integral role in the republic. By focusing on key decisions that concubines, wives, mothers, and daughters of African descent made to seek privilege and eliminate the stigma of their blackness, *Hiding in Plain Sight* joins other works whose authors argue that women protected and cultivated the family in the postcolonial period (1810–1840), just as they did in the colonial period (1776–1810), and became guardians of an increasingly whiter nation.[37]

This book concentrates on Córdoba from the late eighteenth century through the early nineteenth century and is the first comprehensive study in English of the history of African descendants outside of Buenos Aires.[38] By focusing on Córdoba, a provincial and prominent small city, I shift the conversation of identity from the more well-known city, Buenos Aires, to the interior of the country. Córdoba is not Buenos Aires, and it is important to recognize that their cultural and political differences directly affected black invisibility. In fact, Córdoba's distinct geopolitical environment, which was based on the strength of the Catholic Church, contrasted greatly with that of Buenos Aires. The Catholic Church justified the Crown's and later the republic's existence. It remained the bedrock of social hierarchy and order and maintained a conservative culture. In contrast, the Church in Buenos Aires did not have the same prestige, especially during the republican period. Moreover, the demography of the cities also differed greatly. Córdoba, in the middle of the pampas, did not experience the demographic changes or the influx of European immigrants and slaves to the same extent as Buenos Aires, on the coast.[39] The lack of demographic changes meant that elite families could sustain their political and economic influence over a small population for generations. These stark contrasts directly influenced the formation of black invisibility.

Looking at the span of the late colonial and early republican periods (1776–1840), I analyze, using a variety of sources, the individual decisions that women of African descent made to escape their blackness and the institutional whitening that elites imposed. My sources include city censuses (1778, 1813, 1822, and 1832), which I transcribed; baptisms, marriages, notarial and probate records that detail the daily activities of free and enslaved people of color during the entire span of my study; and more than four hundred ecclesiastical and civil court courses, which detail the legal strategies African descendants employed to socially ascend. These sources reflect not only the social reality but also, as George Reid Andrews emphasizes, the "construction of that reality."[40] This wide array of sources provides information about how women of African descent lived, formed relationships, survived enslavement, gained their freedom, cultivated their family, and, when possible, achieved whiteness, which contributed to black invisibility.

Chapter 1, "Miscegenation, Marriage, and Manumission in Córdoba," and chapter 2, "Regulating and Administering Freedom in Córdoba," examine the political and social context of black invisibility in Córdoba. These chapters provide the background to explain how and why women of African descent chose to escape their blackness. Chapter 1 explains how Spanish privilege in Córdoba came about during the conquest that subsequently put Indians, Africans, and their descendants at a disadvantage socially, economically, and politically. This chapter also details how, conversely, Indians and Africans constantly defied the contours of Spanish privilege. Chapter 2 delves into the reestablishment of order and tradition via the Bourbon Reforms from 1776 to 1809, the wars of independence from 1810 to 1819, and the beginning of the republican period from 1820 to 1830. Ultimately, Córdoba offers a unique place for examining how international political and social factors affected a small interior city rather than a large metropolis such as Buenos Aires. The sources include civil and ecclesiastical edicts, the censuses of 1778, 1813, 1822, and 1832, and notarial and probate records from 1776 to 1840.

Chapters 3 and 4 examine how extrajudicial and judicial interrelationships between prominent and influential Spanish men and African-descended women afforded these women access to privilege and status. These chapters demonstrate that when possible, women of African descent used both legal and illegal means to escape their blackness. Chapter 3, "'Her Best Performance': From Slave to Señora," shows how African-descended concubines sought social mobility and to improve their status, often by taking on the persona of a Spanish woman. It centers on a case of cohabitation involving a slave named Bernabela, a woman whom witnesses described as "the color of a Spanish woman," and don José Lino, a vicar. While cohabitating, Bernabela whitened her identity by breaking sumptuary law and dressing above her status. She emulated an elite woman to such an extent that, over the years, slaves referred to her as *la señora* (the lady of the house).

Chapter 4, "'A Woman of His Class': Contested Intermarriages," discusses the legal means that African-descended women used to achieve social mobility through marriage. It centers on the Royal Pragmatic of 1776, a decree that stipulated that unequal couples could not marry without parental consent. Unequal marriage equated in Córdoba to differences in calidad status. But the Royal Pragmatic of 1776 also allowed betrothed couples whose parents negated their right to marry to appeal to secular authorities. Women accused of being African descendants argued and proved that they were in fact Spanish or Indian and had the right to marry. This chapter primarily utilizes marriage dissent cases involving women accused of having mala sangre.

Chapters 5 and 6 focus on motherhood in the republican period. Chapter 5, "(En)gendering Freedom: Maternity and the Manumission Process," provides a survey of the importance of motherhood and familial networks in the manumission process during the colonial and republican periods. Moreover, the chapter details how women and children threatened with enslavement sought freedom in the courts. To evade enslavement, they proved that they had Indian ancestry based on their maternal lineage. This chapter incorporates notarial and probate records that documented the manumission process and contested freedom court cases.

Chapter 6, "Lessons of Motherhood: The Beginning of Institutionalized Whitening," examines how motherhood became not only a legal conduit to freedom but also the basis for social grooming. It focuses on the Free Womb Act, which led to a new understanding of the role of free African-descended women in the republic. Ecclesiastical and governing authorities tasked these women with the responsibility to teach their future children the love of country, morality, and obedience, characteristics that could be learned only in school. Attempts to educate all girls, especially girls of African descent, became imperative for two reasons: as future mothers, they would uplift generations of freed people by teaching their children love for their country, civic responsibility, and virtuous behavior, and the increasing freed population had to receive the proper education so that they could be integrated into republican society. This chapter utilizes notarial records, census data, and newsletters.

My narrative answers the question of what happened to blacks in Argentina by detailing the origins of black invisibility in Córdoba. It reveals how women of African descent, be they concubines, wives, mothers, or daughters, through personal and intimate decisions, contributed to the making of a white Argentina.

ONE

Miscegenation, Marriage, and Manumission in Córdoba

My research for *Hiding in Plain Sight* conveniently took place in Córdoba's historic downtown. The Historic Archive of the Province of Córdoba was three blocks from Plaza San Martín, formally known as the *plaza mayor* (main public square) and the oldest plaza in Córdoba.[1] On sunny days, after I completed my work, I sat in the plaza overwhelmed by the cathedral and cabildo (town hall) that survived four hundred years of conquest, colonization, independence, and urbanization (figure 1.1 and figure 1.2). These buildings represent cornerstones of Spanish civilization: the Church and the Crown. Their presence points to Córdoba's Spanish heritage. I often questioned what they also mask. The answer— Indians and African slaves who constructed and maintained these buildings—remains hidden under the cloak of Spanish domination. Ironically, the more I visited the plaza, the more thoughts of these hidden histories

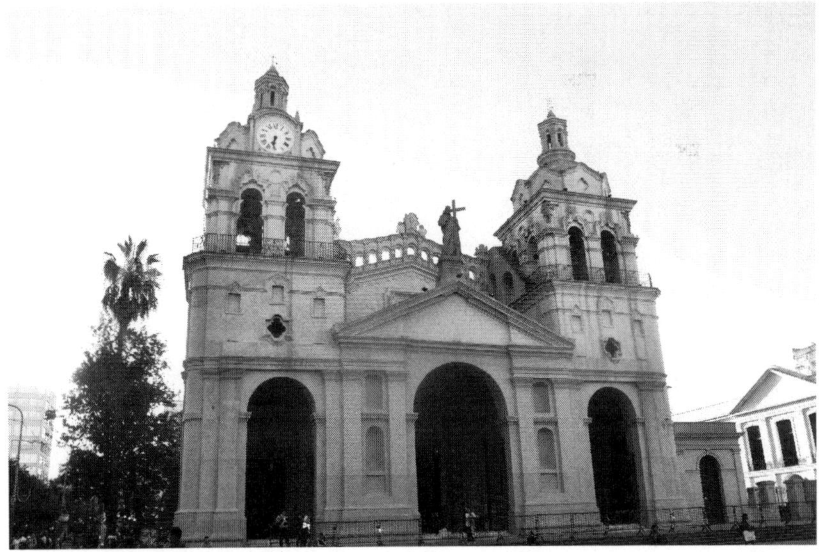

Figure 1.1. Cathedral of Córdoba, 2018. Photograph courtesy of Natalia Verónica González.

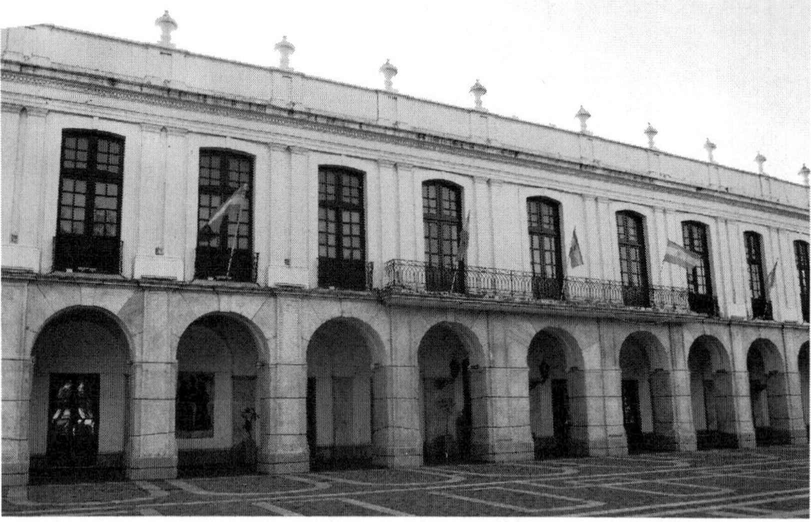

Figure 1.2. Cabildo (town hall) of Córdoba, 2018. Photograph courtesy of Natalia Verónica González.

energized my desire to unearth the reasons for black erasure, which began with the construction of these buildings in the sixteenth century.

In this chapter, I contextualize black invisibility in Córdoba. I focus on the interactions, relationships, and associations between Spaniards, Indians, and African descendants from the sixteenth through the nineteenth centuries. These diverse encounters led to a plethora of calidades that governing authorities, both civil and ecclesiastical elites, used to create social hierarchy. The ruling elite divided those with privilege, Spaniards, from the rest. But Indians and African descendants often blurred these divisions to achieve privilege. Their ability to subvert customary practices and legal codes that privileged Spaniards constitutes the basis of black erasure in Córdoba.

THE CONTOURS OF PRIVILEGE

The contours of privilege began during the era of Spanish conquest and Indian subjection. Jerónimo Luis de Cabrera founded Córdoba de Nueva Andalucía, or Córdoba, in July 1573. The city lay in a valley surrounded by a natural barrier of hills and modest mountains and canyons. A river ran to the north and east and a *cañada* (narrow glen) to the west. These natural barriers—the mountains, canyons, and the river—served as a symbol of Spanish domination and civilization amid the unsettled areas that Indians inhabited.[2] Shortly after colonization, in 1588, African slaves arrived in Córdoba to meet local demand. This legal slave trade continued for 224 years. Together, Spaniards, Indians, and Africans constituted Córdoba's population during the late sixteenth and seventeenth centuries. To ensure that they remained in a privileged position, Spaniards constantly sought policies to assert their superiority in ways that discouraged Indian and African social ascent.

SPANIARDS, INDIANS, AND AFRICANS IN THE EARLY COLONIAL PERIOD

The city's urban layout marked Spanish settlement and evangelization efforts in 1577. Lorenzo Suarez de Figueroa, lieutenant general of the governor of Córdoba, designed a city organized into a *traza* (city layout in a grid-like pattern) of seventy blocks: seven blocks from east to west and ten blocks from north to south (figure 1.3).[3] He also designed each block and street to be the same size, with the exception of the Convent of San Francisco, which equaled two blocks, and the cathedral and the cabildo

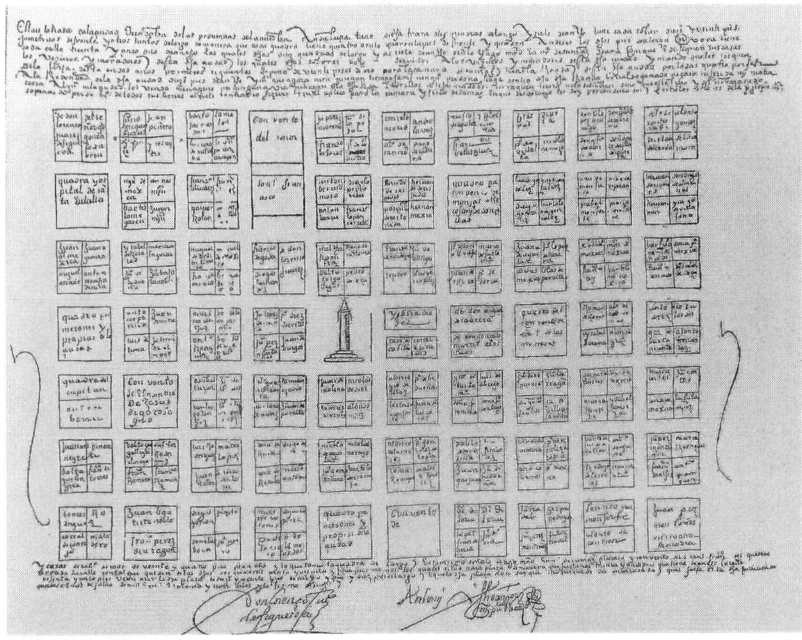

Figure 1.3. Foundational layout of the city of Córdoba by Lorenzo Suarez de Figueroa, 1577. From Carlos A. Luque Colombres, *Orígenes históricos de la propiedad urbana de Córdoba: Siglos XVI y XVII* (Córdoba, Argentina: Universidad Nacional de Córdoba, 1980), 31.

that shared a block divided by the Santa Catalina alleyway.[4] To make room for other religious orders, Suarez de Figueroa labeled one block on the city's design *convento de el nombre de Jesús digo colegio* and the other simply *convento de*. The cabildo assigned the *convento de el nombre de Jesús digo colegio* to the Jesuit order, but when the Jesuits arrived in 1589 they settled in the block labeled *cuadra para monjas o recogmiento de doncellas* and it adjudicated the *convento de* to the Dominican order. However, when the Dominicans arrived, they decided not to move into the assigned block and in 1640 bought another block owned by the *convento de nuestra señora de las Mercedes*.[5] Suarez de Figueroa divided the remaining blocks into 225 *solares* (plots of allotted land in the city) and assigned them to conquistadors, settlers, and their family members, such as doña Juana de Abreu and doña Jeromina de Albornoz, the mother and sister of conquistador Luis de Aberu Albornoz, independent of their nationality, social status, and occupation.[6] Suarez de Figueroa's urban layout symbolized social order. The cabildo, the cathedral, and the Franciscan holdings' larger sizes signified Spanish domination and settlement.

By the end of 1590, a trade network composed mainly of regional Spanish and Portuguese merchants engaged in a vast Andean interregional economy in the Río de la Plata that connected the silver-producing region of Potosí, a city in present-day Bolivia, to Buenos Aires.[7] In response to the rich trade, Córdoba, and to a lesser extent Tucumán, Salta, and Jujuy, created urban economies that sold agricultural products, such as olives, grapes, and vegetables and livestock, textiles, and slaves, to Potosí. By 1801, the three main items of production and trade included the mule trade, which muleteers bred and/or fattened in Córdoba on their way to Potosí, leather products, and textiles.[8] Within the city of Córdoba, these Spanish and Portuguese merchants along with small dealers and grocers traded agricultural products, livestock, textiles, and slaves in the city's main plaza. Small-time dealers, often mestizas, resold products on the corners or house to house, while grocers in the market sold products from their stores to residents through barter or on credit.[9] Within the city, Spanish and Portuguese merchants formed a social aristocracy of the sixteenth and seventeenth century, as many had familial or social networks that linked them to conquistadors or to ecclesiastical authorities. These merchants and other members of the social aristocracy created a Spanish identity that privileged their existence over Indians and Africans.

At the time of the city's foundation, most of Córdoba's Indian population consisted of four major ethnic groups: Comechingones, Sanavirones, Diaguitas, and the "Pampas," a generic label for Indians who lived in the south.[10] The most populous groups, Comechingones and Sanavirones, numbered thirty thousand divided into six hundred settlements and had a semisedentary lifestyle.[11] These groups formed settlements politically organized into families or clans ruled by a cacique.[12] The Diaguitas lived in the sierras, and a subsection of this ethnic group, known as the Calcahquíes, later settled in the outskirts of the city in El Pueblito or La Toma. The Pampas lived a seminomadic lifestyle and resisted Spanish conquest and colonization, earning a reputation for being "infamous warriors."[13]

After conquest and various epidemics that decimated the Indian population (accounts estimate that the indigenous population dropped 88 percent, from fifty thousand preconquest to six thousand by 1582), Cabrera converted Indian settlements to *encomiendas* (royal grants of Indians who are obligated to provide tribute and labor) and granted these to others in his expedition.[14] In exchange for Indian service and tribute, *encomenderos* (holders of an encomienda) had to evangelize the Indians.[15] However, a vast encomienda system comparable to that in the Andean region did not develop in Córdoba. Recent estimates by historians and anthropologists cite twenty-one encomiendas developed during the seventeenth and eighteenth centuries.[16] By 1759, only two encomenderos, Joseph Moyano and Carlos de Olmos y Aguilera, remained in the city and few Indians lived on their encomiendas.[17]

Before the encomienda system ended in roughly the 1770s, the remaining encomiendas converted to *pueblos de indios tributarios* (Crownsanctioned Indian settlements). Indians who lived on pueblos had become tributaries of the Crown and were obligated to pay an annual tribute of five pesos. In the province of Córdoba, the pueblos included the following: La Toma, located close to the city; Soto and Quilino to the north of the city of Córdoba; Nono and Pichana in Traslasierra, where the majority of the population resided; and San Antonio de Nonascate, San Jacinto, Cosquin, and Salascate, the smaller pueblos.[18] Only 29 percent of the total Indian population in the 1770s lived in these pueblos de indios tributarios, and tribute proved difficult to collect.[19] In 1775, of the calculated 226 tributary Indians who owed 1,330 pesos, the *tributo al recaudador* (tribute collector) received fifty pesos and four reales.[20] After years of receiving less than expected financial returns, the governor intendant, Rafael de Sobremonte, more commonly known as the Marqués de Sobremonte, allowed other products to serve as tribute. These products included horses, mules, wheat, corn, linen, and cotton.[21]

Most slaves in the Río de la Plata arrived through the Portuguese slave trade, which began with Pedro Reynel.[22] The Portuguese supplied slaves to the Río de la Plata through both legal and illegal routes. For example, although Reynel had an *asiento* (a formal contract granted by the Spanish Crown to an individual or a company to import slaves), widespread smuggling and fraud caused the Crown to end his contract in 1604.[23] The Crown's attempt to curb contraband did not have a positive effect. Instead, traders found ways to circumvent customs officials with more creative strategies. One strategy that shipmasters used to legally disembark slaves included labeling them *arribadas forzosas* (forced arrivals). Captains often insisted that storms or enemy ships prevented them from disembarking at a designated Brazilian port and forced them to disembark in the Río de la Plata. Once Buenos Aires authorities deemed the disembarkation fair, shipmasters could sell some of their slaves. *Manifestos*, another contraband strategy, allowed individuals who had purchased slaves illegally to pay a pardon (a fee). Individuals also claimed to have found *negros descaminados* (unaccompanied disembarked slaves) wandering the countryside, often because a ship had disembarked in a location to avoid the authorities and sold them.[24] Estimates from the period between 1587 and 1640 suggest that roughly forty-five thousand enslaved Africans disembarked in Buenos Aires.[25] Because Buenos Aires remained a small town with a population that did not exceed ten thousand in the seventeenth century, slave traders sold the majority of the slaves to the interior of the Río de la Plata, stopping first in Córdoba on their way to Potosí or other interior cities such as Mendoza, Catamarca, Jujuy, and Salta.[26]

From 1588 to 1610, six trading companies sold in the city of Córdoba 561 slaves (318 male slaves and 193 female slaves, aged between one year and sixty years old) for a total of 149,195 pesos.[27] Most slaves originated from Africa, and records describe them as Angolan or Guinean, but two slaves, both named Pedro, came from Congo, and one slave, named Gaspar, came from Benin. Brazil was the second most recorded place of origin.[28] Mexico City was another place of origin, revealing the extent of the inter-American slave trade.[29] Slave purchasers overwhelmingly bought male slaves aged sixteen to thirty-five, but on four occasions they bought mothers and their children. For example, Balthasar Perez, a Portuguese merchant, bought María, a negra, from "Loanda, land of Angola," and her five-year-old son, Juan, and two-year-old daughter, Beatriz, both born in the seller's house.[30] Research about the first forty years of the slave population in Córdoba shows that slave traders preferred African male slaves, whom they resold to work in Potosí's silver mines.

The foundational years of Córdoba marked the arrival of Spaniards, the decimation of the Indian population, and the forced migration of Africans. To maintain their privilege and prestige, Spaniards asserted themselves as the dominating group, subjugating Indians and enslaving Africans. Spanish domination manifested in the city's traza, which organized the city into seventy blocks with a plaza mayor that contained two prominent buildings, the cabildo, which represented Spanish governance, and the cathedral, which represented the only acceptable religion, Catholicism. Its design stood in stark contrast to what many Spaniards considered the wilderness and barbarism that embodied unconverted and aggressive Indians. With time, Spanish domination represented a coveted whiteness that the Spanish elite furiously guarded and prohibited Indians and Africans from obtaining.

SPANIARDS, INDIANS, AND AFRICANS: LATE COLONIAL PERIOD

By the end of the eighteenth century, a new wave of Spaniards and, to a lesser extent, Portuguese had migrated to Córdoba and married into local families. These families preferred recently arrived Spanish and Portuguese men as marriage partners because they possessed *pureza de sangre* (purity of blood, referring to Spaniards).[31] Of the 224 foreigners listed in the 1778 city census, the majority, Spanish men, came from the province of Galicia.[32] The prefixes don or doña denoted a Spaniard in the census, which numbered 2,697 in 1778 (table 1.1). Individuals belonging to this social aristocracy owned most of the slaves, ranches, and urban real estate, along with various elements of production and distribution. They also taught or obtained their education at the Colegio Maximo, the Jesuit university, and Real Colegio Convictorio de Nuestra Señora de Monserrat, a Jesuit preparatory school for boys. However, not all people in this group were wealthy. Some worked as manual laborers, but their Spanish heritage granted them access to education, government, and militia careers.[33] Spaniards guarded their privilege closely by creating a tight-knit group of elite families who influenced the political, social, and economic laws and customary practices in the city. Whenever possible, they asserted their privileged status to the detriment of Indians and African slaves.

For some Indians, the precarious and difficult reality of life on the pueblos de indios tributarios caused them to migrate to the city, where they could find employment. An estimated 535 Indians lived within the city (table 1.1).[34] The 1778 census listed only eight Indians as heads of household, six of them men, and two women, Josefa Suasnabas and Juana. Most of the Indian households consisted of immediate family members only. However, the household of forty-eight-year-old Josefa Suasnabas included her family and a free negra named Felipa. Most Indians lived in large households among slaves and free African descendants and worked as *conchabados* (contracted Indian laborers).[35] They often exchanged their labor for a small profit and a place to stay. In the city, Indians remained at a disadvantage in comparison to the Spanish elite but had slightly more privilege than slaves because of their free status.

By the end of the eighteenth century, census takers enumerated 4,038 African descendants, an estimated 56 percent of the city's population. They included 1,795 free and 2,243 enslaved people (table 1.1). The sizable free population marked an important transition over the course of two centuries. Initially, most if not all Africans came to Córdoba as slaves, but because of manumission and miscegenation, a free and mixed population became so sizable and visible that census takers could not ignore them and labeled them "castas." Within the slave population, the census counted 937 single women and 579 single men in the city, a change from the sixteenth century when male slaves outnumbered female slaves.[36] This shift occurred because labor demands shifted from supplying laborers, mostly African men, for the mines in Potosí to fulfill the local demands of domestic service, which consisted largely of cordobés-born African-descended women, in Córdoba.[37] Free and enslaved women of African descent labored as maids, cooks, wet nurses, and textile workers. Given the opportunity, female slaves also sold food and produce in the

TABLE 1.1. POPULATION BASED ON CALIDAD IN THE CITY CENSUS OF 1778

Calidad	Number	Percentage
Spaniards	2,697	37
Indians	535	7
Free (mulatos, zambos, negros)	1,795	25
Slave (mulatos, zambos, negros)	2,243	31
Total	7,270	100

Source: Archivo Histórico de la Provincia de Córdoba (AHPC) 1778 census of the city of Córdoba

market or on the streets.[38] Conversely, free and enslaved men of African descent labored in the city in artisanal occupations such as shoemaker, blacksmith, silversmith, carpenter, and tailor.[39]

Within the city, the majority of slaveholders were members of the Spanish elite, followed by the Church, which possessed 27 percent of the slave population. The Church, especially the Jesuit order, invested in slave labor, which allowed them to maintain a self-sufficient economy, until, that is, the Crown expelled the Jesuits from their territories in 1767.[40] According to the 1778 city and provincial censuses, 32 percent of the slave population had belonged to the Jesuits.[41]

DEFYING PRIVILEGE IN CÓRDOBA

Despite the Spanish legal codes and customary practices that privileged their status, Indians and Africans throughout the colonial period defied those laws and practices through illegal and legal familial and social networks that included miscegenation, marriage, and manumission. Miscegenation created new calidades such as mestizo, mulato, and zambo that blurred the strict lines of Spanish pureza de sangre. Marriages between Spanish men and Indian women and later Spanish men and African women also gave these women and their children a means to social ascent. Later, African slaves manumitted themselves and their family members, creating a large free casta population. African slaves also challenged the definition of labor, which enslaved them but freed Indians. Beyond manumission, freed African descendants also sought privilege by buying it, which further protected and cultivated their families. Defying privilege began shortly after conquest and continued throughout the eighteenth and nineteenth centuries.

Miscegenation occurred during conquest and continued throughout the colonial period. The results of sexual relationships between Spaniards and Indians created the new calidad label "mestizo." Governing authorities applied these new categories to create "order" in colonial society.[42] Mestizos no longer fit the labels indio or negro, and their mixture did not equate them to a Spaniard. Often mestizos were born through acts of violence such as rape or to unmarried couples who became pregnant. Their illegitimacy prevented most from accessing government positions, education, or religious vocations. Still, if their fathers acknowledged them, mestizo children became a part of elite society during the first generation of conquest.

Once accepted into Spanish society, mestizas, such as Isabel de Nadal, succeeded in rejecting all aspects of their Indian past and became fully integrated into Spanish society, adhering to the lines of social hierarchy. For instance, Isabel had Indian servants to whom she bequeathed dresses and animals in her will as a reward for their loyal service.[43] Moreover, as seen in mestizos' wills, they had houses in the city, estancias, small farms, and slaves.[44] Mestiza daughters for instance could receive large dowries, which assured that they would marry other conquistadors. These husbands at times had little or no capital, but mestiza wives inherited Spanish entitlements and privileges, such as the coveted title "doña," and their children became Spaniards, with all the attendant privileges and status.[45] Additionally, mestizo sons recognized by their fathers formed a part of the elite network, worked for the cabildo, attended university, and joined the clergy.[46]

Mestiza daughters could escape their Indian origins, achieving the title of doña, faster than mestizo sons could, in part because of the lack of Spanish women during the initial years of conquest. This imbalance favored mestizas, who were eligible as wives, and disadvantaged mestizos, who often lacked the option to marry Spanish women during the initial years of conquest.[47] For that reason, mestizas sought Spanish men who could support them and their future children.[48] Mestizas such as Isabel de Vega, who married Juan Rodríguez Cardero, a wealthy encomendero, had children who fully integrated into Spanish society. Her daughter married an encomendero and her sons became clergymen.[49] This social ascent lasted only for the first generation and became more restricted when their ascent endangered the tributary system.[50] Later generations of mestizos would not have the same advantages without the aid of marriage, which meant that they were the offspring of a legitimate union. Still, first-generation mestizos, often children of Indian women and Spanish men, blurred the barriers of Spanish purity because of their adoption into Spanish society.

Intermarriage also defied Spanish entitlement and privilege. Although very rare, the Church and Crown did allow marriage between two calidades. An estimated twenty-one marriages between Indian women and conquistadors occurred during the years of conquest and settlement. Examples include Juan de Lepe and María, an Indian, who raised sheep and goats, and Pedro de Chaves, a Portuguese slave trader, whose second marriage was to an Indian named Lucia.[51] These marriages not only gave Indian women social mobility but also benefited the conquistador, because the Crown threatened to take encomiendas from conquistadors who did not marry. Conquistadors were therefore encouraged to marry, as marrying allowed them to stay in the newly acquired territory.[52]

Marriages between Spanish men and enslaved women, also quite rare, took place throughout the colonial period. During the seventeenth century, six marriages between enslaved women and Spanish men occurred.

The number rose significantly in the eighteenth century and early nineteenth century, with twenty-five marriages.[53] These marriages provided slave women and their children with a means of social ascent. Catalina, a slave from the Santa Catalina monastery, for example, married Pedro Escobar, a Spaniard, in 1735. The cathedral registered their marriage in the Book of Spanish Marriages and two of their three children's baptisms in the Book of Spanish Baptisms.[54] Her marriage not only whitened her existence but also benefited her children.

Both miscegenation and marriage provided avenues for social advancement, especially during the early colonial period. Miscegenation created a new calidad, mestizo, that, provided their Spanish father acknowledged them, granted them Spanish privilege and status. However, these advantages applied only to the first-generation mestizos. Marriage between Indians and Spanish men and between enslaved women and Spanish men also granted these women a privileged status. These marriages gave Indian and enslaved wives a legitimacy that they could pass on to their children, who at times could adopt a Spanish identity.

BAPTISM AND MARRIAGE: THE CHURCH
AND SLAVE FAMILIES

From their arrival in the late sixteenth century, slaves formed familial networks that aided in the manumission process. The Church facilitated slave family networks through the sacraments of baptism and marriage, which created social networks that served as survival mechanisms for those enslaved and later freed. Baptism sanctified their existence by acknowledging their spiritual being. Baptismal records also recognized a mother's connection to her child. Slaves also had the right to get married. Marriage, a sacrament, formed the basic unit of the family. Before their expulsion in 1767, the Jesuits promoted marriage among their slaves, in part to ensure that their slaves did not cohabitate. But marriages among slaves also reduced the chance of slaves running away.[55] Together, baptism and marriage formed the foundation of social networks within slave families that led to manumission.

Both godparents and witnesses formed a real and fictive family that extended beyond blood ties.[56] When a child received the sacrament, the parents, designated godparents, and on occasion the slaveholder witnessed the event.[57] Friends and family, freed and enslaved, served as godparents. They took on the important task of teaching their godchild the gospel and agreed to raise the child if anything happened to the parents. Baptism guaranteed that a child had been officially welcomed into the Christian family and allowed to participate in future sacraments such as marriage.[58] In 1816, a man named Jacinto, born in Angola, wanted to marry Micaela, a free African descendant from Córdoba. But first he had to find his baptismal records to prove his Catholic status. Jacinto estimated that he received the sacrament of baptism in 1806 or 1809 and that Church officials had registered his baptism, but the Church could not find his baptismal information. Without this information, Jacinto could not marry Micaela. Other slaves who lived with him in doña Teresa de Allende's household—Juan, José, Mercedes, and Prudencia—came forward as witnesses and testified that Jacinto had served as a godparent for Matias, another slave, who died. The slaves did not remember the year of Matias's baptism, but they did remember that the priest who baptized Matias, don José Julian, named Jacinto as the godfather, a role that required prior baptism, and "for that, they [the slaves] were certain that he [Jacinto] was a Christian."[59] The shared experiences of slavery in doña Teresa de Allende's household created a real and fictive familial network among the slaves, who vouched for Jacinto's Christianity and character, helping him meet the basic requirements to marry.

Once proven a Christian, Jacinto had to present witnesses who established his character and confirmed his ability to marry. Often, extended family members and friends of the fiancés served as witnesses. During their testimony, witnesses declared how long they had known the fiancés and in what capacity. In other parts of the Río de la Plata, these familial connections traced back to time shared on slave ships hailing from Africa or Brazil.[60] In Córdoba, these connections also prevailed. One of Jacinto's witnesses, Domingo Allende, a negro slave from Guinea, testified that he had known Jacinto from the time that their slaveholders had bought them, almost fourteen years ago, and accordingly they came "from the same land of Guinea." These links revealed a larger familial network that extended beyond relatives. Thanks in part to the testimony of the witness who revealed that he had known Jacinto for so long and thus attested to his character, the court ruled in Jacinto's favor.[61]

The Church not only promoted marriage but also guaranteed it as a right. By granting the sacrament of marriage to slaves, the Church encouraged slaves to live a moral life rather than participate in what the institution considered to be an immoral lifestyle of cohabitation. In addition to bestowing the right to marry, the Church permitted slaves to live with their spouses.[62] This practice stemmed from Siete Partidas, a Roman law continued in Spanish America. It stated, "Where two slaves who are married have two masters . . . and they are so far apart that where they serve their masters they cannot join one another and live together; the church can compel one of the masters to buy the slave of the other. Where they are unwilling to do this, whichever of them the church selects can be compelled to sell his slave to . . . a resident of the town or community where the master of the other slave resides, and if no one wishes to buy him the church should do so in order that the husband and wife may not be separated."[63] This ecclesiastical law not only stated that married enslaved couples had the right to live together but also established the parameters to ensure the law's completion. It put the responsibility on the slaveholders to first negotiate and decide who would sell their slave and allow them to live a conjugal life. When slaveholders did not agree, or when both were unwilling to sell their slave, according to the law, the Church should buy the slave.

In Córdoba, this law held through the early nineteenth century, when doña Eugenia Gutiérrez attempted to prohibit her slave Marcos from marrying Pabla, a slave of don José Matias Torres in 1818. Doña Eugenia stated she had raised Marcos since childhood. As an elderly woman, she financially depended on her slave's daily earnings. Upset that he did not seek her permission to marry, which she testified she would not have granted because she depended on him, she asked the court to annul the marriage. The ecclesiastical court, however, argued that "there was no cannon impediment for this marriage [between slaves] nor did the laws require slaveholders' consent."[64] The Church's commitment to allowing slaves to live a married life revealed the pervasiveness and power of ecclesiastical law in Córdoba during the nineteenth century.

If slaveholders negated the law, slaves could seek their freedom. In the case of Martín de la Fuente, a slave, the defensor de los pobres pointed out that Martín's slaveholder did not permit him to live with his wife. For seven years, he lived apart from his wife, Rosa de Valeriana Funes, also a slave, as his slaveholder had not allowed him to see her or have a married life. The defensor de los pobres argued that the slaveholder denied Martín the right to have a Catholic marriage. Moreover, the defensor de los pobres argued that "the laws of our Sovereign Catholics [were] prone to relieve the harshness of slavery," and for that reason Martín and his wife must live together. Lastly, Martín stated, "I am an unhappy slave, miserable person," under the conditions set forth, and for that reason he argued that he deserved a *carta de libertad* (manumission paper).[65] Martín's quest for freedom reveals the lengths slaves went to in order to work within the boundaries of the law to formulate a family.

Intermarriages between enslaved women and Spanish men could also lead to manumission, as in the case of Claudio Ribero Araujo, an "español" from Rio de Janeiro, and his wife, María Fructuosa Seña, a slave of the Monastery of Santa Catalina. They married in 1783 and had two children, a son, Ambrosio Antonio, born in 1784, and a daughter, Juana Tomasa, born in 1786. The children inherited their mother's enslaved status. Interestingly, although most baptismal records denoted the mother's status, María Fructuosa's condition did not appear on their baptism records.[66] In 1784, shortly after Ambrosio's birth, Claudio Ribero Araujo freed his son, paying twenty-five pesos to the monastery.[67] Two years later, María Fructuosa received her manumission. Doña Damiana del Corazón de Jesús, her slaveholder from the Monastery of Santa Catalina, had noted that for some time she had wanted to give María her freedom. She had remembered that when she had received María at four months of age, María's father had tried to free her, noting that he did not want his daughter to live as a slave. He had given doña Damiana money, but she had opposed the manumission. However, in 1786, Claudio Ribero Araujo again approached doña Damiana, asking that doña Damiana grant María manumission, as he no longer wanted his wife's status to be an impediment or a stain on their marriage. Noting the just causes expressed with much love by her husband, Claudio Ribero Araujo, and that María had served them well, the monastery granted María Fructuosa manumission.[68] In marrying Claudio Ribero Araujo, María Fructuosa Seña gained freedom not only for herself but also for their child. This example reveals the importance of familial networks and why enslaved women would benefit from marrying Spanish men.

The sacraments, baptism, and marriage strengthened and created real and fictive family networks that played an integral role in the manumission process. Family cultivation began with baptism, which officially welcomed slaves into the Church's family. From that point, the baptized child entered a familial network that included their parents and godparents. Later, if they chose, slaves could enter the sacrament of marriage. Marriage formed the basis of a nuclear family. Together, these sacraments fostered an emotional bond between family members that helped them survive the harshness of slavery and eventually led to freedom.

FAMILIAL NETWORKS AND MANUMISSION

The Church facilitated and cultivated slave families.[69] They saw the family unit as a way to indoctrinate the teachings of the Catholic faith and ease the harshness of slavery, which also led to the unintended effect of increased manumissions. Mothers and fathers, aunts and uncles, brothers and sisters, and even grandparents went to great lengths to manumit their loved ones. By accumulating wealth via their crafts and social networks, individuals ensured that family members, especially their children, had a better life. These strategies reveal that gaining freedom in Córdoba was a family affair.

Third-party manumissions, that is, manumissions paid by an individual other than the slaveholder or the manumitted slave, outnumbered self-manumissions. Grandparents, parents, siblings, children, and spouses enacted third-party manumissions.[70] In particular, maternal third-party manumissions highlighted a mother's willingness to free her children. Mothers paid up to twenty-five pesos to ensure that their children would be born free, as evidenced by notarial records from the late eighteenth through the nineteenth centuries.[71] In some cases, despite a mother paying for her unborn child's freedom, the baby did not immediately become free. In 1778, Phelipa de la Asumpcion, a nun of the black veil and prioress of the Monastery of Santa Catalina de Seña, accepted Margarita's payment of twenty-five pesos for her unborn baby's freedom, provided she agreed to the following conditions: that her child (boy or girl) would remain with Margarita and be at the disposal of Phelipa to raise in the monastery until the child reached a competent age. If Margarita miscarried or the baby died within seven days, the agreement was void.[72]

African-descended husbands and fathers also sought ways to free their family members. Husbands most often freed their wives, although in 1791, María Orellano, a free African descendant, paid 120 pesos to free her aging and sick husband, Blas Davila.[73] Fathers also purchased their children's freedom, although they did not free their unborn children as often as enslaved mothers did.[74] In 1784, Juan Nuñez de Olivera, described as a free Brazilian mulato in the 1778 census, purchased his son Josef Pedro Martín's freedom for twenty-five pesos from doña Gregoria Soria in 1782.[75] A few months later, Juan Nuñez de Olivera purchased his wife, María Mercedes, and mother of Pedro Joseph Martín from doña Gregoria Soria for 200 pesos.[76] Because Juan Nuñez de Olivera was a shoemaker, he had accumulated the funds to purchase his family members' freedom. Likewise, in 1789, Joaquín Olivera, a master shoemaker who accumulated wealth from his craft, bought a piece of land in the city and later, in 1802, paid thirty-three pesos to free his newborn daughter, Josefa, from the Hospital of Belemnites.[77]

Once some freed African descendants had garnered enough wealth, they also purchased and sold slaves.[78] Don Pedro Arias manumitted Isidora Arias, a seamstress, and granted her 200 pesos to construct an additional room in his house in 1803.[79] Although it is not clear whether she constructed the room, that same year Isidora also sold Cathalina, a twenty-three-year-old negra slave, to don Nicolas Carmona for 288 pesos.[80] Three years later, she sold another slave, Tadea, to doña Marta Martina Almada for 263 pesos.[81] In 1810, she bought eighteen-year-old Teresa Antonia from don Julian Rodríguez for 307 pesos, only to sell her for 312 pesos three years later.[82] A widowed slaveholder, Isidora raised her four children by herself and cultivated a social network that most likely benefited her son Mariano, who became a merchant, a profession that few non-Spaniards attained in 1813.[83] Isidora's life revealed that although rare, freed women of African descent could accumulate enough wealth based on their manual labor and on financial gifts from their former slaveholders to also invest in slave labor.

Other examples of free African-descended women purchasing and selling slaves included María del Sacramento de Llanes, who did this to feed and clothe her family. María del Sacramento's underage niece and nephews, Bernarda, José María, and José Manuel Lujan, owned thirteen-year-old Andres Llanes. Before she could sell Andres for 170 pesos, she had to seek permission from the *defensor de los menores*, a lawyer tasked with representing and protecting minors, informing him that she needed the money to feed and clothe the three children. For her petition to succeed, María del Sacramento had to provide proof of poverty. Two witnesses—Pedro Barbosa and don Pedro Vasquez Nobia—certified her impoverished state and the fair price of 170 pesos, after which the court granted her the right to sell Andres to Juan Nuñez de Olivera in 1801, who had recently freed his wife and son and achieved the rank of a master shoemaker in the shoemaker's guild in 1802 and later in 1807–1808.[84] In this case, selling a slave provided financial stability and enabled María del Sacramento to provide for her family.

Enslaved fathers also learned to navigate and attend to the social ascent of their children. Enslaved men who learned a craft (such as blacksmithing or playing music) often taught them to their children to ensure that the next generation would have skills that could possibly earn them enough wealth to gain their freedom. José Salguero learned to play the organ along with other instruments while a slave of the Jesuits. After the Jesuit expulsion, the cathedral purchased him because of his musical ability. His child, Hipólito Salguero, learned most likely from his father how to play the violin and worked for the cathedral even after he achieved his freedom. For his efforts, the cathedral gave Hipólito a house and paid him twenty-five pesos a year.[85] Like his father, José Salguero, Hipólito also introduced music to his sons, Tiburcio and Sebastián, who played the clarinet and the horn, respectively. In 1798, Hipólito Salguero paid 217 pesos to free his mulata wife, Josefa Gigena.[86] Seventeen years later, he paid 150 pesos to free his son Tiburcio, a cheap price for a slave who played an instrument, who on average could be sold for 295 pesos. This was likely due to Hipólito's dedication to the Church.[87] Sebastián, his other son, stayed a slave of the cathedral until 1832, when he bought his freedom for 150 pesos, but he continued to work there until 1839.[88]

The story of the Salguero family reveals how craft and talent could transfer from generation to generation in ways that enabled some enslaved African descendants to become free and to free their family members. It further shows the importance of family that extended beyond the nuclear setting. Families' commitments to freeing their members began in utero and extended for generations. Freedom in itself was not enough without the skills to build wealth and uplift the family.

SLAVE OR INDIAN LABOR: CHALLENGING LEGAL CONDITIONS

Recognizing the difference between the legal conditions of slaves and those of Indians, slaves sought freedom by seeking Indian status. In 1795, José Eugenio Ascanibí argued before ecclesiastical officials that his recently deceased owner, Dr. don José Antonio Ascanibí, had freed him in his will. To assess his accuracy, the defensor de los pobres read the provision in the will. It stated, "Item 16: It is my will that the referred mulato [José] Eugenio stay *agregado* [attached to a household and often fulfilling labor obligations] to the referred my nephew don Pedro Arrendondo and throughout remain a musician for the Cathedral." The label "agregado" applied to free people such as Indians, while *esclavo* (slave) applied to African descendants.

Both José and don Pedro Arrendondo agreed with don José Antonio Ascanibi's will, which stipulated José's lifelong commitment to the cathedral. But they did not agree on the status of his service; would he serve as a free person or as an enslaved person? As the case developed, it came to center on the label "agregado." In an effort to prove that José's agregado status did not mean slavery, the defensor de los pobres claimed that the label was equivalent to that of the Yanacona Indians in Peru and "[could not] say with truth, that the Indians are slaves, but free and voluntarily agregados to the haciendas." But don Pedro Arrendondo countered with the irony of a free person serving an owner. What exactly did it constitute "that free men would serve an owner, and live off the fruits of their haciendas. . . . It was comparable to the Yanacona Indians . . . who were semi-slaves and freedom was perpetually conditional."[89] Specifically, José's appeal displayed the dubious application of agregado.

After both sides concluded their arguments, the decision ultimately boiled down to the definition of labor. The court granted José his freedom, but he would remain in service to the cathedral.[90] By equating his labor with that of the Yanacona Indians, he aligned himself with a legal Indian identity that kept him attached to employment of the Church but not enslaved. This court case revealed that despite lacking the Spanish privilege, African descendants threatened with enslavement turned to definitions of Indian labor to remain free.

Other instances reveal that free African descendants sought solace in Indian pueblos. By the end of the eighteenth century, free African descendants made up 15 percent of the nine pueblos' population. In the San Jacinto pueblo, which was home to thirty-eight people, African descendants accounted for 31 percent. In the Soto pueblo, which with 117 people was the largest pueblo, African descendants accounted for 20 percent of the population.[91] For example, Joaquín and Pedro Ochoa, both labeled negros, lived in the pueblo because they had married women from Soto. Marriage to Indian women from Soto also allowed Spaniards, such as Francisco Heredia, a soldier in the militia, to live in Soto.[92] Over time, these interrelations between Indian and African descendants produced children, known as zambos, such as Simón Quintero, who blurred the right to hereditary positions such as the cacique.[93]

In 1811, Indians demanded Simón Quintero's dismissal as their cacique in Cosquin, an Indian pueblo. The pueblo led by Pedro Ortiz argued that Quintero's lewd behavior, which included illicit livestock slaughter and adultery with Francisca Alberadano (the wife of Pedro Busto, another member of the pueblo), made Quintero unfit to rule. Moreover, Ortiz and other members of the pueblo argued that Quintero did not have a right to lead their pueblo because of his slave ancestry. Quintero's lack of Indian heritage meant that he did not inherit the job as members such as Pedro Ortiz did, who had blood ties to the pueblo. Although they allowed non-Indians to live with them, they would not permit an outsider such as Quintero to control the pueblo. In response, Quintero claimed that he did belong to the pueblo because his mother was a member. His father, however, did not come from the pueblo. He argued he had a right to rule, which the court later confirmed.[94] Living among Indians on their pueblos benefited free African descendants and, in some cases, permitted them to rise to cacique.

The difference between the legal conditions of Indians and those of slaves proved to be another avenue to freedom in Córdoba. By challenging labels such as agregado, African descendants threatened with enslavement negotiated their working conditions. In the case of José, he would remain a laborer in the cathedral but gained his freedom. Other African descendants sought solace among Indians who lived in the pueblos de indios tributarios. By 1785, 31 percent of San Jacinto's population were African descendants, and Soto had the second-highest African-descended population at 20 percent. Their large presence suggests that they benefited from living outside of the city.

CONCLUSION

Within the seventy blocks of Córdoba, Spanish conquistadors, clergy, and government officials established the contours of privilege, which granted them access to education, governance, and control of a vast interregional trade to the determinant of Indians and Africans. Surviving Indians and enslaved Africans labored and served Spaniards. After conquest and diseases had ravaged the Indian population, Spaniards incorporated Indians into the encomienda system and later into pueblos de indios tributarios to serve their population and pay tribute to the Spanish Crown. Many Indians fared poorly in this labor system and migrated to the city to find employment. However, despite their precarious reality, Indians had a slight advantage because of their free status. Spanish and Portuguese slave traders transported the Africans, the majority of whom were men, to Córdoba during the late sixteenth century to be resold to other slave traders, who in turn transported them to Potosí to fulfill the demand for labor in the silver mines. By the late eighteenth century, the slave population in Córdoba had shifted to a majority of women born in Córdoba who labored as domestic workers followed by men who worked as artisans. Slave status meant Africans could not dictate or control their lives, which encouraged many of them to seek to change their reality and find ways to gain access to Spanish privilege.

Throughout the colonial period, miscegenation, marriage, and manumission led to an increasingly mixed and free population that disrupted social hierarchy and defied the contours of Spanish privilege. New calidades, such as mestizo, that appeared during the years of conquest no longer fit the mold of the original calidades and blurred Spanish privilege, especially because of the familial and social networks that often granted them social ascent. Spanish and Indian or Spanish and African marriages, although rare, also provided a legal and sanctioned union by the Church. Familial and social networks formed from miscegenation and marriage benefited Indian and slave women more they did than men, mainly because of gendered realities. Similar to miscegenation and marriage, familial and social networks also led to manumissions. Despite the Crown's attempts to create a society that promoted Spanish domination and privilege, Indians and Africans and their descendants, labeled castas, constantly defied social hierarchy.

TWO

Regulating and Administering Freedom in Córdoba

By the end of the eighteenth century, miscegenation, marriage, and manumission had created a heterogeneous population in Córdoba, and census takers counted a quarter of that population as free. Together, free castas, slaves, and Indians outnumbered the Spanish population, 63 percent to 37 percent.[1] The governing authorities' reaction to these numbers was not to stop the freeing process but rather to regulate it so that the free and freed population could serve their larger political objectives. Regulations on the free and freed population most noticeably began in 1785 with the Edicts of Good Governance and continued during the wars of independence (1810–1819) and the republican period (1820–1840). These governing initiatives marked the beginnings of institutionalized whitening, as they constantly proposed a dichotomous reality of emulation, which uplifted and socially groomed the casta population, and condemnation, which reinforced Spanish privilege and social hierarchy.

REGULATING FREEDOM IN THE CITY

After the 1778 city census documented that 25 percent of its population were free African descendants, Spanish elites begun to behave "as if they were under siege from other racial groups."[2] To quell the fear of a casta takeover, governing and ecclesiastical authorities implemented a series of reforms aimed at reestablishing social hierarchy. These reforms were part of the Bourbon Reforms, which were ongoing throughout the Spanish Indies. These policies consisted of economic, political, and social reforms aimed at reestablishing order to increase revenue.[3] Governor Intendant Marqués de Sobremonte established the Edicts of Good Governance, which implemented surveillance on the streets and in private dwellings. Bishop Joseph Antonio San Alberto, a Spaniard and ardent follower of King Carlos III, established the only girl's school and orphanage to instill morality and civility in the city's most vulnerable population: children. Together, Sobremonte and San Alberto formed a vanguard defense of Spanish privilege at the end of the eighteenth century.

The Edicts of Good Governance focused first on bringing order to public spaces to transform the city into a formidable society that adhered to the larger political, economic, and social goals of the Bourbon Reforms. The edicts strengthened and regulated the corporate nature of the city, which encompassed various institutions that played integral roles in maintaining order. Among these institutions were convents and monasteries, guilds, confraternities, schools, and the university, but the most significant institution, the household, formed the basic unit of social control and discipline. Everyone in the household performed a specific role that ensured its function and order, and similarly everyone in society performed their role to ensure civil order and social peace. By enacting the Edicts of Good Governance, Sobremonte reinforced Spanish privilege, discipline, and morality on the street and in the home.

To control the streets, Sobremonte divided the city into six districts overseen by six *alcaldes de barrio* (city district magistrates).[4] Alcaldes policed their district and arrested anyone suspected of gambling, prostitution, and vagrancy. They also enforced a nightly curfew that forbade anyone to walk the streets "without precision and without light" or to ride a horse in the streets after dark.[5] Anyone caught on the streets without proper identification risked incarceration or conscription into the militia. The exception was abandoned children, whom alcaldes sent to guilds or public schools where they could learn a craft and become productive members of society.[6] The alcaldes focused primarily on occurrences in the street, often treating "internal domestic dissensions between parents and children or between masters and [*criados* (domestic slaves or servants)]" that did not cause a scandal as private affairs.[7] They intervened in the investigation only if they found that the actions in the home amounted to a scandal (transgression of customary values in the neighborhood). These interventions included suspected cases of cohabitation. Alcaldes on the street ensured that surveillance happened at all levels of society.

Sobremonte's policies largely targeted the nonelite and free African descendants because, according to Sobremonte, the root of all evil was idleness, which perverted "many unsuspecting [people] who lack knowledge or are governed by their natural inclinations to insolence . . . [leading them] to commit murder, robberies, and all kinds of evil."[8] Consequently, he instituted various edicts that restricted castas' movement and gathering. Edicts restricted their physical movement through a series of changes. Conchabados and free castas had to carry a *papel de conchabado* (proof of employment/identification paper) so that when questioned on the street by governing officials, they could prove they had employment.[9] If caught without their papeles de conchabados, free castas faced imprisonment and sentencing to four months of labor.

The edicts also regulated public spaces because, according to

Sobremonte, these spaces promoted vices and immoral acts. He prevented female hawkers from congregating on street corners and more than five castas from gathering in public spaces such as the local *pulpería* (grocery store).[10] These edicts dovetailed with the Church's goal to instill morality. A policy prohibited dancing in public spaces close to religious images and relics, because, according to Sobremonte, those dances were no more than "illicit diversions" celebrated on religious holy days. If castas wanted to proceed with those "diversions," the edict instructed that they do it in another place away from any religious image or relic. If people continued to dance near religious images and relics, they risked a fine upward of twenty-five pesos.[11] Overall, Sobremonte's edicts prohibited the free movement of castas to instill social order and to reinforce the social hierarchy, as well as morality, civility, and productivity within the city.[12]

Bishop Joseph Antonio San Alberto's concerns about the city became intertwined with Sobremonte's Edicts of Good Governance, which aimed to eliminate idleness and to target the majority casta population at the end of the eighteenth century. San Alberto was a contemporary of Sobremonte, and these men adhered to the goals of the Bourbon Reforms. Both agreed that to reassert Spanish privilege and social hierarchy in Córdoba, they had to eliminate ignorance, which disproportionately affected people who resided on the outskirts of the city and the pampas (countryside).[13] San Alberto further explained that the pampas's rustic landscape led to vices such as idleness, something that Sobremonte feared and used to justify his enactment of the Edicts of Good Governance.

Yet San Alberto did not blame people for their ignorance. Instead he questioned, "Is it their fault to have been born in the country [the pampas] not to [have been able to study] in schools [other than] their humble huts, not to have teachers other than the trees . . . ? This is not guilt but misfortune . . . [and its] gravity increases with days . . . and its results are pitiful to Religion and the State."[14] He found it unacceptable that "each neighbor forms his own separate pueblo, where he is the Father, Señor, Judge, Lawyer, Doctor and Teacher. [Moreover, if] they find someone among them that knows how to somewhat read, write, and answer some religious questions . . . that person is looked upon as a phenomenon and venerated as a Doctor or Teacher of Law."[15] According to San Alberto, formal education could uplift the barbaric and ignorant state of the people in the pampas, which remained affiliated with Indians who resisted colonization. More specifically, San Alberto's goals of education targeted those whom he considered the most vulnerable: orphans.[16]

Many of San Alberto's educational ideas, such as combating ignorance and Sobremonte's attempts to eliminate idleness, stemmed from Enlightenment *ilustrados* (advocates of the Spanish Enlightenment who sought to draw the Hispanic world into the European cultural mainstream) such as Gaspar Melchor Jovellanos, who promoted childhood education focused on *crianza* (building a child's character and overall development). Jovellanos argued that education must transform from a useless formality to one focused on the child's well-being, because formal education per Jovellanos taught children only the following: "to present themselves, sit and stand gracefully, speak with modesty, greet with kindness and politeness, eat with a napkin, and spend a lot of time teaching music, dance, fencing, and cultivating other nice useless talents, meanwhile the science of virtue, the basis of their natural and civil duties, [were] forgotten and . . . ignored, [which were] principles from which honesty proceeds."[17] Childhood education, he argued in his writings, had to promote more than just those superficial qualities. It had to instill the virtue that projected decency, modesty, and honesty, ending what Jovellanos defined as "moral ignorance." Moral ignorance led to all manner of evil and disorder, and these, Jovellanos said, "threaten equally the throne and the altar."[18] Moreover, education should not only teach logic and reason but also, he argued, instill desirable behavior: "It is certainly very important to illustrate their spirit, but even more important to rectify their heart. Important to direct them to use their ideas, but much more important [to direct them to use] their feelings and affections. . . . That is the objective of ethics, or the science of good behavior."[19] Ultimately, Jovellanos emphasized that "skills can bring states abundance . . . prosperity, but [only an education can give] peace, order, and virtue, without which all prosperity is precarious."[20] Jovellanos proposed an education that would concentrate on a child's well-being and instill ethical behavior in individuals. As vanguards of the Enlightenment, San Alberto and Sobremonte proposed these ideas when they created public schooling at the end of the eighteenth century.

Many of their ideas about public education would later be attributed to the well-known intellectual Domingo Sarmiento, the author of *Facundo: Civilization and Barbarism*, who would revisit these ideas in an effort to "civilize" Argentina in the mid-nineteenth century.[21] Sarmiento proposed that people in rural areas represented levels of barbarism, or ignorance, because they lacked basic levels of education, order, and work ethic, leaving the developing country destitute.[22] To combat this systemic problem, he proposed and supported European immigration to transform the pampas in the nineteenth century.[23] San Alberto and Sobremonte did not propose such extreme measures, as they still believed that most rural residents needed moral education, which would ultimately provide society with obedient children.

In 1782, San Alberto created the Real Casa de Niñas Nobles Huérfanas (the Royal House of Noble Orphaned Girls) and el Colegio de Niñas
Educandas (the School for Girls), an institution that served as both an
orphanage and a school.[24] As a man of God, he felt he had to rescue Spanish orphaned girls from the ills and vices of society and to give them a
good upbringing in the Church.[25] He targeted girls because of their vital
role as wives and mothers in the household. According to San Alberto,
a woman counseled not only her husband but also the entire family.[26]
Entrance requirements for the orphanage showed his commitment to res-
cuing orphans. He prioritized how orphan girls were chosen, giving pref-
erence to Spanish girls from honorable backgrounds who had lost both
parents, followed by those who had lost just one parent, and finally by girls
whose parents could not sustain them. They had to be poor, but he also
accepted a few girls who could pay their way. Moreover, he allowed up to
eight mulata orphans to join the school and "serve the rest." In turn, the
mulatas received "the same education, care and substance as the rest of
the girls."[27] They could not be younger than five years old or older than
fifteen and had to be free of all diseases and defects.[28]

By 1785, a total of thirty-six orphaned girls and seven girls who paid
for their stay had come from the city and various parts of the diocese to
attend.[29] The following year, Sobremonte founded the first public school
in the city, which he put under the direction of the Franciscans in 1786,
and quickly other schools followed throughout the province. Between 1791
and 1792, rural schools began to flourish in the most remote corners of the
province. Some were initiated by the government, and local authorities such
as small parishes started other schools.[30] San Alberto's institution served
the Edicts of Good Governance instituted by Sobremonte to eliminate idleness and ignorance and to create ideal obedient, docile women who would
become ideal mothers and in turn instill those lessons in their children.

But parents, accustomed to being in control of their children's education, objected to public schooling on practical and ideological grounds.
Within the more practical realm, the authorities' frustrations did not
consider that many parents depended on their children's labor. Ideologi-
cally, Sobremonte's schools intruded into the private sphere of the family,
causing parents to object because schools usurped parents' coveted role as
the guardians and caregivers of their children. In response, Sobremonte
ordered increased "vigilance to sustain the schools and win over the
opposition of the parents who wanted to raise their children as they were
raised."[31] This was meant to break the cycle of ignorance that Sobremonte
argued created idleness.

Despite parental opposition, Sobremonte and San Alberto remained committed to upholding and fostering social control, morality, and civility in an increasingly violent and turbulent period. In the midst of their reforms, the American Revolution ended, resulting in the birth of the first independent republic in the Americas. As well, the Tupac Amaru Rebellion of 1782 had just taken place in Peru. These events marked an ongoing Age of Revolution that at the beginning of the nineteenth century arrived on the Río de la Plata's shores.

WARS OF INDEPENDENCE: A NEW MEANING OF FREEDOM

The wars of independence in the Río de la Plata brought a new meaning of freedom. Freedom not only equated to personal release from bondage but also took on a political meaning, as the success of the wars of independence resulted in the end of Spanish rule and ushered in the republican period. The wars began in 1810 after two tumultuous years of debating and discussing what to do with the Spanish Crown, which the French had overtaken in 1808. The collapse of the Spanish Crown ignited Buenos Aires merchants, who had profited heavily from ties to the Atlantic economy, to push for sovereignty in 1810.[32] The resulting governing body, the United Provinces of the Río de la Plata, abolished the slave trade, instituted gradual abolition, and ended tribute, which institutionalized the freeing process, making individual freedom a sign of the new political body.[33]

The formation of the United Provinces of the Río de la Plata did not initially garner support from all provinces in the Río de la Plata. Instead, in Córdoba, former viceroy Santiago de Liniers and Governor Juan Antonio Gutiérrez de la Concha led the counterrevolution during the first months of the insurgency. However, a military expedition from Buenos Aires arrived in Córdoba and defeated them, beginning the wars of independence. In response, Liniers and other royalists fled northward and once captured were executed by the insurgent army.[34] After that confrontation, Córdoba officially joined the United Provinces of the Río de la Plata. But that did not stop cordobeses from thwarting the insurgency's efforts to recruit.

Under the rules of conscription, all able-bodied slaves between the ages of thirteen and sixty, the years during which a man was considered to have the most rigor and agility for the military, could serve. Slaveholders had to give "one for every three slaves, or two for every six." In exchange for their slaves, slaveholders would receive compensation prorated over three years with interest. But if slaveholders were found to be hiding their slaves, they would be condemned to losing all of them over four years of age. Once in the army, slaves were granted their freedom on the condition that they served for five years.[35] Both measures proved difficult to enforce. Slaveholders' compensation was complicated by the disagreement over jurisdiction. Provincial officials forwarded owners' requests for compensation to Buenos Aires because their slaves were used to satisfy the needs of the national government. Moreover, the lack of resources after the wars "make it doubtful" that compensation was granted to slaveholders.[36]

As a vast number of slaves in Córdoba belonged to the Church, an ardent defender of the Crown, the conscription of its slaves proved difficult. To comply with the Comisión de Rescate in Córdoba (commission responsible for the recruitment of slaves for the insurgency), the Church sent its sick and elderly slaves. In 1814, Santa Catalina presented two slaves, one of whom was sick. Frustrated, the Comisión asked that Santa Catalina replace its sick slave. In response, the convent argued that it had no additional slaves. Deeming the convent's response an act of insolence, the Comisión ordered an inventory of the convent's slaves. If necessary, it would send soldiers to conduct a head count. In response to this threat, Santa Catalina produced an additional ten slaves.[37] Similar attempts at evasion occurred among the elite. Dalmacio de Allende reported to the governor of Córdoba in 1814 that his slave would be of no use because "he lacked teeth . . . [so] he could not take out bullets [from the gun]."[38] Sickness became a clear defense mechanism against losing able-bodied slaves to war. Other slave ailments reported by the Comisión included an acrimonious disposition, epilepsy, fractured bones, two inguinal hernias and a cyst on the left knee, an internal abscess, an aneurism in a vital cavity, a dislocated knee and incapacitated arm, polyps on the base of the nose, and a fever caused by infection of the liver.[39]

Additionally, slaveholders proved a major impediment to the military recruitment of slaves. Widows argued that their slaves were given to them in their dowry and so were exempt from taxes. Others argued that their slaves were in the process of seeking their freedom and so could not be taken.[40] Still others went so far as to suggest that slavery remained a stable institution. In a letter written to the insurgent government, one petitioner shared his grievances about the burden that arose because of slave recruitment: "Slave ownership is the only source of wealth for inhabitants who are located in a resource poor country. [The inhabitants] need the union of many hands to provide themselves nourishment. . . . His Excellency [supreme director of the United Provinces of the Río de la Plata] knows very well that the sweat of an individual cannot produce the necessary land for the lives of many."[41] The petitioner's position was clearly a reflection of his way of life. Slave labor was an integral factor in this small city, and recruitment was starting to take its toll, as the petition noted: "The recruits [were] already up to more than five thousand, which had almost annihilated the subsidiary class of mercenaries. . . . [how could] owners cover the lack of their slaves. . . . It is a less favorable state for those inhabitants of the villages. . . . These are people with widespread poverty that make meager wages. . . . The good of the state cannot be in opposition to the comfortable existence of its members."[42] This petitioner further pointed to the stark differences between Córdoba and Buenos Aires. He argued that Buenos Aires "had become the emporium of America and its countryside, the granary of foreign countries, [and had] many lucrative occupations as well as inhabitants; Córdoba had converted into the image of backwardness and its countryside threatened to desolate all workers." The petitioner stressed that Buenos Aires was ignoring the impoverished reality of Córdoba in taking their slaves to fight in a war.[43]

Despite attempts to thwart slave recruitment, conscripted slaves proved their loyalty on the battlefield and set into motion revolutionary legislation that began the process of gradual abolition. During the wars of independence, the Buenos Aires–based government, the United Provinces of the Río de la Plata, abolished the slave trade in 1812 and enacted gradual abolition.[44] The process of gradual abolition was ultimately invested in enslaved African-descended women's reproduction. In 1813, the United Provinces of the Río de la Plata passed the Free Womb Act, which privileged maternity in the freeing process throughout the Río de la Plata. Before the Free Womb Act, children born to enslaved mothers were also slaves. But from 1813 onward, enslaved mothers produced free children, though slavery did not end for the mothers or any children born before that date because "the legal metaphor 'free womb' represented a separation between the unborn child and the womb that gave life: the first was freed while the latter remained enslaved."[45] Nonetheless, this law overturned the centuries-old practice of partus sequitur ventrem, which meant that children inherited the legal status, slave or free, of their mother. The new law granted freedom to all children born to female slaves in the Río de la Plata.[46] Enslaved mothers became progenitors of freedom. The United Provinces of the Río de la Plata labeled these freed children *libertos*.

Libertos achieved freedom in theory, but in practice they continued to serve their patrons. Various articles of the Free Womb Act, however, guaranteed various protections to the libertos. A patron had to report the birth of a liberto to the mayor within thirteen days and all the churches had to provide free baptisms and burials for libertos.[47] The act also required infants to be suckled for one year. Article five required a liberto under the age of two to accompany his mother if she was sold. For example, in 1837, don José Justo Garay bought Juana de la Vega and her children, five-year-old Fauvario and two-year-old Francisco, both noted as libertos, for 200 pesos.[48] These provisions acknowledged that slave motherhood also helped to cultivate slave families.[49] Other provisions, such as articles sixteen and fifteen, obligated libertos to live in the house of their patron until they reached the age of reason, twenty for boys and sixteen for girls, or until they married. They had to serve their patrons without pay until the age of fifteen for boys and fourteen for girls; after this, they would earn a peso per month. The money collected for their service, per article sixteen, would result in land, the tools to build a house, and seed for the first cultivation.[50]

Nonetheless the Free Womb Act proved hard to enforce. Many abuses occurred, such as separating infants from their mothers, mistreating libertos, attempting to deny their freedom once they came of age, and the most egregious act, selling them. Some owners sold libertos outside of the province of Córdoba, which made it difficult to find them and enforce their rights as libertos. In 1823, Córdoba's provincial governor, Juan Bautista Bustos, responded to owners who evaded the law that gave libertos eventual freedom. His decree stated: "Some owners [have] prostituted a ridiculous interest, having transferred and sold various libertos of those favored by the law of 1813. To attack this excess . . . I have resolved that no one is permitted to extract [from the province] said libertos."[51] The legal protections and recognition granted to libertos meant that Córdoba took steps to enforce the process of gradual abolition.

Libertos were more than slaves, but they were not quite free. This label became particularly important in cases where libertos appealed to courts to gain their freedom. Libertos' birth dates became a principal issue as they tried to prove their cases. In 1836, with evidence from baptismal records, the defensor de los pobres successfully demonstrated that Prudencio Calderón, a liberto, had the right to be free. His baptismal record stated: "Prudencio Calderón, one year of age and son of María Juana Nieva, slave of Doña Cruz Nieva, baptized on March 14, 1814." The proof provided by the parish established Prudencio's liberto status.[52] The Free Womb Act of 1813 served as a crucial element of gradual abolition in the Río de la Plata. In creating a freer republic, enslaved women became conduits of freedom and in turn assisted in the overall distancing and ending of slavery.

African-descended women in turn continued to be leaders of the manu-mission process, but instead of having to pay for freedom, as they did in the colonial period, they literally and figuratively give birth to it.

In 1813, the United Provinces of the Río de la Plata also abolished Indian servitude of all types.[53] The law acknowledged its previous elim-ination of Indian tribute in 1811 and extended it to include "the mita, encomiendas, the *yanaconazgo* [an indigenous labor system during the pre-Hispanic period], and personal service of Indians" and declared Indians "free and [endowed with] equal rights to all other citizens."[54] This legislation by the leaders in Buenos Aires recognized Indians' new role in the republic. They would no longer be servants, and according to the law they would enjoy the same rights as other free citizens. More-over, the law would "take immediate effect, [and] it would be published in all cities and towns . . . in Spanish, Guarani, Quechua, and Aymara for common intelligence."[55]

As with the Free Womb Act, the act abolishing Indian service proved hard to enforce throughout the provinces. In 1813, Feliciano Díaz, an Indian *juez pedáneo* (commissary) for the Las Lagunas, a former encomienda, emphasized that Father Balthasar Ponce de León, a vicar who worked in Las Lagunas, excessively threatened and punished the Indians.[56] Witnesses' testimonies agreed that Balthasar "threaten[ed] [Indians with] desertion, shackles, whipping and excommunication," and the witness Pedro González testified that Balthasar had put "shack-les on José Morales, a blind Indian" and that he had "whipped an Indian woman."[57] In the end, Díaz decided that rather than continue his peti-tion, he would work with Balthasar to correct these abuses. Francisco Antonio Ocampo, the governor of Córdoba, enacted a series of reforms that he noted "the despotic Spanish government" had introduced in 1814. These abuses, he further stated, are "no longer compatible with the liberal and beneficial ideas of the patria, and the natural and civil freedom that all inhabitants of this continent must enjoy."[58] His reforms stipulated the following:

> Every neighbor, inhabitant, or landowner who by himself and without express permission from the territorial judge, . . . whipp[ed] naturales [Indians] who are conchabados or listed in their haciendas will be fined for the first time in the amount of 100 pesos half applicable in favor of the whipped, and the remaining for the benefit of the poor families of that class residing in the district, for the second [offense] 200 pesos with the same distribution [as the first offense,] and for a third [offense] at the discretion of the government, and if they could not cover that amount[,]

they would be destined [to labor] in the public works of this city for a term of six months. [If and when necessary] only jueces pedaneos would be permitted to administer the lash.[59]

His stipulations granted conchabados who caused little problems for the governor protection from abusive patrons. The monies earned from the fine went to the victim as well as the community to provide some financial support, especially to the victim for lost wages if he or she could not work and to support his or her family. Moreover, his policy made clear that only *jueces pedaneos* (commissaries assigned to the countryside) could administer corporal punishment. Considering that some jueces, such as Felicano Díaz, were Indian, the stipulation gave them more autonomy to administer justice as they saw necessary. These provisions revealed that an emerging cordobés republic would no longer tolerate slavery or tribute because these represented a tyrannical past, while freedom represented an enlightened future.

The gradual abolition of slavery and the end of indigenous servitude as influenced by Buenos Aires exemplified a rejection of the colonial tradition of social hierarchy and an attempt, at least rhetorically, to create a republic based on liberalism. But it is important to note that slavery was already in decline in Córdoba. Unlike Buenos Aires, Córdoba did not experience a surge in its slave trade during the late colonial period, and this ultimately meant that the abolition of the slave trade in 1812 had little recourse in the city as few slaveholders bought or sold slaves from Africa or Buenos Aires. The slave trade ended in 1812, as is reflected in Córdoba's city census of 1813, which noted 105 slaves (fifty-four men and fifty-one women) from Africa and eleven slaves (four men and seven women) from Buenos Aires.[60] In 1822, the census listed forty-six slaves (twenty-eight men and eighteen women) from Africa and four female slaves from Buenos Aires.[61] By the 1832, the census listed only eleven slaves (seven men and four women) from Africa and none from Buenos Aires.[62] Moreover, the number of slaves sold decreased after 1813 largely because of the insurgent armies' demands for conscripted slave soldiers and a shift to a more militarized economy, which left little capital for the buying or selling of slaves in the private sector.

Nevertheless, there is no denial that the Free Womb Act enlarged the free population in Córdoba. Per the 1813 census, census takers counted 1,715 slaves and 3,060 free African descendants, which was a notable change from the 1778 census, which listed 2,243 slaves and 1,795 free African descendants. This trend continued in the 1822 and 1832 censuses, which each revealed a larger free population than an enslaved population (table 2.1).

The wars of independence did not originate in Córdoba. Instead the United Provinces of the Río de la Plata, based in Buenos Aires, led this movement and instituted the freeing process for enslaved individuals and Indians. This institutionalized freedom held political significance, because this new republican government intended to differentiate itself from its colonial predecessor. It became a republic of freedom, while the Spanish colony remained a reminder of coerced labor. Moreover, these reforms were aimed at garnering further support among enslaved and Indian populations in the fight for freedom and at garnering political

TABLE 2.1. LEGAL CONDITION OF AFRICAN
DESCENDANTS, 1778, 1813, 1822, AND 1832

	1778	1813	1822	1832
Condition	Number / %	Number / %	Number / %	Number / %
Free	1,795 / 44	3,060 / 64	3,765 / 77	3,192 / 85
Slave	2,243 / 56	1, 715 / 36	1,136 / 23	546 / 15
Total	4,038 / 100	4,775 / 100	4,901 / 100	3,738 / 100

Sources: AHPC, 1778, 1813, 1822, 1832 censuses of the city of Córdoba

allegiance for the republican project. In Córdoba, this resulted both in a freer population and in a society determined to maintain its colonial way of life.

ADMINISTERING FREEDOM IN THE REPUBLICAN PERIOD

Despite the outbreak of the wars of independence in 1810, colonial culture continued to shape the daily lives of the residents of Córdoba. The Church, and a few leading families such as the Cabrera, Funes, and Allende families, still dominated the city's social and economic landscape. From 1778 to 1832, Córdoba remained quite small, and the population increased only slightly, from 7,270 to 11,228.[63] However, one clear change did develop in the nineteenth century: the transition from slavery to freedom. Manumission had always been a possibility, but the new republic's stance on slavery and indigenous servitude accelerated the freedom process. Still, the culture of Córdoba in which freedom proliferated largely mirrored that of the city's colonial past.

One clear continuation of Córdoba's colonial past was the size and

shape of the city, which was relatively unchanged since its original con-
figuration in 1577. The 1813 map shows that the traza remained, as did
the significance of the cabildo, the cathedral, and the religious order the
Franciscans. The Franciscans controlled the Jesuits' former holdings: the
Jesuit block (university, church, and preparatory school) and their original
block, which had existed since 1577. Slight changes included the growth
of the city's sections from six to twelve, which reflected the population's
distribution according to status (figure 2.1). Most elite Spanish heads of
household lived north of the city, in sections six through ten, the exception being section twelve, the area closest to the cañada, the only section
in which there were more free casta heads of household than Spanish
heads of household. The free casta population included Indians, mestizos, and African descendants.[64] The sections south of the plaza, sections
one through five, had a more equal distribution of Spanish and free casta
households. Most slaves lived in section nine, which included the Church
of La Merced, and section four, which included Santo Domingo, Santa

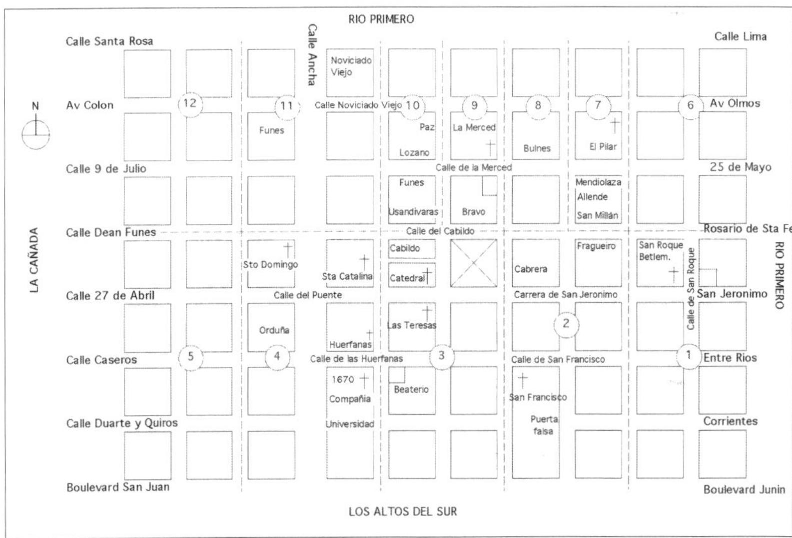

Figure 2.1. Layout of the city of Córdoba in sections, 1813. (1) San Roque; (2) no information; (3) Santa Teresa; (4) Santo Domingo, Santa Catalina, Monserrat; (5) extreme south-
west; (6) extreme northwest; (7) Church of Pilar; (8) between Church of Pilar and Church
of La Merced Section; (9) Church of La Merced; (10) between La Merced and the Old Novi
ciado; (11) Old Noviciado, Ancha Street; (12) extreme northwest. Courtesy of Federico Sartori Moyano. Reproduced by permission of Federico Sartori Moyano, from Alejandro Ali-
aga Moyano and Federico Sartori Moyano, "Los 12 'cuarteles' de la ciudad de Córdoba en el
padrón de 1813," in *Población y sociedad en tiempos de lucha por la emancipación*, ed. Sonia
Colantonio (Córdoba, Argentina: CIES-CONICET, 2013), 80, 279.

Catalina, and Monserrat, reflecting the Church's vast slave populations.[65] In general there tended to be a "darkening" to the south and the west of the city toward the outskirts and the cañada, which tended to flood.[66]

Calidad continued to mark a person's social status, which in turn determined their access to whiteness or privilege. However, from 1778 to 1832, new calidad labels appeared in the censuses, revealing a streamlining of calidad. Because of the war of independence, the Spanish label was practically nonexistent in the census of 1822. In 1813, during the fight for independence, the term "Spaniard" remained a clear demarcation of whiteness that separated white people from the rest of the population. However, after Córdoba's republic came into being in 1821, the term "noble" replaced "Spaniard," because "Spaniard" no longer encompassed the republican ideal.[67] The Spanish identity was associated with a former colonial status that had become criminalized. For example, in 1817, it was illegal for Spanish men to marry *americanas* (a label used to describe white women in Argentina after the wars of independence) or, according to the Reglamento Provisorio of 1821, Córdoba's first constitution, to vote or hold office as long as the Spanish government did not acknowledge the independence that the constitution claimed.[68] Because of the negativity associated with the label "Spaniard," census takers did not label those who affiliated with whiteness with that term, choosing instead overwhelmingly to use the term "noble," which also described a person's honor and reputed whiteness. Moreover, in the censuses from 1822 to 1832, the label *blanco* (white) also increased in use along with "noble." "Blanco" also revealed a hardening in calidad. The flexibility and fluidity of whiteness that characterized the eighteenth century started to give way at the beginning of the nineteenth century to a more fixed definition affiliated with color or an inherited trait.[69]

Like blanco, pardo (brown) marked a clear shift in calidad from an identity based on reputation and social and moral attributes to an identity based on inherited traits as the nineteenth century progressed. In the eighteenth century, ecclesiastical documents, such as the 1795 census and baptism and marriage records, frequently used the term "pardo," which most likely referred to mulatos. This is most likely because in the 1778 city census, the label "pardo" was practically nonexistent and the label "mulato" was more often used. But in the nineteenth century, census takers increasingly used the label "pardo" (table 2.2).[70] Most likely, pardo continued to refer to mulatos, along with those formerly labeled castas, such as mestizo, indio, zambo, *moreno* (dark brown; referring to an African descendant), and negro. Those designated by these casta labels experienced a decrease in population compared to pardos, who from 1813 to 1832 consistently constituted a large proportion of the population (table 2.2). The category "pardo" marked calidad's transition to a more permanent identity because it streamlined those formerly labeled as castas into one common group in an increasingly free population. The slow disappearance of these calidad labels collapsed these identities into a single category of "nonwhite." It also marked a concerted institutionalized effort at whitening; as with the decline of slavery, census takers no longer distinguished people who had once been labeled as castas.

With the elimination of tribute and the slow demise of slavery, free and freed people were not quite blancos/nobles but nor did they belong to their former calidades such as negro, which continued to be associated with slavery. Instead, they all became pardos. This shift did not mean,

TABLE 2.2. POPULATION BASED ON CALIDAD IN THE CITY
CENSUSES, 1813, 1822, AND 1832

	1813	1822	1832
Calidad	Number / %	Number / %	Number / %
Spaniard/ blanco/noble	3,511 / 42	3,857 / 40	4,777 / 43
Mestizo	19 / 0	16 / 0	5 / 0
Indio	56 / 1	32 / 0	480 / 4
Pardo	4,123 / 49	3,877 / 40	5,686 / 51
Mulato	61 / 1	0 / 0	0 / 0
Zambo	6 / 0	0 / 0	0 / 0
Moreno	14 / 0	51 / 1	0 / 0
Negro	524 / 6	648 / 7	100 / 1
Unknown	126 / 1	1,187 / 12	180 / 1
Total	8,440 / 100	9,668 / 100	11,228 / 100

Sources: AHPC 1813, 1822, 1832 censuses of the city of Córdoba

however, that former slaves were ready to be free and equal to blancos. The growth of the free population in Córdoba that began in the late eighteenth century did not make Córdoba a more egalitarian society. The year before the 1822 census, Córdoba's government enacted the Reglamento Provisorio, which defined a *ciudadano* (citizen). The Reglamento Provisorio, stated: "All free men who were born and reside in the province are citizens, but they will not enjoy the right to vote until they are 18 or to run for office until they have completed 25 years."[71] But the constitution imposed further restrictions on the free population. It stipulated that an African descendant had to be two generations removed from slavery to vote. The constitution also stipulated that free male African descendants could hold office only if they could prove that at least a great-great-grandparent had obtained his or her freedom.[72] According to governing authorities, two generations assured the removal of the stain of blackness and moral ignorance that was largely associated with slavery and provided free African descendants with enough time to learn virtuous behavior, civility, and morality. This requirement was very hard to prove, as a very select number of free African descendants could claim that their family had been free for four generations.

By subjecting free African descendants to additional qualifications, Córdoba's governing elite secured its status. To differentiate between those with and without privilege, this legal code put limitations on those who did not fit the prescribed notions of whiteness found in the definition and enactment of citizenship. This code benefited the elite republican families who could trace their social, political, and economic influence back to the end of the colonial period. Although these restrictions did not allow many free African descendants to enjoy citizenship fully, they still strove to better their lives and the lives of their children, as they had done in the colonial period.

CONCLUSION

In Córdoba, moral ignorance, defined as the lack of morality and obedience, posed a constant threat to Catholicism, social hierarchy, and order. By working together, Governor Intendant Marqués de Sobremonte and Bishop Joseph Antonio San Alberto, who represented the Crown and the Church, respectively, sought to instill Enlightenment ideals of crianza. In doing so, they focused on creating schools to teach children the qualities that would make them ideal, hardworking, and disciplined members of society. Through edicts and education, Sobremonte and San Alberto reestablished social order, control, and hierarchy in the small but prominent city of Córdoba. This small population in Córdoba created a privileged group of elite families who formed social and familial networks to protect their influence during the era of conquests and colonization. But more than two hundred years of miscegenation, marriage, and manumission in the city had created a large free and mixed population that no longer fit into this social hierarchy. It was within this milieu that Sobremonte enacted the Edicts of Good Governance and San Alberto created an orphanage and school for girls to reinstitute social hierarchy even as slavery began to disintegrate.

The transition to freedom accelerated because of the declaration of independence, which founded an insurgent governance, known as the United Provinces of the Río de la Plata, committed to ending what it defined as past colonial abuses, such as slavery and indigenous labor. It abolished the slave trade in 1812 and declared the Free Womb Act and the end of indigenous labor in 1813. The movement toward freedom was evident especially over the course of the republican period in which freed people outnumbered slaves. Even though Córdoba adhered to a gradual abolition of slavery, it did not create an egalitarian society. Instead, it maintained the colonial legacy of social hierarchy that privileged those who possessed whiteness and disenfranchised those who possessed blackness. Freed people could not hold government positions or vote unless they could remove the stain of their blackness. Despite these restrictions, African descendants, especially women of African descent, continued to accumulate wealth and free themselves and their family members. When whiteness became attainable, African-descended women redefined themselves to fit that model, even if it meant breaking laws, as we will see in the next chapter. They did so to create a better life for themselves and their children.

THREE

"Her Best Performance"
From Slave to Señora

On December 26, 1793, the ecclesiastical notary Tomás Montano informed don José Lino de León, a vicar of the Catholic Church in Córdoba, that he had caused a scandal of paramount proportions. According to the formal accusation, don José Lino had defamed his position "with little fear of God" by partaking in a scandalous relationship with his slave, Bernabela, treating "her less like a slave and more like a concubine." The prosecutor presented four pieces of evidence to support his accusation. First, he argued, Bernabela had a child out of wedlock. He revealed that don José Lino had purchased Bernabela and her eight-year-old daughter for 400 pesos from don Benito Cevallos.[1] Second, while a slave of don José Lino, Bernabela had another child, although the child later died. The identity of the child's father remained a mystery, but the prosecutor suspected don José Lino. Third, Bernabela wore clothes and accessories that were prohibited prohibited by the Edicts of Good Government. Fourth, don José Lino manumitted her, and she managed the household as if she were the señora (lady of the house).[2]

Don José Lino had cohabitated with Bernabela for ten years, and the ecclesiastical court found him guilty. However, don José Lino proclaimed his innocence, asking "how was it possible for him to engage in such acts as he was a priest and man of the Church?" Besides, don José Lino queried, "what proof did the court have?" If he truly had been in a known relationship with Bernabela, the Church would have stripped him of his title and position. Yet he remained a "practicing priest, [and] a representative of Christ's love" for Córdoba's residents.[3] His defense made no difference. The court placed don José Lino under house arrest, ordered him to participate in spiritual exercises, and forbade him from seeing Bernabela. The court further ordered Bernabela to stay at the Colegio de Niñas Educandas (School for Girls) and later banished her to Buenos Aires. Scared of never seeing Bernabela again, the priest dropped to his knees and, through his sobs, begged the bishop's forgiveness for the "scandal he had caused." While his implorations did not deter the court, don José Lino continued to try to be with Bernabela. In fact, her forced banishment only encouraged their scandalous affair. In response to her forced removal from Córdoba, don José Lino granted Bernabela her freedom, and she was no longer beholden to anyone. She could reunite with don José Lino provided they could avoid capture.

Superficially, this case describes a crime of passion that many priests succumbed to during the colonial period. The case involving Bernabela and don José Lino, however, went beyond an ordinary love affair. On closer examination, their illicit affair revealed important themes: women of African descent actively sought the privilege and status reserved for elite Spanish women by forging sexual relationships with elite Spanish men. Over the course of their relationship, Bernabela transformed into a señora, a title reserved for elite Spanish women. She no longer dressed like a slave (in functional skirts and shirts), and she frequently took pride in wearing forbidden silk clothing and gold accessories in public. Moreover, Bernabela managed the priest's household by giving orders to other slaves. Her transformation proved to be the most damning to both ecclesiastical and civil authorities because her social ascent broke moral and social codes: she cohabitated with a priest and she pretended to be an elite woman. Because of her actions and those of other African-descended women who emulated Spanish women, Marqués de Sobremonte, the governor intendant of Córdoba, targeted cohabitation and implemented sumptuary laws to bring order and obedience to Córdoba, then a small city of roughly eight thousand people comprising primarily castas.

Through the Bernabela case study, I argue in this chapter that women of African descent shaped their own status despite the hardening of calidad identities through sumptuary laws during the late eighteenth century. This case study represents everyday decisions that African-descended women such as Bernabela made in Córdoba. Bernabela's transformation reveals how a woman born into slavery could ascend to be a señora. It also illustrates the extrajudicial means African-descended women used to escape their blackness and to seek the privileges reserved for elite Spanish women. This escape did not derive from a physical manifestation caused by miscegenation but hinged on an African-descended woman's ability to ascend existing social hierarchies through distinct performative actions. Considered by ecclesiastical and governing authorities to have little or no morality because they lacked honor, women of African descent sought ways to secure the privileges they wanted.

COHABITATION: INTIMACY AND THE HOUSEHOLD

The early details of Bernabela's life reveal that she had always sought ways to escape the stain of her blackness through the intimate connections she cultivated with men. The 1772 baptismal records list Bernabela as María Gregoria's mother. However, unlike most castas, ecclesiastical authorities record María Gregoria's baptism in the Book of Spanish Baptisms, which suggests that her father, not listed, was likely white.[4] Based on these few details, it appears that Bernabela did not let her enslaved status stop her from bettering the life of her daughter. By having her daughter listed in the Book of Spanish Baptisms, Bernabela ensured that her daughter would be regarded as Spanish. In any or all future inquiries into María Gregoria's status, ecclesiastical authorities could reference her baptismal records and find that she was a Spaniard.

Six years later, the 1778 census takers recorded don Benito Cevallos as the slaveholder of a thirty-two-year-old mulata slave, Bernabela, and her daughter, María Gregoria, an eight-year-old mulata.[5] Two years later, don José Lino purchased Bernabela and her daughter for 400 pesos.[6] Despite the fact that Bernabela had a child out of wedlock, don José Lino testified that he had bought Bernabela because of her good reputation. Witness testimony suggests, however, that her physical attributes also played a role. Witnesses testified that Bernabela was "good looking, and so light she appeared to be a Spanish woman."[7] This description fit the ideal of female beauty in the eighteenth century, which an eighteenth-century dictionary defined in the following terms: "just proportion amongst the features; the union of one with others . . . in the vividness of the colors, imperceptibly embellished with white and flesh tones, which form the facial complexion."[8] This description equated female beauty with whiteness. Bernabela's light skin made her appear Spanish physically, and based on this description she also had the physical qualities that made her attractive and, according to witness testimony, seductive.

Shortly after Bernabela's purchase, the relationship between don José Lino and Bernabela turned sexual. Sexual relationships between Spanish slaveholders and slave women, such as don José Lino and Bernabela, illustrate the intricate relationship between attraction and inequality. Slaveholders expected slaves such as Bernabela to dutifully serve them and reproduce the slave population. For instance, a male slaveholder who owned a female slave of childbearing age, namely, sixteen to twenty-four years old, would expect her to bear more slaves. Some of these children may be the slaveholder's children, which he could beget with his female slave with few or no repercussions. Slave women could not protect their virginity and thereby maintain their honor; as a result, men "presumed [their] sexual availability," especially to those who resided in the household.[9] Consequently, the sexual abuse of female slaves was frequent, and these abuses remained within the household and rarely were reported to local authorities.[10] Conversely, as in the case of Bernabela, some slave women's presumed sexual accessibility transformed into a loving and intimate relationship.

Bernabela's early life as a domestic slave revealed how the household created an intimate space for her relationship with don José Lino to transform from one of a sexual attraction to one of cohabitation. According to historian Michelle McKinley, daily intimate relationships—both "domestic and sexual—were forged with soiled bed linens, fever-soaked rags, chamberpots, and breast milk."[11] These intimacies developed because of the gendered labor conditions in the household. As historians Pamela Scully and Diana Paton have argued, female slaves "performed conventionally feminine jobs."[12] Female slaves in Córdoba often worked as seamstresses, washerwomen, and maids and performed various domestic chores.[13] These tasks tied enslaved women directly to domestic labor, which solidified their physical presence in the house and created intimate relationships with members of the owner's family.[14] Over time, Bernabela and don José Lino's intimate relationship developed into cohabitation.

Cohabitation described a consensual sexual relationship in which a couple lived together without being married. It had similar characteristics to marriage, as it reinforced gender roles in the family, but it did not have the sacramental and legal protections of marriage, which proved especially vital in matters of inheritance, when the husband died. In Córdoba, casta women and elite Spanish men often cohabitated because marriage proved difficult, owing to the social stigma attached to being married to a woman with no honor.[15] Often, cohabitating relationships would last for long periods. José, a slave, and Juana María, an Indian, revealed in their court testimonies that they had lived together for eight years. For five years, José and Juana María had lived without intervention from or harassment by the authorities. This example revealed that as long as cohabitation did not affect more than the individuals involved in the sinful act, authorities left them alone. In fact, most people knew when cohabitation took place, and provided their relationship did not affect or hurt others, most authorities left the cohabiting couple alone.

But after authorities found out that José had a wife who resided in the city, their cohabitation caused a scandal. The court placed Juana María in a *casa de depósito* (a punitive boardinghouse for women).[16] This penalty, however, did not stop the couple from reuniting. After two days of being in the casa de depósito, José abducted Juana María and they ran away to the pampas, far from the watchful eyes of the city authorities. However, authorities apprehended José and put him in jail. When his owner, don

Esteban Palacios, posted his bail, he again broke the law, found Juana María, and lived with her in the pampas for another six months.[17] José and Juana María's cohabitation revealed the lengths people took to be with whom they chose regardless of legal ramifications or moral stigmas. Cohabitations that caused scandals carried a moral dimension that required authorities to intervene because the cohabitating couple's behavior affected other individuals.[18]

Similarly, the cohabitation of Petrona Funes, an African-descended woman, and don Maríano caused a scandal throughout the city, and authorities intervened to set an example and discourage similar crimes.[19] José Justo Rojas, a witness to their inappropriate relationship, testified that he had heard that Petrona was spending days and nights at don Maríano's house, which happened to be near where she lived. Moreover, Rojas testified that the relationship had lasted eight to nine months and was well known throughout the barrio. The alcalde also stressed how many people had complained about don Mariano and Petrona's relationship because Petrona did not set a good example for her children. By order of the governor, the alcalde put Petrona under doña Margarita Arguello's supervision for two months. To plead her innocence, Petrona came before the court and first confessed that while in the past she and don Maríano had "lived sinfully[,] . . . for over a year she had been separated from this unacceptable affair." The prosecutor countered, noting don Maríano's frequent visits to her house both day and night. She responded that he had, indeed, come to her house but that she only allowed him in because he passed her house on the way to his home. The prosecutor then asked if her daughters knew of her actions, which she affirmed. Finally, the prosecutor asked, "How could she not try . . . to repair her reputation?" Petrona replied that she "could not remedy it [the scandal] because of their [the barrio's] violence and nonsense [toward her] such as on various occasions not wanting to [respond to knocks on the door] they [the barrio] threw stones at her door." These actions reveal that the barrio administered its own justice to temper the actions of one of its members. In this case, the barrio found Petrona's actions unforgivable and deserving of public shame and disgrace.

Ultimately, the court ruled against her, sentencing Petrona to one year in the casa de depósito and depriving her of the ability to see her children so that her illicit affair did "not scandalize them" and banishing don Maríano from the city for two years.[20] This punishment affirms that the city would not tolerate scandals that would lead to further social disruption. Rather than risk the chance that don Maríano and Petrona would reignite their illicit affair, the court physically separated them. Ideally, Petrona would learn the error of her ways and become a moral example for her children.

Unlike Petrona and don Maríano's illicit affair, Bernabela and don José Lino's relationship caused a scandal not because of their choice to cohabitate but rather because they did so publicly and "with little fear of God."[21] Witnesses constantly noted that when he visited her, he would often go to the front door rather than to the back or side door. Going to the front door proved they did not care to hide their relationship. Moreover, according to the prosecutor, don José Lino allowed Bernabela to "ride publicly in his carriage (while he rode on the horse to give Bernabela and her daughter more room) and would allow her to use his bed in an intimate way along with other gestures of affection . . . such as visiting her during the day, providing her with a place to stay, sending her abundant food on the night of his arrival, visiting her during suspicious hours at night . . . giving her silk dresses, sending her money, and . . . gifting a house to her."[22] Don José Lino publicly displayed his affection for all to bear witness. In doing so, he treated her less like a free casta and more like his equal, which broke codes of social conduct.

Moreover, he had no intention of ending his affair with Bernabela. While reading a summary of his crime, the court further noted, "don José Lino proposed to continue the same behavior and way of life, with such determination that it had not been enough to contain [their relationship] with public censorship."[23] What made it worse was that don José Lino had begged the bishop for forgiveness, falling to his knees; however, per the court, he did not live up to his own promises to behave himself and end his relationship. Every chance he had, he sought to be with Bernabela. For example, doña María Garcia Díaz testified that, in exchange for travel to Buenos Aires, don José Lino contracted her to bring Bernabela on her return to Córdoba. To show his love for Bernabela and convince her to come back, don José Lino, according to doña María, gave Bernabela various gifts such as a "box of butter, 1 to 2 dozen hides, 10 to 12 silver pesos, and 1 to 2 half dozen pieces of candy and sweets."[24] These actions, the prosecutor argued, proved his disingenuous apology. He did not care about the consequences of his actions if Bernabela chose to return to him.[25] By publicly displaying their relationship, they legitimated its existence and challenged social hierarchies.

If Bernabela and don José Lino had attempted to keep their relationship secret and confined it to the private sphere, more than likely they could have continued their cohabitation without the intervention of the Church, as priests often solicited sex.[26] In Córdoba, inquisition cases revealed that priests solicited sexual relationships from women who lacked a male guardian in their lives, such as poor Spanish women between the ages of twenty-five and thirty, casta women between the ages of thirty and forty who were single widows, and orphans.[27] Priests solicited married women only when their husbands were of lower status; for example, Baleriana accused the Jesuit Joseph Mena of soliciting sex from her despite her being married.[28] Most of the priests accused of soliciting sex had affiliations with religious orders such as the Jesuits and Franciscans. The priests' religious affiliations were revealed in the court cases when slave women attempted to take on their sexual solicitors. Again, Baleriana, who worked on the Jesuit ranch in Alta Gracia, was an example, as was Manuela, who was a servant in the Convent of San Francisco.[29] In most cases, the slaves did not gain much, but they at least had the ability to publicly shame and dishonor the priests.

Don José Lino, a vicar and a prominent member of the Church community in Córdoba, risked everything to be with Bernabela.[30] At first, he found ways to correspond with her, even though that was strictly prohibited by the ecclesiastical judge. He also violated his house arrest by visiting her. On one of their escapades, he wrote to Bernabela, letting her know not to go to the city but instead to "go to his ranch in [Rio] Segundo, located eight or ten leagues from the city." Don José Lino continuously evaded authorities often escaping to his ranch, which always put him a step ahead of capture.[31] Unable to contain don José Lino's reckless behavior, the bishop sought the assistance of the commander of the militia to arrest him and place him in the seminary school, where they could better control his movements. There, the ecclesiastical judge allowed don José Lino to continue his priestly duties, such as celebrating mass and hearing confession. However, the bishop forbade him from seeing Bernabela.[32]

EDICTS OF GOOD GOVERNANCE: REESTABLISHING SOCIAL HIERARCHY

In the 1780s, Marqués de Sobremonte promulgated a series of polices known as the Edicts of Good Governance as part of his civilizing and modernization project for the city of Córdoba. His edicts sought to eliminate idleness because it provoked other immoral activities that took place in the streets, such as gambling, prostitution, and cohabitation.[33] To civilize the city, Sobremonte worked closely with the Church to eliminate immorality such as cohabitation, which, according to historian María Emma Mannarelli, constituted "the work of the devil" and "a crime against social order."[34] The edict ordered authorities "to guard vigilantly to avoid public cohabitation, [giving until the third violation] for those with no fear of God or respect for real justice [and who] lived wantonly and disorderly." After the third violation, the alcalde could consult "the priest and vicar for the most appropriate means to impede those sins, with prudence and moderation . . . [in regard] to the nature, condition, and state of the accomplices."[35] Together, the Church and the governor looked for various clues that would lead them to rid the streets and homes of immoral activities and reinforce order, discipline, and obedience.

To clean the streets of disruptive activities, alcaldes often conducted *visitas* (official visits into the homes or private dwellings suspected of engaging in immoral activities) to prevent domestic disturbances from becoming a scandal. For instance, authorities conducted a visita at don Josef's home at one thirty in the morning under suspicion that Segunda Estela, a free African descendant and married woman, was there to have sex with don Josef. When authorities found Segunda Estela with don Josef in his bedroom in the middle of the night with the door locked, the alcalde suspected that their actions could cause a scandal.[36] Segunda's free status signified that she did not have the constraints of a slave woman. She chose to go to his house even though she was a married woman. Moreover, according to the prosecutor, don Josef and Segunda Estela actively attempted to conceal their actions because they locked the door and their activities took place in the dark.

Within the small city of Córdoba, people lived very close to one another and movements between the house and the outside (e.g., streets, markets, plazas, or general stores) would not escape the eyes and ears of interested neighbors.[37] The night of the arrest, Martín Partanza, who slept on the patio behind don Josef's house, testified that Segunda had gone to don Josef's home with hopes of sleeping with don Josef; however, his wife already occupied the bed, so don Josef told Segunda that he could not have her that night and that she should look for another place to stay. Instead of leaving, Partanza argued, Segunda found her way into the bed chamber and hid in the closet. When the alcalde found her there, he arrested both don Josef and Segunda and placed them in jail. Another witness, a slave named Santiago Saldana, corroborated Partanza's testimony, stating that he saw Segunda in don Josef's room. However, the most damning testimony came from the minister of justice who had accompanied the alcalde. He testified that when he knocked on the door, Segunda ran out of the room, with "her skirts loosened and untied to Martín Partanza's room on the patio, but he did not want to allow her in, so she returned to the bedchamber, where the alcalde found her when he opened the door."[38] These testimonies reveal that public and private spheres often blended in Córdoba.

Both don Josef and Segunda countered the witnesses' accusations that they had an illicit affair with the claim that they shared domestic activities. Don Josef claimed that Segunda often frequented the house, sharing meals and, on eight occasions, coming for a siesta. But don Josef proclaimed that she never slept at his house at night. During the night of question, he stated, "Segunda was sick and [he] was taking care of her with the lights on, until very late." In making clear that their interactions occurred "with the lights on," don Josef stressed that appropriate activities took place. Finally, he testified, once she felt better he opened the door and they continued to converse.

Segunda's testimony followed, and she explained that these intimate activities did not indicate an illicit affair. In general, her testimony verified don Josef's story. Segunda mentioned that she had eaten at his house a few times and that she often delivered dinner and medicines for his aunt, whom she assisted, in the evening. Segunda stated that her visits always occurred in the presence of others and that the door always remained opened. The night in question, according to Segunda, was just another occasion in which she went to his house and people were there. Moreover, she did not know "who was knocking on the door" the night of her arrest and she did not "run out of [don Josef's] room." She remembered that don Josef told the slave Santiago to open the door, and she returned to the bedchamber, where the alcalde found her. But the court remained unconvinced because of these personal domestic activities.

In the case of Bernabela and don José Lino, the prosecutor also cited domestic activities as proof of cohabitation. While Bernabela remained in Buenos Aires, don José Lino could not control his sexual passions and so he found another woman, doña Francisca Bejarano. Doña Francisca, the prosecutor argued, served as a temporary replacement until don José Lino could be with Bernabela again. Witness testimony pointed to shared intimate activities as proof of this second illicit affair. During an unexpected visit, Tomás Montano, the notary who went to don José Lino's house to confirm future witnesses for the ongoing case, found doña Francisca at don José Lino's house at ten thirty in the morning. Doña Francisca was "alone and in domestic attire," and she told the notary that she "had been shaking out don José Lino's clothing."[39] The notary then returned two hours later and found doña Francisca still at the house, eating with don José Lino. Don Josef Antonio Roman, another witness, stated that doña Francisca had warned don José Lino that the notary would be stopping by and corroborated these intimate activities. Sharing meals with another woman who did not live in the household and having that woman do his laundry indicated an illicit relationship. According to historians María Emma Mannarelli and Eugenia Ambroggio, if a woman who did not belong to the household performed domestic chores such as washing a man's clothes or cooking, it provided enough proof of an illicit affair or cohabitation.[40]

The alcaldes' unannounced investigations in the household revealed the intrusive nature of the government under Marqués de Sobremonte. Under his rule, the Edicts of Good Governance sought to monitor the social behavior of the city. By administering the alcalde position, Sobremonte created direct oversight not only in the streets but also in the homes, as this case reveals. On more than one occasion, governing authorities entered the private home of don Josef to catch the suspected affair. Witnesses and governing authorities proved their cohabitation based on intimate activities such as sharing food, conversing, and doing domestic chores.

HER BEST PERFORMANCE: LA SEÑORA

Bernabela's relationship with don José Lino allowed her to transform into a señora. Born a slave, she attained a higher status that transcended racial and social norms, until ecclesiastical and civil authorities caught her. Her transformation demonstrates the performative nature of the roles that African-descended women undertook to escape their blackness. Bernabela did not rely on miscegenation to attain whiteness but on the ability to act as if she were a señora. However, there is no doubt that her light skin, which the prosecutor described as "white colored like a Spanish woman," made her performance more believable. Through emulation, Bernabela perfected the look and attitude of a señora.

A señora possessed lineage, reputation, and virtue.[41] These components described a Spanish woman's honor in eighteenth-century Córdoba. Lineage stemmed from the notion of pureza de sangre, which encompassed not only religion but also physical traits such as skin color.[42] Over time, calidad became associated more with skin color.[43] Spaniards possessed white skin, while castas, the nonelite, often had darker skin resulting from Spanish, Indian, and African miscegenation. Castas who had white skin and are described in documents as "taken for white" or "the color of a Spanish woman," such as Bernabela, possessed the physical characteristics of a señora.[44] This, however, did not make a casta woman a señora without a perceived reputation and status.

The second component of an honorable señora was a good reputation that others confirmed and recognized. According to historians Lyman Johnson and Sonya Lipsett-Rivera, honor defined "your very being. For in an honor-based culture there was no self-respect independent of the respect of others unless confirmed publicly."[45] All levels of society, from elite merchants to petty hawkers in the street, valued a good reputation because a good reputation allowed them to access economic, social, and political spheres of influence. For that reason, honor took on a performative quality. What a person wore and how others greeted them publicly confirmed or denied honor. Having already possessed the physical characteristics of lineage, Bernabela confirmed her perceived reputation as a señora of the house by dressing in clothes that only señoras could wear, such as silks, and wearing gold accessories.

The third component of honor was virtue.[46] Among women, and especially Spanish women, an honorable woman remained chaste until married, after which her honor was based on performing domestic duties, being a supportive wife, and being a good mother. This description did not extend to casta women, and especially not to enslaved African-descended women, because of their presumed sexual promiscuity. However, women of African descent did value honor, which they expected their peers to acknowledge, even if ecclesiastical officials or elites did not recognize it. Bernabela, who physically possessed the color of a señora and dressed like a señora, demanded that other slaves refer to her as the señora.[47]

As in the case of Bernabela, African-descended women who adopted these performative notions of honor achieved whiteness in Córdoba. In doing so, they disrupted a society built on social order and hierarchy because, as the historian Rebecca Earle has argued, "a mixed-race woman dressed in elegant European clothing truly belonged to a different racial [calidad] group from the same woman dressed in rags."[48] Clothing and adornment also played an integral role in shaping calidad, because they contributed to the "negotiation of reputation and of self-definition."[49] Clothing, according to historian Cecilia Moreyra, could be understood as both the most intimate apparatus within material culture, as it covered and protected the body, and the most public, because it projected to the outside world an image of the person.[50] In other words, clothing was a way to display calidad and a means by which to interpret others.[51] African descendants such as Bernabela, who fit the description "white colored like a Spanish woman," often had an advantage in manipulating their identity, mainly because they already possessed the physical traits of whiteness. Therefore, Bernabela's ability to become a señora marked her most ambitious and egregious act because her affiliation with don José Lino made her transformation a reality.

Cohabitating with don José Lino gave Bernabela the financial and moral support she needed to achieve whiteness. In turn, the prosecutor argued that don José Lino "conserved all . . . criminal passion for Bernabela and demonstrated it by correspondence and giving her installments of money, and other forms of maintenance and assistance."[52] Don José Lino's willingness to support Bernabela facilitated her transformation from a former slave to a señora. Witnesses such as Teresa, a slave of the household, stated, "[Don José Lino] demanded that the other slaves serve and respect her like a señora. . . . Every day they had to give her chocolate in bed and treat her with the same distinction as don José Lino de León."[53] When he visited Bernabela, a witness also commented that he gave her silk clothing and a train suitable for señoras. Another witness, don Manuel Uribe, remembered that while in Buenos Aires, Bernabela was treated like a lady and that both Bernabela and her daughter dressed liked señoras, which he found sufficient "to censure their conduct." These testimonies reveal that don José Lino served as an accomplice who broke societal hierarchies and thus his actions contributed to the breakdown of order. His disconcerting choices bothered governing authorities because they threatened their privileged status in a small city with a majority casta population.

Don José Lino's choice to adorn Bernabela in prohibited clothing and to encourage her performative actions was but one example of a trend that occurred throughout the colonial period.[54] Historians such as Nicole von Germeten note that slaveholders involved in loving relationships with their female slave often encouraged their transformation. In seventeenth-century Cartagena, enslaved Paula de Eguiluz's access to luxurious clothing "due to her relationship with her master, disrupted accepted social and racial hierarchies." She, like Bernabela, benefited from her relationship with her slaveholder and, according to von Germeten, "mocked the costume of proud Spanish doñas, who were obligated to keep their affairs slightly more private or risk public shame and dishonor."[55] Paula's choice to wear luxurious clothing suggested that she too had privilege, and that insulted elite women. Paula, a slave, did not have the right to wear the clothing reserved for those who possessed honor.

Slaves and free castas wore basic and functional clothing, which reflected their lower status (figure 3.1). Their clothes consisted of shirts and skirts with a large variety of fabrics, colors, adornments, designs, and prices. Shirts could be made of brittany, chambray, cheesecloth, and cambric. Some cost only one peso, while others cost up to ten pesos each. The difference in price depended on the embroidery, ruffles, and lace in the finest fabrics.[56] The simplest skirts consisted of coarse varieties of cloth, such as chintz, linen, and thin wool, and ranged in price from five to twelve pesos. Notably, these fabrics, especially linen, were also used for making curtains and bedspreads.[57]

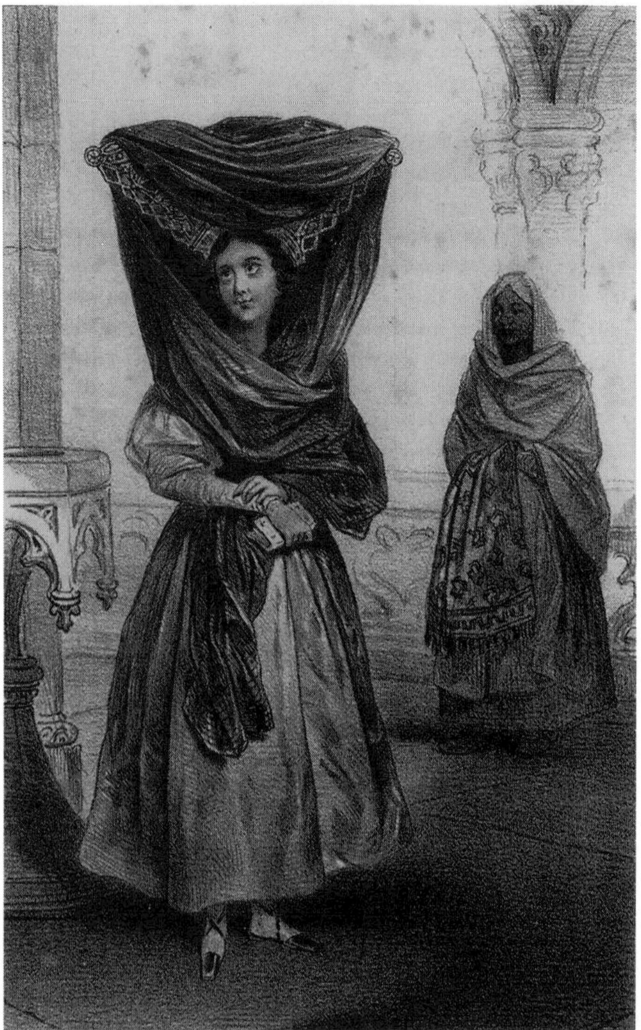

Figure 3.1. *Porteña, Costume di Eglise,* by Arsène Isabell, lithograph, 1835. Elite Argentine woman in foreground dressed for church in an elaborate headdress and expensive garments, and her black servant wearing typical garments for a woman of her status. Illustration courtesy of the John Carter Brown Library.

The use of expensive apparel and accessories fed into the idea of public reputation and ultimately represented whiteness and the privileges and societal superiority of elite Spanish women.[58] More expensive skirts consisted of silk, satin, taffeta, damask, velvet, brocade, and alpaca and valued between thirty and sixty-five pesos, although in some cases they cost up to 120 pesos. Those skirts always had some detail in other fine fabrics, at times even in gold and silver, and were preferred by elite women who wore them for public outings to display their wealth.[59] Dresses, the most expensive piece of women's clothing, consisted of two pieces, a skirt and a jacket made of taffeta, silk, or brocade, adorned with ribbons, galloon lace made of silver, gold, or silk, and buttons enameled with gold and silver. These garments exceeded one hundred pesos and were worn for special occasions.[60] These expensive garments proved an effective means for Spanish women to "jealously [defend] their prominent status."[61]

Spanish women's jealousy over their privileged status resulted in quick and fierce condemnation of casta women who deliberately wore expensive clothing. To stress this point, Concolorcorvo, a chronicler who visited Córdoba at the end of the eighteenth century, noted that "a certain bedecked mulata . . . was sent word by the ladies of the city that she should dress according to her station, but since she paid no attention to this reproach, they endured her negligence until one of the ladies, summoning her to her home under some other pretext, had the servants undress her, whip her, burn her finery before her eyes, and dress her in clothes befitting her class."[62] Concolorcorvo's example reveals the lengths to which Spanish women went to protect their status. These women sent "word," which more than likely meant that the ladies gossiped about the mulata. Their gossip, which eventually reached the mulata, recommended that the mulata stop wearing certain clothes. However, social policing through gossip did not work, as the mulata "paid no attention." Therefore, the elite women sent their servants to publicly shame the mulata. The use of servants to undress and whip the mulata, burn her fine clothes, and replace them with clothes "befitting her class" sent a message to other casta women to beware of their actions. Using servants also demonstrated that they too could be jealous of the social ascent of others in their community. By burning the mulata's clothes and replacing them with clothes that fit her class, they reminded her that her social ascent was fleeting.

Further questioning by the prosecutor in the case of Bernabela pointed to the problem of these performative transformations in which African-descended women tried to emulate something they were not. He noted that "señoras in Córdoba were very jealous of their rights and for that motive mulatas and other castas should never introduce the custom of dressing in silk or other things." "What people," he questioned, "could get used to seeing a carriage pass by with a mulata who appeared to be a woman of quality that little before had been known as a slave?"[63] The prosecutor's observation spoke to the entrenched culture of social hierarchy in Córdoba. Señoras valued the privilege and honor their whiteness garnered and had no intention of sharing it with lower classes, let alone with a former slave. Moreover, he posed the rhetorical question to emphasize the threatening nature of Bernabela's emulation, which disrupted and disregarded centuries of social hierarchy in the small, quaint city. Still, those who did not have the "inborn qualities" required for Spanish honor, such as Bernabela, chose to dress as if they did, putting on some of the greatest performances of their lives, as clothing provided not only social distinction but also a means of appropriation and emulation.[64]

African-descended women such as Bernabela who willingly chose to dress above their status despite harsh social condemnation were one catalyst for sumptuary laws, which according to historian Rebecca Earle were "employed only in cultures which consider it possible to disguise one's status via clothing."[65] In Córdoba, Marqués de Sobremonte passed a sumptuary law as part of his Edicts of Good Governance, which further restricted the use of certain adornments: "I order and command that no mulata or free negra woman or slave wear gold, pearls, or silk, and if she is married to a Spaniard, she can use earrings and chokers with gold in them, and a skirt with a border of silk, but cloaks of this genre [are not permitted under] penalty of losing everything."[66] Although the law gave casta women married to Spaniards some leeway, such as in the case of Eugenia, an African descendant and wife of Juan Bruno, a Spaniard, Spanish women in Córdoba continued to monitor their actions. The ostentation of Eugenia's dress alarmed so many elites that they called on the alcalde to get involved. The case reported that Eugenia wore forbidden garments such as a cloak and silk wardrobe to Church and in public. Moreover, her Spanish husband supported Eugenia's performative transformation because he bought the forbidden garments that she wore. Spanish women would tolerate only so much, as they emphasized that these clothes "only pertained to the nobility" and that to have a "mulata raised in the streets wear those clothes would be a grand prejudice to the government and result in various scandals," which is why they asked that "the matter be considered with the most prudent agreement and determination for the good government, peace, and quiet of" society. The alcalde threatened her husband, Juan Bruno, with a fine of 500 pesos if he did not correct the excessive luxury in her clothing.[67] Despite having been granted some leeway, Eugenia still had to abide by the rules of social hierarchy.

During the case against don José Lino, references made to the edict revealed that despite the sumptuary law's attempts to uphold racial and social hierarchies, the law often weakened those power structures. Sumptuary law, according to historian Alan Hunt, facilitated "competition and imitation since it was cheaper (economically and politically) for all parties to compete over the symbols than over what those symbols represented."[68]

During the questioning of various witnesses, the prosecutor demonstrated that authorities such as Sobremonte knew that Bernabela and her daughter, María Gregoria, "wore silk dresses and with excess, confusing them with señoras in rebellion of the governor's edicts."[69] Dressing in clothes made of silk hinted that Bernabela was a señora, and the governor intendant expressed that Bernabela should abstain from wearing those clothes in rebellion and instead use the clothes that befitted her status.[70]

Clothing allowed African-descended women such as Bernabela to mask and manipulate their identities, which in turn enabled them to dress the part and put on their greatest performance. Such actions by enslaved and freed women also allowed them to recover levels of femininity that had been denied to them.[71] Many enslaved and free women worked in arduous and dirty conditions. Their clothes reflected their labor. Rarely did they have the opportunity to wear elegant clothing, but by subverting the law they reclaimed their femininity because they dressed like señoras, the quintessential example of femininity. The willingness to seek the honor and privilege granted to señoras only fueled African-descended women's emulation.

This emulation was made possible because of the malleability of identity further revealed in Bernabela and don José Lino's relationship. Don José Lino continued to give Bernabela the authority to govern the daily routines and business of the house and demanded that his slaves respect and serve her. These actions embodied those shown to a señora. Bernabela went from being a slave to being a señora, with the support of her lover, don José Lino. One witness, don Pedro Josef de la Quadra, claimed he had known don José Lino since the latter had arrived in Córdoba in 1781 or 1782. He further stressed that Bernabela had lived in the same house as don José Lino as his slave "who manifested into his woman of affection, giving her dominance and superiority over the other slaves who only called her señora Bernabela because he demanded it." Moreover, a fellow slave in the household, Teresa, corroborated don Pedro de Josef's account, stating that "even the black women from Guinea and the *criadas* [female domestic slaves] called her señora Bernabela." Having the respect of the slaves made it clear that Bernabela had escaped her previous life as a slave, and for women like her, according to historian Junia Furtado, it was essential to show "herself to be the owner of a 'grand mansion'" and "remove[d] from the world of work."[72] If she was going to be a señora, she had to act like a señora.

Over time, her attitude also had to change from that of a slave and concubine to that of a señora who demanded respect from others. Acting like a señora marked Bernabela's final transformation and revealed how

African-descended women could escape their blackness and the stain of their former slave past. In Bernabela's case, it was not a physical manifestation that took place because of racial mixture—although the description of Bernabela as "white colored like a Spanish woman" suggests that her white skin came from earlier generations of miscegenation—but the performance she gave that whitened her identity. Formerly a slave, she had risen to become the de facto lady of the house, and that is how she completed her transformation. Spanish women, the governor, and even her former peers recognized that she had transgressed social hierarchies.

CONCLUSION

The case involving Bernabela and don José Lino highlights how a relationship between a slave and her slaveholder could develop into cohabitation and later a scandal. Bernabela began her life as a slave who had a child out of wedlock, but her early life revealed that she had taken steps to socially ascend by having her daughter's birth recorded in the Book of Spanish Baptisms. A few years later, don José Lino purchased Bernabela and her daughter. Over time, the dynamics of their slave and slaveholder relationship grew into cohabitation. This relationship largely developed because it took place within the confines of the household, which ensured their daily interaction. Bernabela and don José Lino's relationship initially did not cause a scandal because many priests solicited sex from their slaves and free castas. Instead the relationship caused a scandal because they chose to publicize their cohabitation. A scandal eventually led to public and social disorder, and that is why authorities such as Governor Intendant Marqués de Sobremonte targeted cohabitation to prevent scandals and reinforced social hierarchies.

Bernabela's transformation into a señora revealed the larger context of African-descended women's assigned blackness through perceptions of their sexuality. Their own nuanced, self-fashioned, and public displays contrasted with how elites, the law, and the Church viewed them. Bernabela, however, did not remain a slave who eventually bought her freedom; rather, she became the señora (lady of the house). Both don José Lino and Bernabela valued their relationship and chose to publicly display it to others. Moreover, Bernabela defied social norms, cohabitating with a priest and portraying herself as an elite woman, which revealed her intentions to seek the privileges denied to her because of her blackness. Although she was not born with honor and privilege, she could emulate and imitate a señora. This constituted her greatest performance.

Once casta women had the look, they then had to embody the

attitude if they were to make the final transformation. Bernabela and don José Lino's case study reveals how these women sought ways to achieve whiteness to better their lives and the lives of their children. But Bernabela's transformation to a señora worked only so long as they were not caught. Indeed, it proved a risky affair. Despite her success at becoming the señora, her illicit affair with a vicar was more than society and the government could handle. If she could have married him, she not only would have maintained her status as a señora but also would have become a woman of his class.[73]

FOUR

"A Woman of His Class"
Contested Intermarriages

In Córdoba in 1798, doña Magdalena López requested that don José Lino, a priest embroiled in an illicit affair with his concubine, Bernabela, serve as a key witness for her court case. She objected to the choice that her son, Ramón Romero, had made in marriage. She argued that María Mercedes Ferreyra, his wife-to-be, came from an inferior linage because her deceased father was rumored to be a mulato from Chile. Don José Lino obliged because he had known Mercedes Ferreyra's parents for some time. He certified that Mercedes Ferreyra came from an "inferior extraction and calidad." He did not state she had African ancestry but instead referenced her calidad as being inferior to Ramón Romero's assumed Spanish ancestry. Despite his own private affair with Bernabela, a woman noted for "being the color of a Spanish woman," and most likely because he remained under the watchful eye of the bishop, he objected to the marriage owing to the apparent inequality.[1]

In this case, don José Lino provided crucial testimony that proved Mercedes Ferreyra had inferior lineage, so the court upheld doña Magdalena's objection to their marriage. But sometimes fiancées accused of having inferior lineage—most often associated with African heritage—could convince the court that accusations of their inferiority were based on a mistaken identity and that in fact they were Spanish or Indian. In this chapter, I argue that women accused of having mala sangre worked within the limits of the law to achieve whiteness by marrying Spanish men. Furthermore, I examine their evasion of blackness through marriage dissent cases.

In Córdoba, marriage dissent cases existed throughout the late eighteenth century and into the nineteenth century, with one of the last cases tried in 1850. A marriage dissent case came about after a parent or guardian denied a betrothed couple the right to marry, which the Royal Pragmatic of 1776, a Bourbon Reform policy continued in Córdoba two years later, permitted, and as a result the couple sought to overturn their negated marriage in court. The persistence of marriage dissent stemmed from ecclesiastical and civil authorities who focused on maintaining social hierarchy in a small city that had a majority casta population. Yet, the verdicts of marriage dissent cases reveal a slightly higher rate in favor of the betrothed's marriage, 52 percent versus 48 percent, than against it.[2] In cases that ruled in favor of the couple, the couple often argued a case of mistaken identity. The woman accused of having inferior lineage was in fact a Spaniard or Indian. By claiming a Spanish or Indian identity, these potential wives appropriated the ideal notions of a wife in Córdoba. In cases in which the fiancée acknowledged her African ancestry and honor, marriage dissent succeeded, mainly because civil authorities did not protect African-descended women's honor. By examining the two strategies put forward, this chapter reveals that the fluidity and flexibility of calidad in Córdoba provided women of African descent who were accused of African ancestry in marriage dissent cases with a means to socially ascend within the confines of the law. Marriage dissent cases also provide a crucial juxtaposition with the previous chapter, which examined women of African descent in cohabiting relationships who resorted to illegal measures, such as wearing prohibited clothing and accessories, to secure privilege and status. But a concubine was also a very precarious status; once caught, as in the case of don José Lino and Bernabela, it could lead to excommunication from the Church and a loss of social and economic influence in society. Marriage, however, had more permanent social and political benefits and clearly was an institution worth fighting for.

INTERMARRIAGES BEFORE THE ROYAL PRAGMATIC OF 1776

During Córdoba's colonial period before the enactment of the Royal Pragmatic of 1776 marriage provided an avenue of social ascent for people of African descent. Despite the small number of free and enslaved women and Spanish men who married—6 out of 947 in the seventeenth century and 25 out of 2,918 marriages in the eighteenth century and early nineteenth century—these marriages often were the means for African-descended women to provide a better life for their children and themselves.[3] Intermarriages also provide insight into upward mobility among castas. Marriages involving Indians and African descendants reveal the extent to which these two groups comingled and lived together in the city and the pampas. They also demonstrate that even when castas could not achieve whiteness, they still found ways to better the lives of their children. Children born from a marriage between Indian women and enslaved men reveals this practice. Indian women provided a way for enslaved men to guarantee that their children would be free and thus removed from the stain of former enslavement.

In marriages in which enslaved women married Spanish men, six slave women successfully achieved the coveted title of doña.[4] In 1765, casta marriage records listed Juan Bautista Ferreyra, also known as José Ferreyra, who originated from Rio de Janeiro, and described as a free pardo, as married to Teresa Sotelo, a slave. Thirteen years later, the census of 1778 noted a meaningful change in their calidades. José Ferreyra transformed into a Spaniard and Teresa a mestiza. The census also noted Teresa as the head of household, which consisted of José Ferreyra, her husband, their five girls, and a free negra named Theodora Romero.[5] Teresa Sotelo made her final transformation to doña after the death of her husband. The widow then married don José Antonio Garcia in 1788. In 1811, the census listed them as Spaniards in the Salcaste, a small provincial town, and she had the title doña. Often married couples such as don José and doña Teresa would leave the city and settle in places where they could start new lives and assume new identities. In this case, Teresa started life as a slave in the city, then transformed to a mestiza, and later became a doña in another town.[6] Her ascendancy revealed that physical mobility enhanced the effects of a fluid and continuously evolving identity at the end of the eighteenth century. Having moved with her new husband from the city where she was known to have been a slave to a small town as a doña, Teresa made the final transformation through the social networks she shared with her husband.

Similarly, Ana Isabel Olmos also achieved the coveted title doña because of her husband, don Joaquín , who had emigrated from Spain. In 1765, don Joaquín freed Ana, a parda, the same year of their marriage.[7] Don Joaquín's will showed that he brought roughly 10,000 to 12,000 pesos to the marriage, while Ana brought "nothing."[8] When they married, both don Joaquín and Ana already had children from other relationships. Don Joaquín had a son named José Gavino and Ana had a daughter named Teresa, and while married they had a son, José Andres. Don Joaquín's wealth, which came from his merchant activities, gave Ana, her daughter, Teresa, and their son, José Andres, a very comfortable lifestyle. While married, Ana received various gifts such as colorful skirts, bodices, gold earrings, and pearls, which assisted in her transformation from slave to doña.[9]

Additionally, when Teresa married in 1773, before don Joaquín's death, her dowry included 265 pesos, clothing and adornments such as petticoats, stockings, skirts, bodices, shirts, ribbons, shoes, silver buckles, and gold earrings, and the more traditional objects such as bedding, a mattress, sheets, pillows, blankets, and some merchandise for sale such as yerba, sugar, and honey. Their shared son, José Andres, received the farm, various items in their rented home in the city, three slaves, and all of his father's clothes (which included French suits).[10] Thirty years after their marriage, the 1795 census described Ana as a forty-five-year-old widowed doña living with two slaves, José Bernardo and Pedro Ignacio, whom she inherited from don Joaquín, along with furniture, several domestic appliances, salt and capers to sell, and silver objects.[11] Because of their marriage, Ana achieved a coveted whiteness and privileges that also extended to her children, Teresa and José Andres.

Between 1720 and 1779, both Indian men and women tended to marry slaves.[12] These marriages did not directly benefit the spouses, but they did guarantee a better future for their children. Because the Royal Provision of 1542 prohibited Indian enslavement, enslaved men sought Indian and free women of African descent to ensure their children's freedom, because their children inherited their mother's free status.[13] In turn, Indian women sought enslaved men because their children would be exempt from paying tribute. This practice took place as early as the seventeenth century in the Río de la Plata, where, according to historian Daisy Rípodas Ardanaz, Indian women often enjoyed certain freedoms after leaving their pueblos to be with African descendants, because their children would be exempted from paying tribute, while enslaved men knew their children would be free.[14] Most likely the trend continued in the eighteenth century and explains why there was such a high rate of marriage between Indian women and enslaved men as the eighteenth century progressed.[15]

Marriages between enslaved women and Indian men also provided upward mobility but not to the same extent as marriages between Indian women and enslaved men. Because a child inherited their mother's status, the children resulting from these relationships would become slaves. However, they would no longer have to pay tribute in Córdoba. Additionally, Indian men who married enslaved women moved to the residence of their enslaved wives, which meant they were no longer subject to paying tribute but would be subject to the discipline of the wife's household.[16] For instance, Thomas Paragaui, whose last name suggests that he had originated from the Jesuit missions located in Paraguay, married a slave. He lived on the same Jesuit ranch, Jesús María, located in the province of Córdoba, as his wife under the "same conditions."[17] Even though marriages between Indian men and enslaved women did not produce the same freedoms, the tendency for Indian men to marry enslaved women in the eighteenth century suggests that social mobility did occur. Social mobility among castas must be emphasized, because despite how ecclesiastical and governing authorities viewed and categorized castas, among themselves, castas had their own qualifications and hierarchies.

THE ROYAL PRAGMATIC OF 1776 AND ITS SUBSEQUENT DECREES: THE REINFORCEMENT OF SOCIAL HIERARCHY

The Royal Pragmatic of 1776 specifically targeted potential marriages that were deemed a threat to social order. Charles III enacted this decree as part of a series of policies known as the Bourbon Reforms to reinforce social hierarchy and order throughout the kingdom. Under the Bourbon Reforms, the Spanish Indies increased revenue, challenged the Church by removing the Jesuits, reorganized political jurisdictions, and strengthened the military. Various policies targeted free castas by controlling their movements, ensuring they had a steady income, and instilling socially and morally correct behavior. These reforms not only governed the public sphere but also addressed the interworkings of the family. The family represented a microcosm of the larger empire; thus, by extension, the King represented the supreme father figure. In his role as the Father King, he safeguarded the social order and hierarchy. He authorized the Royal Pragmatic to guarantee that at the most basic level, marriage would remain an institution that protected the elites' interests.

To ensure that children did not make a mistake in choosing a marriage partner, the Crown reinforced the usurpation of the family's interest over rash individual choices.[18] According to the Royal Pragmatic, children, often influenced by emotion, contracted marriages with "unequals" without waiting for parental consent or guidance.[19] Their rash decision resulted in "the perturbation of good order . . . [and] continuous discord and prejudices in the families."[20] Charles III's decree protected the family and by extension social order. It required sons and daughters younger than twenty-five to receive permission from their parents (or those in their place) to marry. Sons and daughters younger than twenty-five were believed to base their opinions on emotion rather than logic, and of course, according to the King, they lacked the experience necessary to "reflect on the consequence and anticipate in time the [possible] troublesome results, prejudicial to the families and the public."[21] Those older than twenty-five were also required to obtain parental consent; however, if the parents did not approve, the marriage would still be valid, although the parents could disinherit their son or daughter.[22] This measure reinforced the Crown's patriarchal rule in the home and private dwellings. In doing so, the Pragmatic preserved "the fathers' regular authority in families, so that all rights belonged to them in the intervention in and consent to their children's marriages."[23] This further ensured that the family's interests came before the individuals' desires.

The Pragmatic also provided the means through which parents throughout the Indies could assert a measure of control that superseded that of the Church, which had traditionally protected an individual's right to choose his or her future spouse. Careful not to anger the Church, the King incorporated the sacrament of marriage in the Pragmatic, stating that he would "leave unharmed the ecclesiastical authority and canon dispositions of marriage," thus ensuring that "the spiritual effects" of marriage remained.[24] This wording allowed the Church to maintain authority over the sanctity of marriage as a spiritual act and thus ensure that marriage would remain within the Church's religious boundaries.

Nonetheless, King Charles III noted that parents should consent to marriages if they did not cause immediate harm to the family's honor or to the Crown. To curb any potential irrational dissent from the parents, the couple had the right to appeal their decision to the Royal Justice and have it resolved within eight days, or to appeal to the Chancellery council or *audiencia* (the highest royal court of appeals within a jurisdiction such as the viceroyalty) in the Indies and have it resolved within thirty days.[25] These appeals would no longer take place within the ecclesiastical system but rather within the civil courts. This switch ensured that the Church's notion of free will would not influence or interfere with the Crown's goal of reinforcing the social hierarchy. This stipulation formed the basis of marriage dissent cases.

Two years later, the Crown enacted the decree throughout the Spanish Indies, which maintained the original Royal Pragmatic guidelines with slight modifications to the cultural and demographic differences in the Indies. First, the term "unequal marriages" remained undefined.[26] However, based on marriage dissent cases in Córdoba, parents often cited *tenía mala sangre* (he or she has tainted blood) or *desigual linaje* (unequal lineage) as reasons to prohibit their son's or daughter's marriage to a person accused of having mala sangre.[27] Second, the Royal Pragmatic of 1776 "included everyone from the highest classes of the State without exception to the most common [classes]."[28] The 1778 decree, however, clearly defined what groups would be included, such as Indians, and what groups would be excluded, such as African descendants. According to historian Steinar Saether, the inclusion of Indians and the exclusion of African descendants in the 1778 decree revealed the Council of the Indies' (the Crown's advisors on the Americas) "enlightened and absolutist eagerness to create order."[29] The Crown sought to reinforce social hierarchy, which in general privileged Indians over African descendants. These differences between the original Royal Pragmatic and its subsequent decree reflected the Crown's understanding of the Spanish Indies as demographically and culturally different from the peninsula and therefore the need to adjust the law.

The king's willingness to include Indians extended his protectionist views over the Indian population, which more than likely dated to the original intent of conquest: namely, to evangelize and civilize the Indian population. Still, the law did not apply equally to all Indians. Tributary Indians had to obtain parental consent. If their parents could not provide consent, then priests who would not receive any duties, gratuities, or recompense had the right to grant consent. Moreover, the 1778 decree stated that because of "Indian caciques' noble status, [they] are considered to be in the same class as distinguished Spaniards for everything forewarned in the Royal Pragmatic [of 1776]."[30] This classification in the 1778 decree may have its roots in the Crown's seventeenth-century marriage policy. According to Beatriz Bixio, a historian who examines seventeenth-century Córdoba, the Crown allowed marriages between Spanish men and Indian women because they secured Spanish settlement.[31] Most importantly, these intermarriages formed political, military, and economic alliances.[32]

The 1778 decree excluded people of African descent, such as "mulattos, negros, coyotes, and individuals of castas and similar races publicly held and reputed to be so," because of their assumed illegitimate status, which ruled out their consideration.[33] However, the decree included African-descended officers in the militia and African descendants who had "distinguished themselves from the rest by their reputation, good operations and services." The law subjected them to the same rules and further suggested that they "should be advised to understand the natural obligation they have to honor and venerate their elders."[34] As with Indians, the Crown did not treat all African descendants in the same way. African descendants who had proven their honor though the virtuous act of service had to abide by the same marriage laws as Spaniards and Indians.

Over the next twenty-five years, the Crown revised the Royal Pragmatic of 1776 because litigation forced further review of the law. A final revision to the Royal Pragmatic occurred in 1805, directly influenced by the intermarriages that occurred in the Río de la Plata. After Marqués de Sobremonte, viceroy of the Río de la Plata and a former governor intendant of Córdoba, expressed concern that "nobles and those of pure Spanish blood were attempting to marry blacks, mulatos, and other castas," the Crown prohibited marriages between the Spaniards and African descendants (which reinforced the original intention of the Royal Pragmatic of 1776).[35] After 1805, all intermarriages involving an African descendant had to receive permission regardless of the betrotheds' ages. Unlike the Pragmatic of 1776 or the 1778 decree, the 1805 decree's revision to the law deemed those who possessed African ancestry to be "unequal," which was grounds for prohibiting a marriage.

Victorino Rodríguez, the governor intendant of Córdoba (1805–1807), reiterated this law two years later. He stated, "They must not allow marriages between those who have inequality, of which one of them has pure origins and the other notoriously of the mulato or negro class."[36] Rodriguez's support of the law reveals intermarriages involving African descendants and Spaniards in Córdoba continued despite the revisions to the Royal Pragmatic in 1805. In Córdoba, eight of the twenty-five, or one-third, of all intermarriages involving African-descended women and Spanish men from 1700 to 1810 occurred after the enactment of the Royal Pragmatic of 1776. These marriages demonstrated the active role of women of African descent in the whitening process. Ignacia, a slave and mother to three children, Manuela, Gregorio, and Bárbara, married José Lorenzo de los Santos, who originated from Portugal in 1786. In the 1795 census, the married couple's household noted some changes. First, the census listed Ignacia as doña Ana Ignacia Roma and wife of don José Lorenzo de los Santos. Second, they had seven children, Bárbara, born a slave but listed as doña Bárbara, Juan, Pedro Pablo, Antonio José, Antonino, María Antonia, and María de la Cruz, who lived in the household. Born a slave, Ignacia not only whitened herself, becoming doña Ana Ignacia, but also whitened the lives of at least two daughters: Bárbara, who became doña Bárbara, and María de la Cruz, whose baptism was listed in the Book of Spanish Baptisms.[37] This marriage, which took place after the implementation of the Royal Pragmatic of 1776, reveals that despite attempts to curb unequal marriages and prevent African-descended women from achieving whiteness, these women still succeeded in changing their status through marriage, thwarting the intention of the law.

Still, intermarriages in Córdoba tended to be more conservative in comparison to other regions of the Río de la Plata. A comparison among regions in the Río de la Plata reveals that Córdoba's more traditional and conservative society produced fewer intermarriages than did Buenos Aires, where intermarriages had increased notably by the end of the eighteenth century and continued to increase into the nineteenth century. Historian Susan Socolow argues that the difference between the rate of intermarriage in Buenos Aires and the rate of intermarriage in Córdoba derives from the cities' respective economies. Since the seventeenth century, Córdoba's economy had strongly depended on its mule trade. By the first half of the eighteenth century, Córdoba had experienced both economic and demographic stagnation. By the mid-eighteenth century, it had become "a net exporter of population both to the north (Jujuy) and to the south (Buenos Aires)." Although the economy improved under the viceroyalty period of 1776 to 1810, Socolow argues that the "economic base of the city was always too small to support the local population." Buenos Aires, by contrast, had experienced steady economic growth since the seventeenth century. As a port city, it served as a commercial entrepôt and focused on processing and exporting hides. It also had a large artisan population.[38] Because of its economic strength and continued growth, Buenos Aires often overlooked calidad differences in marriages, provided that the fiancé could economically support his wife. The difference in intermarriage rates in the Río de la Plata shows how the political and economic environments shaped notions of whiteness, which in turn granted an individual privilege and honor.

The examination of the Royal Pragmatic and its subsequent corollaries revealed the Crown's attempt to introduce the Bourbon Reforms' goals of social order and discipline into the home. In doing so, the Crown attempted to curb all social disorder at its root, namely, the family. As the supreme father figure, the king enacted the Royal Pragmatic to protect and preserve the patriarchal government and instill social order, morality, and obedience. The Crown extended the age of consent for young adults to ensure that they sought parental guidance. This served two purposes: it curbed rash decisions, which according to the Crown contributed to discord, and it limited free will, which the Church promoted and protected within the realm of marriage. Nevertheless, the Royal Pragmatic provided a small but significant qualification. The law did not take away a couple's right to contest their parents' objection. Throughout the remainder of the colonial period and into the republican period, marriage dissent cases, which are the appeals of these couples, reveal the lengths to which individuals would go for the right to choose whom to marry. By specifically examining marriage dissent cases involving women accused of having mala sangre, this analysis provides an intimate look into how African-descended women worked within the limitations of the law to achieve privilege.

ATTEMPTS TO MARRY: BECOMING SPANISH, INDIAN, AND HONORABLE

The 1778 decree's inclusion of Spaniards and Indians and exclusion of

African descendants revealed the Crown's attempt to protect and perpetuate Spanish privilege. Therefore, a marriage partner could either enhance or diminish not only an individual's social standing but also their family's status. In a small city like Córdoba, in which very few elite families ruled, it was imperative that elites marry the right people, lest they suffer social descent. For African-descended women, however, marriage to Spanish men provided a legal mechanism for achieving social ascent. To do so, they claimed to be a Spaniard or an Indian. Claims of whiteness are unsurprising, as the previous chapter demonstrated that sumptuary laws were put in place because African descendants often emulated whiteness. But claims of indigenous heritage also proved to be another strategy that women accused of having mala sangre used to gain the right to marry and distance themselves from slavery and their accused blackness. The following testimonies from marriage dissent cases involving those accused of having mala sangre reveal that once women accused of mala sangre proved their Spanish or Indian identity, they could marry their fiancés.

In general, dissent cases pitted parents against their children's choice in marriage. Parents objected to their children's choice to marry women of mala sangre because of the larger societal and political repercussions. Parents feared that their honor and lineage would be tainted by mala sangre. Don Juan de la Peña went before the court in hopes of quelling the discord that his son had brought to the family in 1825, revealing that colonial legacies such as the Pragmatic continued to shape cordobés society during the republican period.[39] Don Juan stated that "a blind passion dominated his son's willingness to go against him and his mother." This quotation referred to his son's choice to marry Ana María Avila, a known free casta. But the father hoped that by citing the Royal Pragmatic, he could prove that his son was under age and needed to abide by his rule. Don Juan provided various witnesses who testified that Ana María "never had the reputation to be Spaniard." He further pointed to the revisions made to the Royal Pragmatic in 1805, which stated that "nobles could not marry a negro, mulato, or coyote (all terms used to describe African descendants)" without the permission of their parents.[40] These declarations demonstrated the lengths to which parents went to protect their whiteness. They defamed the fiancée and argued that due to passion their child only thought of the immediate or individual satisfaction and remained blind to the collective consequences to the family and society. Don Juan de la Peña realized that his son's rash decisions could affect the family's reputation and access to crucial social and economic networks.

His son, don Lorenzo de la Peña, countered his father first by stating he did not need his father's permission because of his age. Moreover, he stated that no inequality existed because Ana María derived from a "legitimate birth" and had pureza de sangre. Don Lorenzo brought forth various witnesses who declared that Ana María descended from Spaniards. And, to end all doubt about his intentions, he told the judge, "My election is made, my commitments [are] public, my honor determined . . . [and] my heart decided." This emotional declaration showed don Lorenzo de la Peña's willingness to go against his father to marry who he wanted. In the end, the judge agreed with don Lorenzo de la Peña, noting that his father's marriage dissent was irrational and that don Lorenzo and doña Ana María had the right to marry.[41] Arguing that Ana María was a Spaniard worked in favor of don Lorenzo. In these cases, in which the fiancée argued a case of mistaken identity, the case came down to whether they could prove her whiteness, which in turn ensured that she epitomized an honorable woman worthy of marriage.

Similarly, claims of Indian identity often granted women accused of mala sangre the right to marry. In 1813, don José Baigorri opposed the marriage of his brother, don Manuel, to Manuela Arrieta.[42] Acting in the name of his deceased mother, he claimed that the marriage could not take place because Manuela, a mulata, was "notoriously unequal to his brother in her birth"; that is, she had mala sangre. In defense, don Manuel noted his age, twenty-five, which meant that he had obtained the maturity necessary to make such a crucial decision. He further stated that he would provide witnesses who could prove Manuela's honor and show that there was "no place for the opposition of his mother (who his brother represented)."

Witness testimony relied on gossip and hearsay and created an informal genealogy that corroborated or denied mistaken identities in marriage dissent cases. Doña Josefa Bustos, a witness, testified that "she did not know the parents of Manuela Arrieta, or her grandparents" but declared that Manuela "was not of the mulato race, just Indian." Furthermore, witness José Juárez declared that Manuela's "parents, named Tomás Arrieta and doña Juana Rosa Molina, and the parents of Arrieta named Santos Arrieta and Francisca, have been known as Indians, and doña Juana Rosa was of don Manuel Molina and doña Mercedes Aguero and they had been known as Spaniards with some mixture."[43] Also, the attempts to trace her lineage linked her to a past of miscegenation between "noble Indians," on the one side, and Spaniards, on the other. The witnesses' use of the label "noble Indians" suggests that Manuela came from Indians with stature, most likely caciques. The use of this label strengthened Manuel's case as the 1778 decree, which had been instituted more than thirty years before, acknowledged that Indian caciques should be considered as belonging to the same class as distinguished Spaniards. Together, these laws and witness accounts revealed that Córdoba maintained much of its colonial culture, which emphasized social hierarchy and order after the declaration of independence.

Believing Manuel Baigorri's supporting witnesses, the court declared that no inequality existed and granted the couple the right to marry. Undaunted, José continued to protest the court's decision and supplied other witnesses, who provided an extensive genealogy to prove her African ancestry. He stated, "Juana Molina mother [of Manuela] was the wife of the Indian or mulato Thomas Arrieta. Theresa, the sister of Juana and aunt [of Manuela] . . . married a slave, and Josefa, another sister of Juana and [aunt of Manuela], married a mulato slave named José in San Roque. The same with the mulata Mercedes, [a cousin of Manuela] who married a slave of the Arrendondos." José Domingo concluded that she was "well-known [as a mulata] and notorious in the jurisdiction of Punilla [a small town in the province of Córdoba]." But despite his attempts, the court maintained its original decision.[44]

Claims of Indian identity did not always come from witnesses. To strengthen her case, Ana Felipa Abendaño, accused of having mala sangre and an immoral lifestyle and as a result deemed unable to marry don Juan Agustín Garay, went before the court to prove her Indian identity and question the pureza de sangre of Juan Agustín's father, don Leonardo.[45] Ana Felipa gathered her own witnesses and asked the following questions: "Is it certain that I am from a legitimate marriage of Antonio Abendaño and Rosa Rearte, my father the son of the now-dead Josef Abendaño[, a] natural of Buenos Aires[,] and Michaela Liendro[, a] natural Indian of the Alta Gracia estate?" Second, she asked witnesses, "Did they know or had they heard it said that . . . my father, Antonio Abendaño, had always been reputed to be a legitimate Indian with no other mixture but Spanish?" An affirmative answer to these questions posed to witnesses would establish that she had come from a legitimate intermarriage, put aside questions of her honor, and ensure that she did not have mala sangre. Her final question to the witnesses was, "Is it true that don Leonardo is . . . [a] known mulato?" This last question redirected accusations of impurity to don Leonardo.

Of the four witnesses, one, María Josefa Paredes, a free mulata of San Xavier of the Valley of Traslasierra, said she had known "Ana Felipa since she was born and knew she was the legitimate daughter of the marriage between Antonio Abendaño and Rosa Rearte naturales [Indians] of . . . San José, [which was a part] of the Jesuit hacienda in Alta Gracia." María Josefa "also recounted that she knew the father and mother of [Ana Felipa] Abendaño[;] the first was a Spaniard and the second a mestiza." Moreover,

María Josefa stated, "Leonardo was known to be the mulato son of Benito, also a free mulato, and grandson to a slave who was owned by the don Pedro Garay who had passed away." Finally, she added that don Leonardo had taken the last name Garay from don Pedro Garay, who had passed away.[46] Ana Felipa's defense posed a series of questions that proved her Indian identity. The witnesses acted as genealogists revealing an important characteristic that defined Indian identity: place of origin. By stating that Ana Felipa's parents came from San José, the witness, María Josefa, pointed to a not so distant past, the Jesuit occupation of Córdoba. Jesuits employed Indian workers, typically as conchabados. Moreover, Ana Felipa also cast doubt on don Leonardo's purity. In proving that don Leonardo did not have pureza de sangre, there was no basis for a case of inequality.

In response, don Leonardo countered with his own evidence that he had pureza de sangre. He argued that Ana Felipa was the daughter of Antonio Abendaño, a mulato, who served in "the company of pardos"—which proved that she came from an inferior lineage. Don Leonardo served in the company of Spaniards. Don Leonardo then presented witnesses to testify to his pureza de sangre and to discredit Ana Felipa's character. The first witness, don Juan Pablo Ramírez, testified that don Leonardo was reputed to be a Spaniard. However, he also claimed that some people in Calamuchita, a city in the province of Córdoba, had also thought that don Leonardo's paternal line had some mulato blood. Additionally, he stated that he "knew Ana Felipa's parents and they were known to be mulatos," and don Juan Pablo went as far as to claim that Ana Felipa "raised two children who were the results of her prostitution." Discounting her accused prostitution, the court ruled in favor of the couple, noting there was "no place of inequality" and asserting "they remain free to marry." Don Leonardo would not accept the court's decision and chose to appeal to the Audiencia of Buenos Aires.[47] This exchange of accusations of mala sangre made by the witnesses who testified on behalf of Ana and of don Juan Agustín reveal the fluctuations of a person's reputed identity.

In both cases, claims of Indian identity permitted the betrothed to marry, because the law considered some Indians to have the same class as distinguished Spaniards. In the case between brothers, Manuela Arietta was not a mulata but a descendant of Indian nobility, so she had the right to marry don Manuel Baigorri. In the case of don Leonardo's attempts to prevent his son, don Juan Agustín, from marrying Ana Felipa, Ana Felipa proved her Indian status and cast doubt on don Leonardo's lineage. Both used genealogies to prove their Indian heritage. Indian identity, at least from the standpoint of marriage, proved to be an alternative strategy for escaping or denying their blackness. Moreover, this case occurred almost thirty years after the 1778 decree's implementation. Córdoba's protection of Indian privilege within the realm of marriage demonstrates that governing authorities maintained a distinction between some Indians and African descendants during the republican period.

However, not all defendants agreed that Indians deserved noble status. Don Joseph Felipe Manvilla, owner of the slave Luiz, did not oppose the desire of Luiz, his slave, to marry María de la Concepción, an Indian from Santiago de Estero, because according to him all castas were equal. In this case, don Joseph Felipe represented his slave to prove that Indians and African descendants had the right to marry. However, María de la Concepcion's sister and brother-in-law would not allow them to marry based on their inequalities. But don Joseph Felipe countered, stating that the Royal Pragmatic did not apply to castas but rather was reserved for "Spaniards or those who are reputed commonly to be of that class." For that reason, don Joseph Felipe argued that María's sister and brother-in-law should prove her pureza de sangre or whiteness or allow the intermarriage to take place. After presenting two witnesses, María's sister proved María's Spanish calidad and the court prohibited the marriage.[48] Instead of proving her Indian identity, her family verified her Spanish ancestry. Upon revelation that she was Spanish, the stark difference between Luiz and María became more apparent, and the court ruled the marriage dissent to be rational because of the proven inequality.

Córdoba remained committed to instilling order, discipline, and obedience. Rash individual decisions in marriage choice did not consider the larger societal, political, and economic consequences, which is why parents opposed their sons' decision to marry anyone with mala sangre. However, once the betrothed proved no inequality existed the courts granted them the right to marry, because these women, whether Spaniard or Indian, conformed to the governing authorities' concept of ideal wives.

ATTEMPTS TO MARRY: AFRICAN DESCENT AND HONOR

Granting a marriage between an African-descended woman who did not deny her blackness and a Spanish man based on honor proved to be more difficult because of the negative association with mala sangre. Mala sangre linked African-descended women to promiscuity, which led to dishonorable acts such as having illegitimate children.[49] These stereotypes also may explain why the Crown did not include African descendants in the 1778 decree. These assumed dishonorable actions stereotyped African-descended women and may largely explain why those who tried to argue that they possessed honor to secure the right to marry Spanish men rarely succeeded. Based on the verdicts rendered in marriage dissent cases, only one out of seven cases allowed couples who appealed to the woman's honor to marry. Most of these cases pitted a father or mother against a son, revealing the lengths to which parents went to prohibit an unequal marriage. Although rare, African-descended fathers also stepped forward to fight for their daughter's right to marry, especially if the husband-to-be had already given his word. Still, in both scenarios, acknowledging the woman's blackness did not prevail. Even in the most extreme case, where an African-descended woman's honor had been compromised, resulting in a pregnancy, the court ruled against her and upheld Spanish privilege.

In 1790, Joaquín Díaz, went before the court to appeal doña Magdalena Villafanes's objection to the marriage of her son, Ramón, to Díaz,'s daughter (no name provided), despite having been betrothed. Joaquín sought to restore his daughter's honor because Ramón had already committed to marry his daughter.[50] Quickly the case centered on doña Magdalena's objection to the marriage. She objected to the marriage because of the "unequal status which went against our Majesty and his Pragmatic of 1776, which mandated children could not contract marriage without asking and obtaining advice and consent from the father, and in his absence mother, to avoid grave hurts and continued familial discord." This statement reveals that doña Magdalena cited the law as both a precedent and the example to follow.

Moreover, doña Magdalena argued that Joaquín and his family came from an inferior lineage. A series of questions, such as if witnesses "knew the class or reputed class [of Joaquín and his mother Rosa Castro] to be honorable or plebeian, what color or aspect did they manifest, and if their treatment by others manifests with privilege or a commoner," demonstrated that she objected to the marriage based on Joaquín's calidad.[51] This question did not name a specific calidad, such as mulato or zambo, but instead asked for phenotype or the color, which suggests that calidad by the end of the eighteenth century was affiliated more with physical appearance than with other characteristics such as wealth.

But a more offhand question, such as whether Rosa Castro had more children and whether one of them, Juana, labored as a *criada* (female domestic slave or servant), hinted not only at a lower class but also at an affiliation with slavery. Don Juan Manuel Ramallo confirmed this suspicion, testifying that "Rosa Castro, was the mother of Juana, and she had been reputed to be a mulata." With this response, and the lack of denial from Joaquín, who had hoped to base it on Ramón's promise to marry his daughter, the court deemed doña Magdalena's dissent rational.[52]

Sometimes, parents sought expert witnesses to prove their pureza de sangre in order to provide further proof that an inequality existed between their son and his fiancée. In 1798, don Pedro Celestino Fernández requested that don José Lino, who remained embroiled in his own scandal, testify on the racial purity of his wife, doña María Maldonado. Don José Lino obliged and certified that he had known doña María's mother and father as "Spaniards free of other races or stains."[53] Don Pedro contested the decision of his son, don Bernardo, to marry María Eugenia González because she had inferior lineage.

In response, María Juana González came forward in her daughter's defense. She testified that María was the product of her own illicit affair with don Joseph, a storekeeper, of Spanish descent. She claimed that don Joseph had promised to marry her but had died of a malignant sickness before the marriage. However, she stressed, "he would have [married her] based on his love and will," and he knew at the time of his death that she was pregnant with María Eugenia. Don José Lino's testimony contributed a key piece of evidence that proved don Bernardo's pureza de sangre (purity of blood), while María Eugenia's background remained dubious. The court ruled in favor of don Pedro and stipulated that Bernardo should obey his father.[54] This case revealed that intended honorable actions, such as planning to marry, did not provide enough proof of María Eugenia's pureza de sangre. Moreover, having a priest such as don José Lino who sided with the parents proved more influential than the mother, who had hoped to gain sympathy for her own plight.

In another example, Manuel Corbera, of African descent with a respectable background, went to court to defend his daughter's honor. He wanted to force Ermenegildo Gaitán to marry his daughter, Norberta. Manuel Corbera, a captain in the pardo militia, intended to prove that Ermenegildo's opposition to marrying Norberta because of unequal lineage could not stand because Gaitán's family did not have pureza de sangre.[55] Manuel Corbera's position in the military qualified him to be included in the 1778 decree. Moreover, being a captain in the militia revealed he had proven his virtue through individual merits. By refuting Ermenegildo's purity, Corbera would prove that no inequality existed.

Through various witnesses, Corbera traced the lineage of Ermenegildo's mother, Inocencia Pérez, to prove her dubious background.[56] His first witness, Estanislao Ferreyra, another sergeant in the urban militia of the pardo squadron, argued that Inocencia's parents, Melchor Pérez and Catalina Ludena, were Indians from the frontier who had returned to the city after being banished. Moreover, Inocencia's relatives, including one of her sisters, were married to free African descendants, and one of her cousins had married a slave. The most damning piece of evidence that Estanislao provided suggested that the single Inocencia already had children when she married don Juan de la Cruz Gaitán, the father of Ermenegildo.[57] Thus, this testimony questioned Inocencia's pureza de sangre and her honor, thereby tainting her son. This witness pointed out that there were various African descendants in her family, which suggested that mala sangre tainted her pure blood. The witness also implied that before marrying don Juan, Inocencia lived an immoral lifestyle, which disqualified her from being honorable.

Similarly, another witness, Anselmo Ferreyra, stated that he knew Inocencia's parents had come from the border but was not "sure if their relocation was based on a voluntary or violent desertion, or if they were Spanish or of an inferior lineage." But what he did know is "Inocencia's relatives were married to naturales [Indians] . . . and a cousin [of Inocencia] named Rosario was married to a slave." Although Anselmo did not know of Inocencia's origins, another witness, Pedro Ferreyra, testified that he knew her parents. He stated that Melchor [Inocencia's father] had been raised on the border and captured by "faithless pampa Indians" and that he had been with them for quite some time. Although he did not know how the father "was rescued, when he did return he had married Catalina, and [they] passed as Spaniards."[58] The witness pointed to Inocencia's father's experience with Indians. But unlike being a descendant of noble Indians, as in previous cases recounted in this chapter, Inocencia's father had spent substantial time with "faithless pampa Indians," and after being rescued by authorities he passed as a Spaniard. This comment suggests that while her father could have descended from Indians, his indigenous lineage did not stem from a Christian cacique but rather from uncivilized and barbarous people who had yet to adopt Catholicism. This testimony further proved that Inocencia and by extension Ermenegildo Gaitán lacked pureza de sangre.

Manuel Corbera, whose father's name was also Manuel Corbera, also appeared before the court to strengthen the case but this time with another tactic. He testified that Ermenegildo had seduced his sister Norberta. They had had an illicit affair that resulted in her pregnancy, which in turn inflicted "incredible hurt on his parents" and caused a scandal in the neighborhood. Manuel testified that "Gaitán confessed to the crime and was convicted, and when they [Norberta and Ermenegildo] tried to marry to restore the honor of his house, some of [Ermenegildo's] relatives alleged inequality." As a consequence of Ermenegildo's actions, Corbera stated that Ermenegildo should either marry his sister to restore her honor or leave the province so that his parents could salvage their honor and avoid further scandal; to him, that would be justice. In this instance, Manuel appealed to the court to consider the dishonor Ermenegildo had caused his family. Norberta, his sister, was pregnant, and the proper thing to do was to marry her now that a baby was on the way. Manuel did not deny the family's blackness. Instead, based on his father's position as a captain in the militia, Manuel expected Ermenegildo to marry his sister. Manuel's testimony highlights the role of honor among African descendants in Córdoba. Corbera's family had higher social status, at least among other castas, because Corbera's father was a captain in the militia and had loyally served the city. Manuel did not have to deny their blackness because he thought he had the protection of his father's honor. Moreover, Manuel expected the court to side with his family to uphold his sister's honor. The scandal Ermenegildo had caused dishonored his sister and the Corbera family, who valued their standing in the community.

Despite two damaging accusations—the first that Ermenegildo did not have pureza de sangre and the second that he had seduced Norberta—the court did not think Manuel Corbera had a case. When Ermenegildo appeared before the court, he argued that the purpose of these civil cases was to counteract a family's rejection of a couple's willingness to get married. He, however, no longer wanted to marry Norberta, so there was no case. Moreover, he denied having confessed to the affair because there would have been a summary and witnesses, neither of which existed; only Norberta claimed it had taken place.[59] Attempts to force a marriage based on the honor of Norberta or her family did not work, largely because according to governing authorities, Norberta, an African descendant, did not possess honor. So, despite her father's position in the militia, the court was not willing to protect her and by extension the Corbera family's honor.

In marriage dissent cases in which African-descended women based their right to marriage on honor, they overwhelmingly lost the case; only 14 percent of the rulings allowed the couple to marry, and 86 percent denied or upheld parental opposition. Most often, the parents cited the Royal Pragmatic, suggesting that their initial dissent worked within the parameters of the law and were quite rational. Their proclamations also hinted that their sons lacked the maturity and knowledge to understand the consequences of their actions. When necessary, parents such as doña Magdalena sought expert witnesses such as don José Lino, who was embroiled in his own scandal, to justify their objection to the marriage. Even in cases such as Norberta's, whose pregnancy threatened her family with shame and dishonor, the accusation of mala sangre could not be escaped. The court remained steadfast in protecting Spanish privilege and hierarchy over forcing Ermenegildo to marry. The court ruled against forcing Ermenegildo to marry Norberta, despite Norberta's father's honorable service in the militia. His honor could not make up for his daughter's actions. These cases reveal that acknowledged blackness did not garner social mobility, as it disputed the basis of social hierarchy and Spanish privilege.

CONCLUSION

Intermarriages before the implementation of the Royal Pragmatic in 1776 provided means for upward mobility. Marriages involving Spanish men and enslaved women of African descent allowed African-descended women to escape enslavement and, as a result, achieve privilege. In some extreme cases, women of African descent, such as Teresa and Ana, could become doñas, revealing the advantages of marriage and the fluidity of calidad. According to historian Michelle McKinley, intermarriage for African descendants signified the "penultimate barrier to completing their whiteness and securing their calidad and that of their children."[60] Unlike concubinage, marriage was a more secure means of economic and social influence that remained even in widowhood, as in the case of Teresa, who later remarried and made her final transformation into a doña. Moreover, intermarriages between Indians and African descendants also achieved social mobility, although not to the same extent. Instead their relationships ensured a better life for their children as they inherited free status. Still, despite their small number, intermarriages caused alarm because they could disrupt social order, which explains why the Crown implemented the Royal Pragmatic of 1776.

By focusing on marriage dissent cases, this chapter unveils how some African-descended women legitimately and legally whitened themselves to secure the privileged status associated with being married to white men. To become the ideal wife, a woman had to be honorable. Spanish women innately possessed honor, and according to the 1778 decree, Indian caciques belonged to the same class as "distinguished Spaniards." Betrothed couples responded to the law by having the fiancée become the ideal wife, which became a successful strategy for marriage.

In these marriage dissent cases involving African-descended women, the fluidity of identity becomes apparent. Because identity remained in flux in eighteenth-century Córdoba, if couples could prove a case of mistaken identity, they could marry and legally escape their accused blackness. Cases in which Indian identity proved beneficial provide insight into how Córdoba's governing officials privileged Indian identity, which signaled another avenue African descendants could use to become free.

FIVE

(En)gendering Freedom
Maternity and the Manumission Process

In 1809, María Guerra, facing the threat of enslavement and of having her family separated, went to court asking that her slaveholder's heirs, doña Rosa Guerra and don Pablo de Acosta, recognize the freedom of her six children, three grandchildren, and herself.[1] Rather than testifying that she had served her owner faithfully and thus justly deserved to be free, she argued that the heirs had mistaken her status. The heirs cited the services that María provided, which made her a slave, but María stressed that she was descended from the Pampas, an Indian ethnic group, and was born free. María maintained that while she had served don Francisco Guerra (doña Rosa's father) until his death, she had always remained free. She challenged doña Rosa and don Pablo, who wanted to sell María and her children into slavery. In doing so, they would condemn the wrong person. To prove her Indian identity, she presented witnesses who attested to her maternal Indian lineage.

Maternity played an integral role in the process of freedom in Córdoba. Based on loyal and faithful service, slaveholders granted slave mothers and their children freedom. Manumission records demonstrate that slave and free mothers also paid for their children and other family members' freedom. In cases of contested freedoms, maternity also played a pivotal role. Through a series of witnesses and declarations, some mothers and children threatened with enslavement argued cases of mistaken identity. Rather than being an African descendant, these mothers and children testified that they were Indians. Other slave mothers argued that they deserved freedom based on honor. This chapter focuses on how both strategies relied on the social and legal bonds of motherhood formulated by family networks to achieve freedom.

THE SIGNIFICANCE OF MOTHERHOOD

Mothers' participation in manumission highlighted the strength of their legal and emotional maternal bonds. From 1776 to 1812, women of African descent—grandmothers, aunts, nieces, wives, and mothers—proved essential in manumitting their loved ones. In 1803, Juana Manuela Echenique and her mother, Marta Echenique, gathered 150 pesos and gave the money to doña Clara Echenique to purchase Juana's three-year-old daughter, Margarita.[2] The most expensive manumission in Córdoba cost 360 pesos in 1802. Josefa, a former slave of the widow doña Mercedes Encalada, who married don Lorenzo Blanco de Sireron, a judge on the Royal Audiencia tribunal in Buenos Aires, paid that price to free her fourteen-year-old daughter.[3] The manumission process represented an extension of that bond.

More than likely, African-descended mothers acquired the money to purchase their children by saving the earnings from their labor. Most free and enslaved women worked within the domestic sphere as cooks, sewers, weavers, spinners, and maids, although the 1813 census noted that one of the two businesswomen listed was a free parda named Andrea Abelina Toledo.[4] Andrea lived with her husband, Miguel Guayanas, who was listed in the census as being unemployed, and their children, in a house located north of the plaza.[5] Elite and privileged Spaniards lived mainly north of the plaza, which demonstrates that Toledo, and her family, had transitioned to an elite status that few parda women could achieve.

Accumulated wealth among African-descended women also came from buying and selling property in Córdoba. In 1785, Thomasina Moyano bought a *solar* (plot of land) from doña Hipolita Ledesma for a reduced price of sixty pesos. Six years later, Thomasina sold a house to doña Marcelina Moyano for 900 pesos.[6] Although most transactions took place between free African-descended female property owners and individuals designated as don or doña, there were also exchanges among free African descendants, such as when Carmen Vilchez sold a solar to Teresa Flores for eighty pesos in 1797.[7] These transactions among free African-descended women reveal that they actively accumulated wealth throughout the city. Probate records mention only one slave, Frutusoso, who labored in the Monastery of the Carmelitas Descalzas, as a property owner. He sold a solar to Juan Castro, a free casta, for 200 pesos in 1785. But before the transaction could be finalized, Frutusoso had to have permission from the Reverend Mother Francisca Antonia de Jesús del Corazón of the monastery.[8] The presence of women buying and selling property reveals a source of wealth for the family, as in the case of Antonia Salguero, a free African descendant who donated a solar to her son, Eusebio Gurmendi, to enjoy along with his successors.[9]

Even when slave mothers did not pay for their children's manumission, intimate relationships with their owners proved vital in freeing their children. Overall, slaveholders granted the most manumissions.[10]

Historian Michelle McKinley, who studies seventeenth-century Peru, has found that the domestic sphere cultivated a relationship based on the "economy of emotion."[11] This economy of emotion defined household relationships established over generations between slaveholders and slaves. McKinley noted that based on cartas de libertad (manumission papers), female slaveholders and domestic slaves "used language of maternal affection, not sexual intimacy."[12] In Córdoba, cartas de libertad overwhelmingly pointed to the "[slave] mother's good and loyal service" as the reason for freeing her son or daughter. Sometimes the cartas de libertad mentioned that both the mother and child served the slaveholder. In 1781, doña María Margarita Lujan freed Theresa Luisa, a sixteen-year-old mulata, because of the loyal and faithful service of both Theresa and her mother, Petrona. Doña María's reasons for her manumission signified that Theresa had served independently of her mother and established a separate relationship with doña María.[13] Manumission based on services by slave mothers or their children reveals the intimate relationships that developed in the household between slaveholders and slaves.

Often slaves received their freedom upon the death of their slaveholder. For example, at the beginning of the insurgency in 1810, María's slaveholder declared that "from the departure of these Kings or until these Kings verified his death," she would be free.[14] This carta de libertad took into account the tumultuous period during the insurgency, suggesting that, whether Córdoba remained a colony or a republic, once he died María would achieve her freedom. Mandating that a slave wait until the owner died ensured the maximum utility of the slave. Even after the death of an owner, the conditions of freedom required slaves to continue to serve. In 1796, doña Antonia Arana, a twenty-five-year-old slaveholder, granted freedom to María Loreto, a seventeen-year-old, after Antonia's death. Moreover, María's freedom hinged on becoming *agregada*: committed to serving and remaining at "a monastery, her niece's house, or a Christian and honorable household of [María's] choosing" and having four masses, likely per year, said for the repose of doña Antonia's soul for ten years.[15]

Having masses said on behalf of the slaveholder's soul also demonstrated that some manumissions were contingent on various stipulations before slaves could fully enjoy their freedom. In 1804, doña Ana Theresa Robles Candelas ordered Rosa and her fourteen-year-old daughter, Josefa, to have one hundred masses said for her brother and slaveholder, don José Ignacio Robles, to achieve the family's freedom, which included Rosa, Josefa, and six-year-old Anselmo. Once they had completed their one hundredth mass, doña Theresa verified it and granted them freedom.[16]

Maternal figures actively sought freedom for their children and husbands, which illustrates the strength of familial networks throughout the city of Córdoba. The Church encouraged and fostered a family bond that extended beyond immediate members. As a result, grandmothers and aunts became active participants in the freeing of the grandchildren, nieces, and nephews. In 1781, Ambrosia freed her granddaughter, one-month-old María de la Ascensión, paying forty pesos; two years later, she freed her fifteen-day-old grandson, Joseph de la Espirtú, from doña Francisca Labayen.[17] While freeing her family members, Ambrosia also bought a solar for 108 pesos in 1783.[18] Such actions reveal that free African-descended maternal figures remained critical to accumulating wealth and freeing their families.

CONTESTED FREEDOMS: SLAVE TO INDIAN

Maternity, the most profound familial connection between a mother and a child, allowed the United Provinces of the Río de la Plata to relieve a growing tension: the right to freedom versus the protection of property rights.[19] To ease the tension, the United Provinces of the Río de la Plata enacted gradual abolition, which consisted of not only the abolition of the slave trade in 1812 and indigenous servitude in 1813 but also the Free Womb Act in 1813, which tied freedom to enslaved mothers' bodies. As mentioned in chapter 2, these children, known as "libertos," marked the transition between slavery and freedom. These gradual abolition laws reflected the larger trend toward a decline in slavery and indigenous service throughout the nineteenth century. But not all slaveholders embraced this legislation, and this ambivalence resulted in contested freedoms. These lawsuits were often pursued by mothers and reveal their willingness to fight for their freedom and for that of their children. Two strategies advanced in Córdoba highlight the role of motherhood in the republic. Under the first strategy, mothers claimed Indian identity, based on their maternal lineage, making them free. Under the second, slave mothers fought for their child's release from slavery.

Of the two strategies, claims of Indian descent proved the more successful in contested freedom cases after 1813 in Córdoba. Córdoba's cultural and political environment contributed to this preferred calidad. Córdoba consisted of a small and concentrated population that held on to tradition and the strength of the Catholic Church. Although the insurgency initially forced Córdoba to fight for independence, Córdoba's culture remained conservative and upheld the social hierarchy well into the nineteenth century. The maintenance of Córdoba's culture meant that strategies to gain freedom in contested freedom cases were more successful, provided they did not disrupt the social hierarchy and order. Claims of

Indian identity, which throughout the colonial period signified free status, did not disrupt or challenge the traditional, conservative culture in Córdoba and explains why this strategy worked. Moreover, claims of Indian identity did not threaten cordobés society, because most Indians who lived in the city had been absorbed into the larger free population and only nine pueblos de indios tributarios existed in the province of Córdoba at the end of the eighteenth century.[20] Proclamations of Indian identity did not challenge the social hierarchy, which elites and governing officials protected. Thus, claims of Indian identity worked for women and children threatened with enslavement.

In 1809, witnesses served as informal genealogists to prove María Guerra's Indian background. Witnesses testified that Don José, whose prominent family could be traced back to the conquistadors, brought María and her sister Josefa to the city. Don José gave María to Rosa's father to serve him, and in exchange he evangelized her. Don José kept her sister Josefa as a servant and she married Bentura, a Pampa Indian and *curaca* (Indian chieftain) of the pueblo de la Toma, an Indian settlement on the outskirts of the city. Witnesses asserted that both María and Josefa were free Indians.

What María wore and where her family lived provided the most convincing evidence. Descriptions of clothing and a person's origin reflected calidad, which remained in flux and depended on the social context. Witnesses stated that they often saw María dressed in *mantas* (blankets or cotton cloth associated with Indian clothing), which suggested her Indian identity. Location also denoted an Indian identity. In María Guerra's case, her sister had married a curaca from the pueblo de La Toma.[21] Other cases that proved indigenous heritage claimed origins as far away as Paraguay, as when María del Transito testified that her great grandmother, Teresa, was Paraguayan.[22] Based on the eighteenth-century marriage records, among Indians who had origins outside of Córdoba's province, Paraguay was the most prominent place of origin, followed by Santiago de Estero, Peru, Salta, Tucumán, and Santa Fe.[23] The 1813 census also recorded Indians with origins in Cochabamba, Suipacha, and Potosí.[24] These places reflected Córdoba's role in regional trade and settlement. The city's ideal location connected the Pacific and Atlantic coasts dating to the period of conquest. But most locations were provincial pueblos, such as La Toma, throughout the province of Córdoba. In another case, Pedro Salgado sought his freedom based on his mother's indigenous heritage. He argued that she came from the pueblo de NoNo.[25] The descriptions of dress and location in this case highlight an Indian identity; they wore mantas and came from provincial towns, such as La Toma.

Not all witnesses supported María's claims of Indian identity. Other witnesses doubted her Indian ancestry and supported doña Rosa and don Pablo, stating that María was a mulata slave whom traffickers had traded for mules. Another heir argued that María had become a slave by way of a dowry and was known as "la Conga," a label that denoted her African origin and thus assumed her slave status. In addition, don Pablo claimed that his family's will proved María's slave status. It dated as far back as his great-grandfather, don Diego González Carrido, who owned María's mother, also named María. It contained the birth and death records of María in addition to those of her daughter, María Guerra. But he could not provide a copy of it, as, he claimed, it had gone missing, which weakened don Pablo's case.

For eight years, María's fate remained undetermined while the wars of independence ensued. It took until 1817 for the civil court to side with María and declare that "María, educated in the house of doña Rosa Guerra, daughter of a southern pampa Indian with the same name, who was educated in the house of don Francisco Guerra, and . . . all of her legitimate and natural descendants on their maternal side . . . [have] the power to enjoy . . . natural liberty, as free citizens in the provinces of South America."[26] Her children and grandchildren inherited her freedom based on her maternal Indian lineage. This decision reflected the larger decline in slavery and indigenous servitude during the republican period.

María Guerra achieved freedom by claiming an Indian calidad, revealing the fluidity of identities during the early republic. As discussed in the previous chapter, Indianness had its advantages for African-descended women accused of having mala sangre. Within the realm of marriage, Indians had the right to marry Spaniards, but this right did not extend to African descendants.[27] Despite the social discrimination Indians faced and their similar labor conditions to those of slaves, another advantage Indians had over African descendants was that they were legally free; according to the 1530 Royal Provision, no one could "capture or make an Indian a slave." Later, the 1542 Royal Provision reiterated that Indians had to be "instructed and taught the things of our sacred Catholic faith, and treated well as free people and our vassals," although they had to serve and pay tribute in the United Provinces of the Río de la Plata until 1813.[28] In choosing to become Indian, María took steps to better her life and the lives of her children and grandchildren and to distance her family from potential enslavement.

Enslaved children also used arguments of Indian identity to achieve their freedom. In 1825, Manuel Monaco argued that he deserved freedom because his mother was a free Pampa Indian. His owner, don Xavier

Burgos, however, rejected his claim, noting that it was strange that he asked for his freedom after thirty years of slavery. After Manuel's mother died, don Xavier Burgos testified that Manuel asked for a *carta de venta* (the legal transfer of the rights to sell a slave), which he gave Manuel, but it was "to trick him and put forward an unexpected and unjust solicitude" for his freedom. For that reason, don Xavier requested that the court "put [Manuel] in jail, demanded they give him lashes, chain him, and sentence him to hard labor for two months."[29] Having already lived life as a slave for many years, Manuel's proof of Indian identity could not be based on mistaken identity as María's claims were, because he had already served as a slave for many years. Instead, the proof of his indigenous identity would be based on the conditions of his mother's labor.

To prove his Indian identity, the defensor de los pobres (a court-appointed official tasked with representing women and the poor in court) questioned witnesses about the origins of Manuel's mother and how she came to work for the Burgos family. Doña Gabriela Burgos, the slaveholder's sister, testified that she knew Manuel to be the son of a Pampa Indian and that Rosa, Manuel's mother, "had been bought on behalf of her mother in the quantity of 200 pesos from Dr. Rosas[,] a priest from Río Cuarto." When her mother bought Rosa, she also came with "a little boy [Manuel] who was two years old. [Rosa later] married and ran away with her husband staying away for three to four years." The next witness mentioned that he had heard from doña Gabriela that Manuel "was free because he was the son of a Pampa Indian." Doña María Francisca Burgos also stated that her "brother now deceased, don Fabian Burgos [the father of don Xavier], had bought a Pampa Indian with a son who was still suckling from don Rosas. The Pampa Indian married another Indian and ran away, leaving the boy with don Xavier Burgos. The boy was named Manuel and he was around 8 months." These witnesses' testimony revealed that the Burgos family had acquired a Pampa Indian woman. As in María's case, the witnesses argued Rosa originated from the Pampa Indians.

The most definitive argument came from the defensor de los pobres who cited a law from the sixteenth century that stated that the Crown did not subject Indians to enslavement. He argued that "the progenitors of the actual King of Spain Ferdinand VII, despite their iron core, have issued decrees so that the infidel Indians would not be slaves, under the desire to make them Christians. . . . When it comes to [Manuel] his physiognomy is an undeniable assurance that he is Indian. . . . The status of the child is based on the mother's womb. The child and the womb were free; consequently, Manuel Monaca rightly [should] claim his rights, and no longer have a reputation as [a] slave." Because his mother was free based on her

Indian status, Manuel inherited her free status. But the defensor de los pobres also hinted at the physical differences between Indians and slaves, stating that Manuel's physiognomy clearly made him an Indian. In the end, the court ruled in favor of Manuel, after which Manuel demanded payment for the time he had spent serving don Xavier Burgos.[30] Cordobés society privileged Indian status, and if enslaved persons could prove their Indian identity, they could earn their freedom.

In both cases, María Guerra and Manuel Monaco proved their Indian heritage through their maternal lineage and as a result became free. These cases, and others like them, illustrate the importance of maternity and its role in the manumission process. Deciding to become Indian allowed women who faced enslavement to fight for their children and ensure that the next generation (or in the case of María, the following two generations) distanced themselves from slavery. In cases such as Manuel Monaco, who argued that don Xavier had wrongfully enslaved him, Indian identity guaranteed his freedom. Manuel, however, still had to trace his Indian lineage through his maternal side. Becoming an Indian, in a society in which only a small population identified as such, did not challenge social hierarchies. Legislation also privileged Indian identity. The Royal Provision of 1542 stated that Indians could not be subject to enslavement. The United Provinces of the Río de la Plata also eliminated all forms of indigenous servitude. Together, these laws linked Indian identity to freedom. In essence, in Córdoba the Indian population within the city limits and designated pueblos did not pose threats of disorder to the ruling elite.

CONTESTED FREEDOMS: SLAVE MOTHERS AND HONOR

When a slave mother went before the court on behalf of her children's freedom, she argued for it on the grounds of mistreatment and dishonorable actions by the owner.[31] But such claims of maltreatment often fell short because of what maltreatment implied in Córdoba. These slave mothers directly challenged a society steeped in tradition, honor, and social hierarchy. As mentioned in chapter 1, Córdoba remained a city of churches and close-knit elite families who jealously protected their economic and political influence. These cultural traditions rendered anyone who challenged the social order a threat to their well-being.

For instance, María de la Cruz de Monserrat, a slave belonging to don Marcos Ariza, a priest of this diocese, filed for her freedom and that of her children, resulting in a long case that took place from 1811 to 1814 during the wars of independence. María claimed "that her owner Don Marcos

Ariza had taken her from her mother Juana de Monserrat, with the pre-
tension to teach [her] to read, [and] took [her] to live [in his house]." While
living there, she stated she "was seduced and [her] purity compromised.
Under this state, he bought [her] from the Colegio [de Monserrat] as it
is known and [she] became his slave. Then with . . . more influence and
empire he enjoyed [her] person."

She argued that she was an innocent child: "I looked on his loving
insinuations like a force that I could not avoid. I concurred with his
wishes and desired in time the effects that had resulted, but not being
happy with this vagrant love, the promise of my freedom and freedom of
his products [children] stopped. He flattered me and forced me to continue our reunion by giving me money, and not giving me my freedom
and the children I bore. There is more! As love is a fire, that quickly
consumes, even though the flames are enjoyable, I started to feel reduc-
tion of these offers. These promises of love converted into lashes, in bit-
terness, in continued work and tears. This tragic metamorphosis made
me implore justice and demand that he not only completes his promises,
but also, he must grant me and my children freedom."[32] The relationship described by María situated her as a victim. Subjected to the control
of her slaveholder, she became his lover but ultimately found that he did
not share her feelings.

In seeking justice, she sought to gain her freedom by publicly sham-
ing her slaveholder for his sexual abuse. This priest not only had an affair
with his slave, but this relationship resulted in two children. In support
of her daughter, María, Juana de Monserrat, another slave of don Marcos Ariza, solicited the court to free her daughter and their two children.
Juana further proclaimed that don Marcos had plans to move her daughter
to Buenos Aires, where he could "without a doubt, circumvent the [legal]
actions of my daughter and the providence of this court."[33] Juana feared
that if they did not prosecute don Marcos for his actions and free María, he
would leave town and move to a city outside the jurisdiction of the court.

Two years later, Juana, desperate because her fears had come true
(don Marcos had taken her daughter to Buenos Aires to sell her), brought
the case before the court. Upset that Juana brought the case before a civil
court, the bishop who presided over the case found it outrageous that after
doing nothing for two years, she wanted the proceedings to conclude in
two days. He also found it upsetting that Juana did not obey the law. She
did not initially use a defensor de los pobres; instead she took it upon
herself to represent her daughter and grandchildren, which the law did
not permit because a slave could not represent another slave. He further
noted, "One cannot conceal how injury envelopes this period or hides the

volume of this offense, if you consider, who is offended, and who is the offender. A black woman from the school has violated a bishop. But [he] promised that [he] would not let her get away with such insults."[34] Rather than considering the actual validity of the case, the bishop found it insulting that an enslaved woman would approach the court with such disregard for his superior status.

Amid the wars of independence, the maintenance of social control and hierarchy took precedence over María de la Cruz's freedom. A woman, moreover a slave, had insulted the bishop with her "capricious illegalities." Moreover, after two years, Juana went to both the civil and the ecclesiastical tribunals, breaking yet another rule by crossing jurisdictions. As this case involved a priest, don Marcos, the bishop in charge of the case argued that it belonged within the Church. During the colonial period, the Church had *fueros* (privileges to have all legal matters heard within the jurisdiction of the Church). Clearly in 1813, three years after the outbreak of war, Córdoba's colonial legacy remained intact.

But that did not stop Juana, whose actions reveal the lengths to which an enslaved mother would go to free her child from bondage. Throughout the case, she constantly reminded the court of the illicit affair that had resulted in illegitimate children. In other words, don Marcos had jeopardized her daughter's honor, and for that reason she deserved her freedom. Worse, when she used a defensor de los pobres, she found him to show partiality toward don Marcos because of the intimate relationship her daughter had with her slaveholder. For that reason, she asked for the defensor's replacement with an impartial lawyer. Juana's disregard of the court and its superior members broke social customs, order, and elements of hierarchy that elites deemed essential to a civil and orderly society.

Ultimately, the court ruled in favor of don Marcos, which meant that María de la Cruz remained his slave. Despite Juana's insolence, she did not produce witnesses who could corroborate her daughter's claims that an illicit affair had taken place. Moreover, don Marcos testified that María de la Cruz had previously run away, abandoning her children to participate in a robbery, which proved she lacked any honor. After the robbery, she hid at doña Pabla Ydalgo's home, where her grandmother lived, and after fifteen days the defensor de los pobres returned her to don Marcos. Juana could not provide the necessary proof to condemn don Marcos Ariza. Don Marcos, however, proved that María de la Cruz was not only a bad mother but also a woman who did not obey the law.[35]

The case involving María de la Cruz and her mother challenged social hierarchies in cordobés society. They attempted to expose a priest's dishonorable actions. Don Marcos, a priest, like don José Lino (discussed in chapter 3), engaged in an illicit affair with his slave. Unlike don José Lino, however, the defamation of his character did not come from ecclesiastical authorities but rather from an African-descended mother. The accusations against don Marcos were more difficult to prove, especially when Juana decided not to follow protocol and approached the court on behalf of her daughter. She was not only a slave but also a woman who disregarded social order in 1814. This course of action was especially sensitive, as this case took place during the wars of independence. What's more, don Marcos emphasized that María acted irresponsibly and argued that she was not a good mother because of her own dishonorable actions such as participating in a robbery. Don Marcos demonstrated that María, having already broken the law by participating in the robbery, would continue to cause a scandal and disrupt the social order and peace.

CONCLUSION

Within the institution of slavery, a mother's ability to claim familial ties to her children strengthened the maternal bond that would later lead to freedom. In most cases, freedom came as a reward for the mother's loyal and dedicated years of service. Mothers continued to fight for their child's freedom in the republican period after the passage of gradual abolition legislation using two main tactics: claiming Indian identity and claiming to possess honor and to deserve manumission. Of the two strategies, claims of indigenous heritage based on the maternal lineage proved the more successful. Slave mothers who went before the court to fight for their child's freedom based on mistreatment, as in the case of María Guerra, fared worse. María not only took it upon herself to seek freedom but also did so for her children and grandchildren, thus seeking freedom for three generations.

In Córdoba, claims of Indian identity worked because they did not challenge traditional social hierarchies. Although these women did not gain the benefits and privileges of whiteness, they did achieve freedom. Becoming an Indian worked in tandem with attempts by governing elites to instill social order and hierarchy. The second strategy, which pitted a slave mother, such as Juana de Monserat, against her slaveholder, proved more difficult because it did not work within the power structures. Claims advanced by slave mothers on behalf of their daughters challenged the patriarchy and social hierarchy and resulted in a less favorable outcome.

Despite the discrepancy between these two tactics in postcolonial society, the bond of mother and child could not be broken. In fact, it was imperative that all mothers became educated so that they could uplift their children from the shackles of slavery.

SIX

Lessons of Motherhood
The Beginning of Institutionalized Whitening

In 1816 in Córdoba, doña Micaela Catalina del Santismo Sacramento y Quintana, a widow of don Santiago Allende, freed the following slaves: Alexo and his wife, Encarnación, and their child, Bernardina, along with Paulina, Felipa, Benito, Antonio, Miguel, and Santiago under various conditions. All of them had to remain obedient, maintain employment, and live honorable lives, but the carta de libertad specifically stated that Alexo and Encarnación "could not take Bernardina out of the Colegio de Huérfanas, where she was being educated."[1] Her instructions for Bernardina's enrollment in school reveal that free status did not equate with ideal behavior. Instead, education institutionalized social grooming, that is, a learned and ideal behavior that uplifted free African descendants from the stigma of their enslaved pasts. Public education rescued freed children and other free African descendants born after the Free Womb Act of 1813 from what threatened society the most: moral ignorance. This was an ignorance that authorities such as Bishop San Alberto and Governor Intendant Marqués de Sobremonte had sought to eliminate.

Doña Micaela's commitment to Bernardina's education most likely stemmed from her background and service. She married don Santiago Allende, who belonged to a prominent and conservative family, and they lived a privileged life, which included owning many slaves. After her husband's death, she became a nun at the Monastery of Santa Catalina.[2] Her involvement in the religious life meant that she most likely knew of the recently created classroom for parda girls, which included African descendants and Indians enrolled at the Colegio de Niñas Educandas (School for Girls) and was geared toward educating poor girls throughout the city. Like Bishop San Alberto, who founded the school in 1782, doña Micaela probably saw the benefit of keeping Bernardina in school, where she would learn civility, obedience, and morality, qualities that would uplift Bernardina's moral character and free her from ignorance. Doña Micaela's commitment to Bernardina's schooling tied freedom to an education that socially groomed and whitened her identity.

In this chapter, I argue that childhood education institutionalized social grooming, which in turn whitened the population. Governing and ecclesiastical authorities tied childhood education to the development of the republic.[3] In cultivating and molding children, governing authorities made education a civic duty that politicized the importance of motherhood, revealing how African-descended girls contributed to the nascent republic. After these girls received their education, governing and ecclesiastical authorities tasked them with the responsibility to uplift their families by instilling in them the qualities they had learned in school: civility, morality, and obedience.

In turn, institutionalized whitening provided an avenue for African-descended women to protect and cultivate their family, especially in the republican period, a period in which calidad became associated less with a reputed identity and more with biological or inherited attributes, such as color.[4] Because of this shift, the attainment of whiteness transformed from merely individual decisions made by African descendants to a combined decision-making process enhanced by formalized institutional social grooming. Within generations, an education marked social advancement. Bernardina, born in 1810 to enslaved parents (Alexo, an Angolan, and Encarnación, a mulata born in Córdoba) not only obtained her freedom at the age of six, through doña Micaela's efforts, but also enrolled in school to learn social discipline and virtue. Her education marked a social grooming that her freed parents did not possess. Within one generation of arriving to Córdoba, Alexo's daughter had gained her freedom and learned the desired behaviors that would help distance herself from her former slave status.

In effect, education fulfilled governing authorities' attempts to produce free individuals who would be correctly integrated into a moral and civil republic and also served as an avenue for social advancement for African-descended girls and, as the century progressed, African-descended boys, who, when possible, also attended school.[5] By focusing on the ideology and implementation of education in the nineteenth century, this chapter reveals that the cordobés elite, both governing and ecclesiastical officials, remained steadfast in maintaining a hierarchical society and required all members of society—but especially girls, who would become future mothers—to do so as well. In turn, African-descended girls such as Bernardina enrolled in school to secure social advancement and the ability to uplift their families.

THE CALL FOR GIRL'S EDUCATION IN THE NINETEENTH CENTURY

The attempts to moralize the city and enact social order through education remained a goal in postcolonial society as schools continued to expand throughout the Río de la Plata. As the century progressed, female education transformed into a political project that fostered the success of the nascent republic. This shift ensured that all girls participated in the making of the new republic. Thus, in addition to eliminating ignorance and instilling good character, childhood education became a means of ensuring a peaceful and loyal citizenry that would adhere to the republic's political agenda. However, commentary began to appear in the newsletter *Telégrafo mercantil: Rural político económico e historiógrafo de la Río de la Plata*, which was shared throughout the Viceroyalty, that education was not meeting the needs of its targeted groups of girls and castas.

In the *Telégrafo mercantil*, two articles pointed to disparities between the rhetoric and the implementation of childhood education. This lack of educational opportunities, the anonymous author wrote, continued to stigmatize girls and castas. In the article "Memoria sobre que conviene limitar la infamia anexá á varias castas de gentes que hay en nuestra América" (Memory of which is convenient to limit the infamy annexed to several castas of people that there are in our America), the author wrote, "Castas, who are degraded by their condition and birth, are not admitted in public primary schools, so that they do not coalesce or interact with [Spanish children]."[6] The author wrote about the disgrace of an enslaved status but also about the condition of blackness, which stay with freed castas despite their having achieved manumission.

Nonetheless, the author argued that if these girls received an education that "removed . . . their infamy," then they could achieve social advancement. The author suggested that these girls could "engage with Spanish ladies . . . and raise their daughters with the same sentiments of honor and virtue [that] they raise and educate Spaniards. They would not see them walking ideally alone in the streets at a very dangerous age or gather[ing] with immoral people."[7] This opinion reflected the ongoing rhetoric about the benefits of public education for an increasingly free population. Given the opportunity, the author stressed, casta girls could be uplifted and "engage with Spanish ladies" and no longer indulge in immoral acts or idleness. The engagement between Spanish girls and casta girls, however, did not establish their equality but rather confirmed that casta girls knew how to behave in public spaces. Education whitened their behavior so that they would understand and further fit into the hierarchical structures of the budding republic. Once they became mothers, they would instill these qualities in their children.

In 1802, another article on the benefits of girls' education appeared in the *Telégrafo mercantil*. "Education: Reflections about Women's

Education," written by "la señora porteña," made a strong plea to educated women: "[Women] are the pleasure of life, the cornerstone of society. They inspire the desire to please, and this obligation is a spring that makes us taste sweet restraint, which paces the tumult of our passions, corrects our extravagances, composes our exterior and covers it with a veil of decency." This quote emphasized the importance of women in the home. The woman was the social fabric of morality. Furthermore, women inspired good behavior in others. The señora porteña further argued, "Where women are ignorant and frivolous, you will see few enlightened and solid men."[8] These observations pointed to the importance of motherhood. As historian Leslie Walker argues, a mother was an "educator, supervisor, and moral center."[9] As a center of morality, a mother shaped and molded her children's character and taught them ethics and good behavior. Educated mothers instilled from an early age a moral principle that contained passions, restrained impulses, and gave boys especially a degree of decency.

The peace and order of society depended on mothers, and for that reason they had to first learn the corrective behavior and moral principals in school so that they could later enrich and edify their families. A mother, according to la señora, possessed such a significant role in the family because her role extended beyond the confines of the home. According to la señora, "The state is nothing more than a region of families, and each family needs a mother who would be a daily sentinel that maintains order and peace and portions this mode to her husband [in order for him] to serve the public."[10] Mothers served as "sentinels" who protected the domestic sphere, teaching children how to contain their passions, which otherwise led to unruly behavior, and supporting their husbands in sustaining order throughout the household and beyond. Moreover, according to la señora, "[if] society needs the men to defend it from exterior enemies, then equally it needs the women to guard the interior. . . . How can a State sustain itself without 'the economic government' of the family?"[11] Without an education, la señora argued, discord in the home would eventually spread to the streets and affect all levels of society.

The girl's status did not matter, because, according to la señora porteña, "the laborer, artisan, all classes of men that work shares with his wife, his works, his cares, his fears, and his hopes, his loses, and his gains, and takes advantage of her teachings and adopts her advice."[12] In agreement with the article "Memoria sobre que conviene limitar la infamia anexá á varias castas de gentes que hay en nuestra América," printed a year earlier, la señora porteña saw the benefit of educating all girls because of their effect on not only their children but also their husbands. La señora pointed to the shared intimacy between a husband and a wife.

A husband who shared his thoughts and most importantly his fears with his wife not only sought solace but also listened, within the confines of the household, to potential solutions. Knowing, as la señora stated, that the husband shared his "cares, fears, and losses" with his wife made it paramount to ensure that she had learned enlightened principles that guided him to make the right decision. But despite the positive rhetoric about childhood education throughout the Río de la Plata, girls, according to la señora porteña, still lacked access to public education "when it is most needed," and as a result the State "condemned [girls] to ignorance and idleness."[13] These articles from the *Telégrafo mercantil* reflected the ongoing discourse and efforts to enhance the education of girls from the end of the eighteenth century.

In 1810, concerted efforts were made to broaden educational opportunities in Córdoba. Despite Bishop San Alberto allowing as early as 1782 up to eight mulatas to enter the orphanage to serve the girls and receive an education, it was not enough, according to Rodrigo Antonio de Orellana, the rector of the University of Córdoba. He proposed that the university board assist in establishing a public school for pardos in the city and its rural jurisdiction, where they could teach pardos the "Christian doctrine and good manners because pardos continued to suffer from ignorance."[14] Similar to commentary advanced in *Telégrafo mercantil*, and more specifically in the article "Memoria sobre que conviene limitar la infamia anexá á varias castas de gentes que hay en nuestra América," de Orellana argued that ignorance remained a common ailment among pardos. By creating a school geared to pardo children, they could indoctrinate these children with Christian values and morality, which especially elevated recently freed African descendants, bringing them more in line with ideal, honorable, and Spanish behavior. Unable to find a separate location for the school, Orellana hoped to use an old Jesuit school building next to the university and the Colegio de Monserrat.[15] But the board of the university denied his request, stating that "although this was a laudable effort, in addition to other reasons against it, they did not have the necessary repartitions for this classroom."[16]

The urgency of the wars of independence in the Río de la Plata brought to the forefront the lack of girls' education and made it a priority for the burgeoning republic. It enhanced the roles mothers played in the home. They not only reared the children and supported their husbands, but they also served a civic duty in the republic.[17] Shortly after the call for independence, Manuel Belgrano, a leader of the revolution, wrote a polemic essay, "The Education of Women," which pointed to the direct role mothers played in the republic. Together, men and women both contributed to the republic's efforts, although one fought on the battlefield and the other cultivated the family.[18] Belgrano further stressed that "nature ensured a woman would be a mother," but he questioned "who should inspire the first ideas [of citizens], and what has she [the mother] taught them if she has not been taught? How have social and moral virtues developed, characteristics that are situated in the profound parts of children's hearts? Who has told them these virtues . . . justice, truth, good faith, decency . . . are so necessary to man?"[19] According to Belgrano, women inevitably become mothers. But that was not enough when it came to child-rearing. The girls had to learn specific values, such as "justice and truth," so that they could instill these values in their children. Without an education, mothers could not instill morality and civility, qualities that ensured the peace and productivity of society.

COLEGIO DE NIÑAS EDUCANDAS: LEARNING THE LESSONS OF MOTHERHOOD

As the wars of independence ensued, the United Provinces of the Río de la Plata had to wrestle with a jarring hypocrisy: how could they fight for freedom from a tyrannical Spain but continue to uphold the institution of slavery? The Free Womb Act served as a compromise that also signified the importance that African-descended mothers would have in the republic. The essence of the law freed slave mothers' children known as "libertos," but these children had to remain with their mothers for the first two years of their lives and within the patron's household until they came of age. This demonstrates that although libertos had gained freedom, they still needed social grooming.[20] The Colegio de Niñas Educandas, which officially opened its doors to parda girls, both African descendants and Indians, played a key role in this grooming in 1811. With Córdoba's adoption of the Free Womb Act and its school for parda girls, slave mothers not only produced freedom but those liberta daughters who obtained an education would edify the next generation.

The exact reasoning or decree for establishing the school remains unclear, but the context in which the school created a classroom for parda girls cannot be ignored. Occurring one year after the call for independence and shortly after the failed attempt to establish a school for pardos in 1810, Colegio de Niñas Educandas opened its doors to parda girls. At school, these girls learned morality, civility, and obedience, qualities of a virtuous girl who would serve her civic duty to raise respectable and cultivated children.

The pardas' education consisted of mass in the morning followed by praying the Litany of Our Lady on their knees. Afterward, the girls started lessons in reading, writing, and manual labor such as sewing, cooking, and cleaning, and they dedicated their mornings and evenings to thirty minutes of singing catechism songs. Sometimes during their chores, the girls would lead a spiritual lesson and the teacher would take advantage of this time to teach them the respect and obedience they owed their parents and the devotion they owed to the Church and to instruct them about the horror of sin.[21] In the afternoon, they would partake in the same activities as in the morning, praying the rosary after they had sung their catechism lesson. The day's instruction ended with a kiss on the teacher's hand and with "much modesty and silence in the streets" as they returned home and kissed their parents' hands.[22]

However, the school did not allow these girls to join the orphanage, which school officials reserved for honorable Spanish girls, and the school segregated parda girls from other poor girls who did not reside in the orphanage.[23] Part of the reason for this segregation stemmed from the school's previous practice of separating "interas" (orphans) from "externas" (girls who commuted). The internas consisted of Spanish girls from honorable backgrounds, while externas consisted of girls from lower socioeconomic means. The parda classroom became an additional classroom for the externas. Having a segregrated classroom suggests that upliftment for those of African descent would remain within the constraints of hierarchy. This is because upliftment did not mean equality but instead perpetuated the existing social hierarchy, which Sobremonte and San Alberto, the founders of public education in Córdoba, espoused. Institutional whitening or social grooming focused more on controlling and ensuring that an increasingly freed population did not fall victim to ignorance and idleness and remained productive and loyal members of society.

In 1825, a citywide school census revealed that, within the orphanage, fifty-seven "niñas blancas," formerly labeled "Spanish," attended one of the schools and forty-six "pardas or castas" attended the other.[24] One half of the pardas paid for their lodging, while the other half received it for free. Fourteen pardas labored as servants within the school, and four served others outside of the school. Pardas continued receiving instruction in domestic arts, basic literacy, and religion, while the niñas blancas received more extensive instruction, which included reading, writing, and Christian doctrine. Additionally, they received lessons in basic history, sewing, embroidery, weaving silk, and arranging flowers.[25]

This curriculum revealed that despite treating motherhood as a shared experience of all women, freed mothers played a different role in the republic than did noble (formerly labeled Spanish) mothers. African-descended girls had to learn how to be industrious and to exhibit moral and ethical behavior. As mothers, they would impart these qualities to their children, which ensured that their children would not fall victim to barbarism that constantly threatened the social order and peace. Noble girls, however, received a more comprehensive curriculum that directly prepared them to become ladies of the house. Their roles in the republic remained quite similar to those of the colonial period. Remaining within the confines of the Church, the school continued to promote the importance of motherhood while maintaining social hierarchies. Historian Silvia Arrom found similar differences in female education in Mexico City. The Spanish girls received lessons in reading, writing, arithmetic, science, history, embroidery, sewing, and music, while for Indian girls the school emphasized basic literacy and household skills, such as washing and ironing. The stark contrast continued to reinforce existing social hierarchies.[26]

Nevertheless, manumitted African descendants enrolled in these schools to whiten themselves. Ten years after Bernardina's manumission and schooling, for example, the 1822 census listed her as free and living at the Monastery of Santa Catalina, where the census also listed doña Micaela residing.[27] Bernardina maintained her free status and most likely benefited from the school's social grooming and from her continued connection to doña Micaela. Their relationship began with Bernardina's mother, Encarnación, who first appeared in the 1795 census, as a nine-year-old mulata slave in doña Micaela's household. As mentioned in chapter 4, these domestic activities created levels of intimacy that benefited slave mothers and their children. Encarnación's service to doña Micaela most likely helped to secure her daughter's schooling.

In another case, a former slave's grandchildren went to school. Based on the 1778 census, Feliciana Martínez and her husband, Clemente Ortega, listed as a free mulato, lived in doña Jacinta Sobradiel's household.[28] By 1813, Feliciana Martínez had achieved manumission and the census takers described her as a fifty-year-old widow and free parda who worked as a baker. Her daughters, Francisca and Dolores Ortega, followed in their mother's footsteps and worked as bakers too. But her granddaughters, Patricia and Francisca, both five-years-old, enrolled in school.[29] Within this family, achieving freedom went only so far. They took advantage of the recently created school, although under segregated terms, and enrolled her grandchildren.

The parda school's acceptance of Indian girls reveals that its efforts to uplift all future mothers extended beyond African descendants. The 1813 census lists sisters Francisca Quijano, eight, and Salome Quijano, ten, as being in school. They lived with their parents José Hilario Quijano, listed as a free Indian who labored as a carpenter, and Marcela Olivera, listed as an Indian seamstress in the city.[30] That Indian girls were enrolled in the school as early as 1813 suggests that social grooming also benefited their status. Even though Indians' free status benefited people threatened with enslavement, as discussed in chapter 5, an Indian status alone did not carry the same privileges as the nineteenth century progressed. Enrolling in class helped to differentiate educated Indian girls from other Indians who lived outside of the city or in the pampas. As noted, governing authorities stereotyped those in the pampas as being savage, ignorant, and barbarous. Over time, the girls lost their Indian identity, because by the 1822 census, Francisca and Salome and their younger sister, Magdalena, had become free pardas.[31]

Some slaveholders—such as doña Michaela, who in 1816 made Bernardina's freedom contingent on her remaining in school—took care to ensure that their female slaves received an education. In 1826, the orphanage admitted Ceferina, a seventeen-year-old criada. The school's ledgers listed her as a criada of don Francisco Antonio González. In this case, the term "criada" alluded to her enslaved status; it was unclear whether she had been a criada since birth or had acquired the position later.[32] This case suggests that education was a vital component of African descendants' uplift and of how some slaveholders, such as don Francisco González, made concerted efforts to ensure that their criadas were taken care of even after they gained their freedom. This example, along with that of Bernardina, reveals the levels of intimacy and care that could develop between slaveholders and their slaves.

Governing and, most importantly, ecclesiastical authorities tasked African-descended mothers with raising their children not only to be good, loyal, and moral but also to know their place in the budding republic. In turn, African-descended girls decided or were encouraged by their family members and sometimes slaveholders to attend school to learn the desired behaviors and implement these behaviors in their homes. In this way, African-descended girls continued to whiten themselves in order to meet the growing republic's definitions of acceptable behavior.

THE GROWTH OF PUBLIC EDUCATION IN CÓRDOBA

From the beginning, Córdoba's republic made education, particularly childhood education, its priority. The Reglamento Provisorio of 1821, Córdoba's first constitution, stated that childhood education "sustain[ed] and inculcate[d] the principles of humanity," which included "industry and fragility, honesty and delicacy in behavior, generous sincere feelings, and social affection." Furthermore, education, according to the Reglamento, taught the morals and civility necessary to establish "a peaceful preservation of men's rights in society."[33] To ensure that all children received an education, the Reglamento Provisorio of 1821 ordered that "all indigent and misfortunate citizens" should have access to education no matter their social condition. Moreover, Congress was responsible for drawing up plans and securing funding to sustain public education.[34] As stated clearly in the constitution, the government had the responsibility to implement education.

To fulfill the goals of education, governors had to create more schools and ensure that young children could attend them. The first governor of Córdoba, Juan Bautista Bustos, shocked that "in all the province only two schools existed, one in the city and the other in the province [Villa del Rosario, in el Río Segundo]," commissioned a governing body known as the *Junta Protectora de Escuelas* (School Board) to increase educational facilities.[35] Bustos ordered the Junta to establish a school in every quarter of the countryside, promote one student from each quarter to the university, and continuously replace that student with another student from the area.[36] Under his leadership (1820–1829), the republic saw a dramatic increase in public education.

However, as in the colonial period, parental opposition hampered some of their efforts to establish schools throughout the pampas. A letter written to the Junta Protectora de Escuelas complained that parents were abandoning their role in ensuring that their children went to school. José Manuel Salguero, a representative of the Junta Protectora, noted that parents did not support "the education of their children, and that they only aspire [for] them to be lazy, and . . . imitate their ignorance and bad manners." Salguero feared that leaving child-rearing to uneducated parents would only perpetuate the cycle of moral ignorance and produce less industrious and virtuous children. Moreover, the only way to combat living in the pampas, which environment, according to ecclesiastical and governing authorities, bred ignorance, was through learned behavior taught outside of the home at school. Nevertheless, Salguero remained hopeful and asked for help in identifying "those children who are capable of receiving an education."[37]

Interestingly enough, parents, especially elite parents, who did subscribe to the goals of an education protested the integration of a public school located in the city. The parents petitioned the Junta Protectora de Escuelas because they did not agree with the integration practices, citing them as "unfortunate abuse[s]" most likely because they did not see their sons as equals to pardo boys. Instead the parents considered it an abuse of power that the Public School of the University had allowed pardo and noble boys to attend the same school, and thus they no longer supported their children's attendance. The Junta Protectora de Escuelas relayed to the governor that under those circumstances of "confusing the classes," the fathers of these families stopped sending their boys to school. Additionally, they had only one teacher, so the excessive number of boys who did attend the school made learning more difficult. To remedy both problems, Bustos decided to divide the school, creating one school for pardo boys and the other for noble boys, each with their own teachers.[38] Bustos determined that all boys needed an education, but to keep the peace and not upset parents, he divided the school based on the boys' status. The governor's agreement to segregate the class indicates that institutionalized whitening was intended not to uplift pardo children and thereby create an equal society but rather to uphold the existing social hierarchy.

Busto's decision was mirrored in the School for Girls' segregated classes. But his commitment to pardo boys broadened the institutional whitening measures because the budding republic relied on all free men to maintain and keep the peace within the province. The Reglamento Provisorio of 1821 stated that "all individuals of the state born in America, every foreigner who enjoys active suffrage in civic assemblies: all Spanish Europeans with a citizen card: and all African and free pardos . . . of the city, town and countryside, from age 20 to 50 . . . are soldiers of the State."[39] As a result, the broadening of institutional whitening to include pardo boys, although under segregated terms, served the larger republic's goal of upliftment, which in turn produced well-trained and industrious citizens who contributed to the making of the republic.

From 1822 to 1829, Juan Bautista Bustos enacted aggressive legislation that made education a cornerstone for Córdoba. He continued the efforts begun during the late eighteenth century to combat the ignorance and idleness found in the pampas. He established schools to reach pardos and nonelites not only in the city but also, and most importantly, in the pampas. Through his efforts, he broadened the institutional whitening begun with female education in 1811 to include boys. The efforts to increase public education would continue with José María Paz, the next governor of Córdoba and also a Unitarian and political adversary to Bustos, who associated with the Federalists. He defeated Bustos in the Battle of San Roque in 1831.

During his brief reign from 1829 to 1831, Paz remained politically isolated. His Federalist political adversaries lay within the city, the province, and the capital, Buenos Aires. Constantly under threat, Paz had to build a loyal following that would defend his political agenda. To entice pardo soldiers, Paz granted their children free public education, finding "no reason for excluding castas [pardos] . . . as they serve in the militia" yet were denied entrance into public schools.[40] This measure secured pardo support because it dealt with the harsh reality of discrimination. Shortly after taking control of Córdoba's province, Paz declared the following measures for the institution of public education for pardos:

1. The doors of public education will be open to all pardo children who have the aptitude and talent.
2. They will be taught grammar and drawing, which is necessary to perfect them in all the arts.
3. The same teacher who teaches white children will teach castas [pardos].
4. Those who have talents and aptitude for the study of mathematics will be directed to the same teachers who reside in the cathedral.
5. Special care will be given to ensure their success.
6. Two of these students will enroll in the school of the Governor's choosing and receive assistance from the State.
7. The General Minister is responsible for the completion of this decree.[41]

These guidelines desegregated institutional whitening but still upheld the goal of social grooming. The first measure acknowledged that all pardo children who had the aptitude and the talent deserved an education. In contrast to Bustos, who had declared in 1822 that boys should attend segregated schools, Paz's third measure dictated that the same teacher would teach both white and casta boys. This stipulation made clear that Paz was determined to socially groom all children in the same manner to live up to the egalitarian ideologies of the burgeoning republic, which first declared itself responsible for educating children. Paz further provided financial assistance for pardo boys to attend public school. In general, these measures spoke to boys' merits and aptitudes rather than the social hierarchy. Paz's decree made him a hero and a champion of slaves and free castas.

Involving himself in the social realities of his constituents ensured their support and loyalty. Paz stated that the goals of denying the children of artisans access to education were to "dominate them . . . [and] submerge them into the most profound ignorance."[42] Paz's desegregation policies not only democratized public education and ensured further support for his regime but also had a lasting influence. In focusing on the child, Paz created lifelong supporters. According to Tomás Anchorena, a prominent politician in the early nineteenth century, education and politics served the larger objective of "plant[ing] the seed of hope that [the children] would in turn support it."[43] In this case, surrounded by political adversaries and enemies, Paz fostered a relationship with free pardos and the enslaved to ensure that he had constant support.

Paz made these concessions only to those loyal to him. In 1830, he allowed masters to reinstate into slavery those former slaves who had fought against him. Owners had to pay only ten pesos for each slave. However, when General Paz fell from power in 1831, the new governor, José Vicente Reynafé, deemed invalid all but Paz's educational decrees and other concessions such as manumission, leaving many slave soldiers in a precarious situation. Manuel Antonio, an African-descended soldier, sought his freedom because of his former service to General Paz. His slaveholder, however, attempted to reenslave him. Even with verification that he had liberto status, the court ruled in favor of his reenslavement.[44] Still, Paz specifically guaranteed that African descendants would have access to education, although this guarantee was politically motivated. Paz fostered a relationship with pardos and slaves that lasted long after his defeat in 1831. In 1840, the Unitarians, Paz's political affiliation, briefly took over the city. The success of the attack, according to the newspaper the *Standarte nacional*, resulted from "600 industrious workers, who formed the virtuous battalion *cazadores de la libertad* [hunters of freedom]."[45] Paz had created the Cazadores de la Libertad battalion, one of three urban militia corps that consisted of "pardos, blacks, and slave artisans" that fought for Paz, historian Seth Meisel argues, "because they received benefits such as pay and uniforms."[46]

In 1832, the census revealed that childhood education had increased dramatically between 1813 and 1832. This increase represented the efforts of Bustos, Paz, and the Colegio de Niñas Educandas. Overall, the census reflected a growth in educational affiliation. Education rose dramatically from 140 people affiliated with schools in 1813, including teachers and students, to 911 people affiliated with schools in 1832. Considering Córdoba's small population, just 11,228 inhabitants in 1832, these numbers are significant, with 8 percent of the population affiliated with formal schooling.[47]

Based on the 1813 and 1832 censuses, a larger percentage of parda girls received more education than boys, despite the fact that more pardo boys attended school. In 1813, 33 percent of parda and Indian girls, in comparison to 12 percent of free pardo and mestizo boys, attended school (table 6.1 and table 6.2). In 1832, while there was an overall increase in education, 52 percent of parda and Indian girls attended school, while only

35 percent of pardo and Indian boys did (table 6.3 and table 6.4). These percentages reflected girls' tendency to gain and maintain their access to education. The creation of the parda school in 1811 contributed to the increase in the number of female students attending the segregated external class that catered to pardas and Indians. Governing and ecclesiastical authorities encouraged female education among all classes because of the influence they would have as mothers over their children. According to historian Carlos Newland, if girls "were ignorant superstitious and unproductive, they would produce sons with the same defects."[48] All future mothers deserved an education, which in turn would ensure the proper upliftment of the recently freed population.

The same trend in education is evident for Indians girls' access to education, in comparison to Indian boys' access, in 1832. That census listed twenty-seven Indian girls and eighteen Indian boys as enrolled in school. Of the twenty-seven Indian girls listed as students, the majority, fifteen

TABLE 6.1. AGE AND STATUS OF FEMALE STUDENTS
AND TEACHERS, CÓRDOBA 1813

Age	Free pardas	Indians	Spaniards	Total
5–9	6	1	10	17
10–14	0	1	7	8
15 and older	1	0	1	2
Total	7	2	18	27

Source: AHPC 1813 census of the city of Córdoba

TABLE 6.2. AGE AND STATUS OF MALE STUDENTS
AND TEACHERS, CÓRDOBA, 1813

Age	Free pardas	Mestizos	Spaniards	Total
5–9	6	1	24	31
10–14	7	0	51	58
15 and older	0	0	24	24
Total	13	1	99	113

Source: AHPC 1813 census of the city of Córdoba

TABLE 6.3. AGE AND STATUS OF FEMALE STUDENTS
AND TEACHERS IN CÓRDOBA, 1832

Age	Free pardas	Indians	Spaniards/ noble/ blancas	Total
5–9	81	12	81	174
10–14	51	15	67	133
15 and older	8	0	7	15
Total	140	27	155	322

Source: AHPC 1832 census of the city of Córdoba

TABLE 6.4. AGE AND STATUS OF MALE STUDENTS AND
TEACHERS IN CÓRDOBA, 1832

Age	Free pardas	Indians	Spaniards/ noble/ blancos	Total
5–9	109	9	149	267
10–14	71	8	180	259
15 and older	7	1	55	63
Total	187	18	384	589

Source: AHPC 1832 census of the city of Córdoba

girls, fell within the age range of ten to fourteen (table 6.3). Some of the oldest girls included Teresa Leiba and María Noriega, aged thirteen. These numbers reflect a dramatic increase from those in the 1813 census, which listed only two free Indians, Francisca and Salome Quijano, eight and ten years old, respectively (table 6.1).[49] Indian boys who attended school also increased dramatically, from none in 1813 to eighteen, including the brothers Candelario and Antonio Guiterres from Tucumán, in 1832 (table 6.2 and table 6.4).[50]

Two factors account for the increase in the number of Indians who attended school. First, the Indian population in the city had increased from 32 in the 1822 census to 430 in the 1832 census (table 2.2). This is most likely because La Toma, one of the few remaining Indian pueblos in the nineteenth century located close to the city, increased its land.[51] Second, Indian status took on new meaning in the republican period. Over the course of the nineteenth century, the label "Indian" did not garner privileges or status as it had in the eighteenth century. Instead, over the course of the nineteenth century, governing authorities argued that a person labeled "indio" represented the ignorance and idleness found in the pampas, because they decided not to acculturate to the city. An education served as an uplifting mechanism for Indians who sought to distance themselves from the increasing negative association with the label "indio." Being tasked with the similar responsibility to educate and reform the next generation may also explain why Indian girls who lived in the city outnumbered their male counterparts in 1832.

Further analysis of the city censuses demonstrates that age played a significant role. In 1813, free parda and Indian girls ages five to nine and ten to fourteen had greater access to schooling than those who were fifteen and older. A similar situation obtained for Spanish girls, for whom there was a slight decrease in schooling from five to nine and ten to fourteen, but at least one Spanish girl more than fifteen years of age had access to schooling (table 6.1). Similarly, free pardo and mestizo boys had access to school at rates comparable to those of free parda and Indian girls, as those fifteen and older were not affiliated with schooling. This is in stark contrast to those boys labeled "Spaniard," where there were an equal number of boys ages five to nine and fifteen and older (table 6.2).

In 1832, free parda and Indian girls overwhelmingly attended school between the ages of five to nine, with a slight growth among pardas who were fifteen and older (table 6.3). Pardas in the five-to-nine and fifteen-and-older age categories were almost equivalent to Spanish/noble/blanca girls. Among the fifteen-and-older age group, four of these women taught classes. They included doña Mercedes and doña Basila, who the census takers noted as noble women, and Josefa Romero and Josefa Sarate, noted as pardas.[52] That year, pardos and Indians younger than fifteen constituted most of those who had access to education, although there is a slight increase from 1813 in access among free pardos and Indians who were fifteen and older (table 6.4).

Throughout the republican period, pardo and Indian parents did not mind supporting a rudimentary education for their children aged five to nine and, if possible, ten to fourteen, but they could not afford for their older children to be in school because they needed them to earn money to contribute to the household. These older children were also barred from attending the university because they lacked pureza de sangre. In addition, conscription had an effect among pardo boys. The wars of independence started in 1810 and continued to affect Córdoba until 1820, and the ensuing civil wars lasted until the 1860s. The constant need for manpower on the battlefield meant that freed boys were not given the same educational opportunities. Notably, the increase in education among Spanish/noble/blanco boys between the ages of five and nine and ten and fourteen and among a sizable number of these boys and men aged fifteen and older in 1832 reflected the continued advantages they possessed in cordobés society, such as attending the university (table 6.4).

CONCLUSION

The Colegio de Niñas Educandas officially opened a segregated class for parda girls in 1811, marking the beginning of an institutionalized whitening process in an increasingly freed population. Not trusting the parenting skills of the nonelite and especially of the castas, the ecclesiastical and governing officials sought to uplift free and freed African descendants from their state of moral ignorance and idleness, to instill in them desirable values such as ethics and civility, and to teach them domestic skills. This instruction did not transform them into white elites; rather, female education gave free pardas the tools to better themselves and their children according to the Church's and the governors' desired behavior. They would become virtuous mothers who would uplift the next generation of citizens, further removing the stigma of their former enslaved status. In promoting education, the Church and government directly shaped the whitening process. As a result, as the nineteenth century progressed, whiteness no longer constituted a series of individual choices made by African-descended women but instead became a marker of class. Freedom without an education did not suffice, and, for that reason, governors Bustos and Paz also permitted free casta boys to attend school, with the intention that they would become virtuous citizens and soldiers.

Together with the Church, which ran the only public school for girls, the republic, under Bustos's rule, remained committed to building schools in both the city and the pampas. His efforts continued the goals set forward by San Alberto and Sobremonte during the eighteenth century, which focused on instilling a desired behavior in children that would lead to a better society. However, by 1831, Paz, a Unitarian, had taken over governance of the province. To maintain a loyal following, composed largely of free pardos and slaves, to protect him from his political adversaries, he granted an important military concession. He desegregated the public schools. The actions of these two men brought about an increase in public education throughout Córdoba's city and province that institution-alized whitening and ensured that the republic uplifted and cultivated an increasingly freed population.

By the second half of the nineteenth century, the Colegio de Niñas Educandas had begun a new phase. In 1858, five years after the abolition of slavery in Córdoba, the school's segregrated class for pardas ceased to exist. Most likely, the pardas were integrated into the *externa* (commuter class) that remained a part of the orphanage throughout the nineteenth century.[53]

Conclusion
Visualizing Black Invisibility

Black invisibility in Argentina stems from individual and institutional efforts to escape, eliminate, or edit out blackness in cities like Córdoba. African-descended women sought and achieved privilege by claiming Spanish or Indian identities, and their claims marked the beginnings of black invisibility dating from the colonial period. Their shift to Spanish or Indian identities came about because of the political and economic realities of this period. Calidad remained in flux despite civil authorities' categorization and quantification of their respective populations. This fluidity made it possible for these women to socially ascend and become Spanish or Indian, which in turn made them protagonists in their own erasure. This may seem problematic and unfortunate, but I would counter that people make decisions based on the choices they are given. In these cases, seeking a better life for themselves and/or their children meant escaping the societal and governmental limitations of blackness when possible.

By examining women's role in black invisibility, the narrative moves from the battlefield to the household, male soldiering to female motherhood, and masculine self-sacrifice to feminine protectors of the home. Rather than focusing on heroic and individual moments of fighting on the battlefield, this book approaches the household as a space of contested and challenged identities. The household is not only where African-descended women monopolized domestic labor but also where intimate relationships between members in the household manifested as intricate social networks and sources of influence that these women used to ascend. Self-sacrifice did not mean an outward bravado but instead a silent strength that kept women hidden in plain sight even as they were protagonists in the formation and cultivation of their families. Ironically, the republic eventually targeted this quiet fortitude, and the result was institutionalized whitening.

Institutionalized whitening took place as part of a concerted effort of republican-sponsored black erasure. Evidence of the republic's efforts to lighten the population is drawn from census data that reveal that the pardo category grew to encompass those formerly labeled "castas" in the republican period, a period of formidable development. The collapse of the casta labels into pardo encompassed a larger movement of eliminating remnants of colonial society such as former calidad labels and of integrating an increasingly freed population into the republic. No longer bound to negra or mulata, the ambiguity of the label "parda" facilitated the social ascent of women of African descent.

As a freer population developed under these conditions, so did governing authorities' willingness to not only control but also mold their actions into what they considered to be ideal social behavior. In other words, freedom in itself was not enough for African-descended children, which is why social grooming was institutionalized in public education. Schools taught the ideal behavior that was associated with whiteness (morality, productivity, and civility) and discouraged behavior that was associated with blackness (promiscuity, idleness, and moral ignorance). Institutionalized whitening also marked an important transformative stage of identity, which no longer had the malleable qualities of the eighteenth century. Instead, the republican period marked a gradual grouping of otherness, which without social grooming would not fit into a developing whitened national identity.

Together, individual and institutionalized whitening during the eighteenth and nineteenth centuries sheds lights on an often-overlooked process of black invisibility. African descendants' attempts to achieve privilege did not mean they sought whiteness only; instead, this period reveals that Indian identity also proved advantageous.[1] In Córdoba, an Indian who lived in the city or remained on government-sanctioned pueblos had the privileged status of freedom, which is what many enslaved African descendants sought to achieve throughout the colonial and early republican periods. This seeking of Indian identity highlights Córdoba's social and political conditions. People in Córdoba maintained a conservative understanding of identity that stemmed from the colonial period well into the republican period. Córdoba's conservative culture remained because of the city's small size and diminished economy, which meant that ruling elites clung to tradition during a very tumultuous and chaotic transition from colony to republic. By including Indians in the narrative of black invisibility, this book has provided a more inclusive and complex notion of identity in Argentina and points to another explanation for black invisibility that is deserving of more attention.

In taking the path less traveled and studying black invisibility in Córdoba, I find that a clear distinction between the interior of the country and the littoral port city of Buenos Aires emerges. Despite the concentration of research on Buenos Aires, Córdoba is more representative of black invisibility during the late colonial and early republican periods. This is because

Buenos Aires was an anomaly compared to the rest of the Río de la Plata. Most of the interior consisted of small provincial towns and cities like Córdoba, while Buenos Aires experienced population growth and became the epicenter of trade. By focusing on a smaller city, I uncovered the intimate individual choices and institutionalized whitening that reflect a more colorful and representative Argentine experience.

At its core, black invisibility in Córdoba is a story about resistance. In general, rebellions and revolutions have encapsulated black resistance. But this book engages "everyday forms of resistance." African-descended women's decisions to transform into Spanish or Indian women or become educated highlight adaptation as a form of resistance. Whether propelled by their willingness to ameliorate their social condition or adhering to institutional definitions of ideal behavior, African-descended women adapted to the choices they were given, signifying that they did not passively rely on others to secure their social advancement. Instead, while remaining hidden in plain sight, they adapted not only to the rules of the household but also to the larger political and social conditions, and as a result they forged their own experiences.

Glossary

agregado/a. Attached to a household and often fulfilling labor obligations.

alcalde de barrio. City district magistrate.

americano/a. Person born in the Americas. Often used after the wars of independence.

arribadas forzosas. Forced arrivals, slaves who disembarked in a different location than originally planned.

asiento. Formal contract granted by the Spanish Crown to an individual or a company to import slaves.

audiencia. Highest royal court of appeals within a jurisdiction such as the viceroyalty.

blanqueamiento. Whitening process throughout Latin America that claimed a white nation was a modern nation and advanced economic and political polices to increase European immigration.

cabildo. Town hall.

cacique. Indian chieftain. *See also* curaca.

calidad. Individual's reputed public persona that often indicates racial background.

cañada. Narrow glen.

carta de libertad. Manumission papers.

carta de venta. Legal transfer of the rights to sell a slave.

casa de depósito. Punitive house for women.

casta. Of African or mixed-race descent. *See also* pardo.

ciudadano. Citizen.

conchabados. Contracted Indian laborers. *See also* papel de conchabado.

criada. Female domestic slave or servant.

curaca. Indian chieftain. *See also* cacique.

defensor de los pobres. Court-appointed lawyer who represented slaves, women, and other castas in court.

don/doña. Title granted to Spaniards or those designated as having pure blood.

encomendero. Holder of an encomienda.

encomienda. A royal grant of Indians awarded to an encomendero to receive tribute and labor.

español. Spaniard, referring to people born in Spain or the Americas and considered white. *See also* pureza de sangre.

externa. Commuter class.

ilustrados. Advocates of the Spanish Enlightenment who sought to draw the Hispanic world into the European cultural mainstream.

indio. Indian.

juez pedáneo. Royal official who served as a local magistrate.

mala sangre. Tainted blood; the opposite of pure blood. *See also* pureza de sangre.

manifesto. Legal strategy that allowed individuals who purchased slaves illegally to pay a fee.

manta. Blanket or cotton cloth associated with Indian clothing.

mestizo. Mixture of Indian and European ancestry.

moreno. Dark brown; referring to an African descendant.

mulato. Mixture between African and European ancestry.

negro. Black; often synonymous with slave status.

negros descaminados. Unaccompanied disembarked slaves.

noble. Noble; replaced the term "Spaniard" after the wars of independence and referring to the white population.

papel de conchabado. Proof of employment/identification. *See also* conchabado.

pardo. Brown. Term used synonymously with mulato during the colonial period and referring to those formerly labeled castas in the republican period.

partus sequitur ventrem. Roman law from the thirteenth century that decreed that a child inherited the mother's status regardless of the father's status.

patria. Country, nation, or fatherland.

plaza mayor. Main public square.

pueblos de indios tributarios. Crown-sanctioned Indian settlements.

pulpería. Grocery store.

pureza de sangre. Pure blood, referring to Spaniards. *See also* español.

Reglamento Provisorio. Constitution during the republican period in Córdoba.

sistema de castas. Racial classification system.

solares. Plots of allotted land in the city.

traza. City layout in a grid-like pattern.

tributo al recaudador. Tribute collector.

yanaconazgo. Pre-Hispanic Andean labor system.

zambo. Mixture of African and Indian ancestry.

Notes

Introduction

1. Alejandro Frigerio, "'Negros' y 'blancos' en Buenos Aires: Repensando nuestras categorias raciales," *Temas de Patrimonio Cultural* 16 (2006): 77–98; María Lina Picconi, "El 'negro cordobés': Formación de alteridad en la ciudad de Córdoba a comienzos del siglo XXI," in *Estudios Afrolatinoamericanos 3: Actas de Las Quintas Jornadas de GEALA*, eds. Eva Lamborghini, María Cecilia Martino, and Juan Francisco Martínez Peria (Buenos Aires: Ediciones del CCC Centro Cultural de la Cooperación Floreal Gorini, 2017), 284–94.

2. The phrase in Spanish is *no hay negros, desaparecieron.*

3. George Reid Andrews disproved these myths in his book. See George Reid Andrews, *The Afro-Argentines of Buenos Aires, 1800–1900* (Madison: University of Wisconsin Press, 1980).

4. The phrase "they disappeared" (*desaparecieron*) references the Dictatorship from 1976 to 1983. More than thirty thousand people disappeared owing to state-sponsored terror, torture, abductions, and death squads. The whereabouts of many of the disappeared, also known as *desaparecidos*, remains unknown. The term "desaparecido" suggests that those who went "missing" may return. I am not suggesting that this term be applied to Argentina's black past. Instead, I acknowledge why some Argentines use the phrase "they disappeared." In the case of Argentina's black history, the phrase more than likely suggests the unknown answer to what happened to the black population.

5. Recent works that deal with black invisibility include: George Reid Andrews, *Afro-Latin America: Black Lives, 1600–2000* (Cambridge, MA: Harvard University Press, 2016); Lea Geler, *Andares negros, caminos blancos: Afroporteños, estado y nación Argentina a fines del siglo XIX* (Rosario, Argentina: Prohistoria, 2010); Paulina Alberto and Eduardo Elena, eds., *Rethinking Race in Modern Argentina* (New York: Cambridge University Press, 2016).

6. Andrews, *Afro-Latin America: Black Lives, 1600–2000*, 4.

7. Despite the historical trend of African descendants deciding to seek whiteness, from the late 1990s to today, advocacy for African descendants has increased tremendously. Various political and activist groups such as Diaspora Africana en la Argentina (DIAFAR) are led by African descendants, who acknowledge their blackness as part of the larger African diaspora.

8. For this book, I use the labels "African-descended women" or "women of African descent" to encompass the varying degrees of blackness, which include labels such as *negra, mulata, morena,* and *parda.*

9. A common misconception holds that African-descended women had no choice in the whitening process. According to this misconception, the wars of independence and the ensuing civil wars killed so many African-descended men that women of African descent could find only white men. Thus, women became biological conduits of the disappearance.

10. Andrews, *The Afro-Argentines of Buenos Aires, 1800–1900*; Marvin Lewis, *Afro-Argentine Discourse: Another Dimension of the Black Diaspora* (Columbia: University of Missouri Press, 1996); Geler, *Andares negros, caminos blancos*; Lea Geler, Florencia Guzmán, and Alejandro Frigerio, eds., *Cartografías afrolatino-americanas: Perspectivas situadas desde Argentina* (Buenos Aires: Biblos, 2016); Alejandro Frigerio, "Los afroargentinos: Formas de comunalización, creación de identidades colectivas y resistencia cultural y política," in *Afrodescendientes y afri-canos en Argentina*, eds. Rubén Mercado and Gabriela Catterberg (Buenos Aires: Programa de las Naciones Unidas para Desarrollo (PNUD), 2011), 1–51.

11. For more discussions on how black women forged their own sexual expe-riences, see Nicole von Germeten, *Violent Delights, Violent Ends: Sex, Race, and Honor in Colonial Cartagena de Indias* (Albuquerque: University of New Mexico Press, 2013), 11.

12. For studies on black invisibility in other countries, see Sherwin Bryant, Rachel Sarah O'Toole, and Ben Vinson III, eds., *Africans to Spanish America: Expanding the Diaspora* (Urbana: University of Illinois Press, 2012); Ben Vinson III and Matthew Restall, eds., *Black Mexico: Race and Society from Colonial to Modern Times* (Albuquerque: University of New Mexico Press, 2009); Matthew Restall, *The Black Middle: Africans, Mayans, and Spaniards in Colonial Yucatan* (Stanford, CA: Stanford University Press, 2009); Lowell Gudmundson and Justin Wolfe, eds., *Blacks and Blackness in Central America: Between Race and Place* (Durham, NC: Duke University Press, 2010); Aline Helg, *Liberty and Equality in Caribbean Colombia, 1770–1835* (Chapel Hill: University of North Carolina Press, 2004); Marixa Lasso, *Myths of Harmony: Race and Republicanism during the Age of Revolution, Colombia, 1795–1831* (Pittsburgh, PA: University of Pitts-burgh Press, 2007).

13. See the following for recent discussions of calidad in the colonial period: Ann Twinam, *Purchasing Whiteness: Pardos, Mulattos, and the Quest for Social Mobility in the Spanish Indies* (Stanford, CA: Stanford University Press, 2015); Jo-anne Rappaport, *The Disappearing Mestizo: Configuring Difference in the Colonial New Kingdom of Granada* (Durham, NC: Duke University Press, 2014); Rachel O'Toole, *Bound Lives: Africans, Indians, and the Making of Race in Colonial Peru* (Pittsburgh, PA: University of Pittsburgh Press, 2012); Robert Schwaller, *Géneros de Gente in Early Colonial Mexico: Defining Racial Difference* (Norman: University of Oklahoma Press, 2016); Ben Vinson III, *Before Mestizaje: The Frontiers of Race and Caste in Colonial Mexico* (New York: Cambridge University Press, 2017); Ale-jandra Araya Espinoza, "Registrar la plebe o el color de las castas: 'Calidad' 'clase' y 'casta' en la matricula de Alday (Chile, siglo XVIII)," *América colonial: Denom-inaciones, clasificaciones e identidades*, eds. Alejandra Araya Espinoza and Jaime

Valenzuela Márquez (Santiago, Chile: Universidad de Chile/Pontificia Universidad Católica de Chile, 2010), 331–61; Carmen Bernand, "El color de los criollos: De las naciones a las castas, a las castas a la nación," in *Huellas a Africa en America: Perspectivas para Chile*, ed. Celia Cussen (Santiago, Chile: Editorial Universitaria/ Universidad de Chile, 2008), 13–34; Carolina González Undurraga, "De la casta a la raza: El concepto de raza; Un singular colectivo de la modernidad, México, 1750–1850," *Historia Mexicana* 60 (January 2011): 1,491–1,525; Norah Andrews, "Calidad, Genealogy, and Disputed Free-Colored Tributary Status in New Spain," *Americas* 73, no. 2 (April 2016): 139–70; William San Martín Aedo, "Colores oscuros y estatus confusos: El problema de la definición de categorías étnicas y del estatus de 'esclavo' y 'libre' en litigios de negros, mulatos, y pardos (Santiago a fines del siglo XVIII)," in *América colonial: Denominaciones, clasificaciones e Identidades*, eds. Alejandra Araya Espinoza and Jaime Valenzuela Márquez (Santiago: Universidad de Chile/Pontificia Universidad Católica de Chile, 2010), 257–84; Verónica Undurraga Schuler, "Españoles oscuros y mulatos blancos: Identidades múltiples y disfraces del color en el ocaso de la colonia chilena, 1778–1820," in *Historias de racismo y discriminación en Chile*, eds. Rafael Gaune and Martín Lara (Santiago, Chile: Uqbar, 2009), 341–68; Florencia Guzmán, "Performatividad social de las (sub)categorías coloniales: Mulatos, pardos, mestizos y criollos en tiempos de cambios, guerra y política, en el interior de la Argentina," in *Cartografías afrolatinoamericanas: Perspectivas situadas para análisis transfronterizos*, eds. Florencia Guzmán and Lea Geler (Buenos Aires: Biblos, 2013), 57–86; Judith Farberman, "Imaginarios sociales en la colonia tardía: Clasifaciones y jerarquías del color en Los Llanos de La Rioja, siglo XVIII y XIX," in *Cartografias afrolatinoamericanas: Perspectivas situadas desde la Argentina*, eds. Florencia Guzmán, Lea Geler, and Alejandro Frigerio (Buenos Aires: Biblos, 2016), 25–50.

14. Colonial documents rarely use the label "blanco" (white). Instead the term "español" (Spaniard) was used to describe the population who possessed pureza de sangre. However, "blanco" was used as a qualifier, especially for castas who could and did pass as Spaniards. The term "blanco" gained in use after independence and replaced the label "español," which applied only to those from the peninsula. The extreme opposite, "negro," often denoted an enslaved status associated with African ancestry. See Guzmán, "Performatividad social de las (sub)categorías coloniales," 59.

15. Undurraga Schuler, "Españoles oscuros y mulatos blancos," 352–53.

16. See the following for recent discussions about the Enlightenment and Atlantic History: Sebastian Conrad, "Enlightenment in Global History: A Historiographical Critique," *American Historical Review* 117 (October 2012): 998–1,027; David J. Weber, *Bárbaros: Spaniards and Their Savages in the Age of Enlightenment* (New Haven, CT: Yale University Press, 2006); Nick Nesbitt, *Universal Emancipation: The Haitian Revolution and the Radical Enlightenment* (Charlottesville: University of Virginia Press, 2008); Marisa Linton, *The Politics of Virtue in Enlightenment France* (New York Palgrave, 2001); Bianca Premo, *The Enlightenment on Trial: Ordinary Litigants and Colonialism in the Spanish Empire*, 1st ed. (Oxford: Oxford University

Press, 2017); Jorge Cañizares-Esguerra, Matt Childs, and James Sidbury, eds., *The Black Urban Atlantic in the Age of the Slave Trade* (Philadelphia: University of Pennsylvania Press, 2013); Jack P. Greene and Philip D. Morgan, eds., *Atlantic History: A Critical Appraisal*, 1st ed. (Oxford: Oxford University Press, 2008); Lyman Johnson, *Workshop of Revolution: Plebeian Buenos Aires and the Atlantic World, 1776–1810* (Durham, NC: Duke University Press, 2011).

17. The Bourbon Reforms sought to increase the Crown's revenue through the enactment of political, social, and economic policies and reforms. See Allan J. Kuethe and Kenneth J. Andrien, *The Spanish Atlantic World in the Eighteenth Century: War and the Bourbon Reforms, 1713–1796* (New York: Cambridge University Press, 2014); Adrian J. Pearce, *The Origins of Bourbon Reform in Spanish South America, 1700–1763* (New York: Palgrave Macmillan, 2014).

18. Gradual abolition first began in Pennsylvania in 1780. See the following for gradual abolition in the United States: Joanne Pope Melish, *Disowning Slavery: Gradual Emancipation and "Race" in New England, 1790–1860* (Ithaca, NY: Cornell University Press, 1998); Gary B. Nash and Jean R. Soderlund, *Freedom by Degrees: Emancipation in Pennsylvania and Its Aftermath* (Oxford: Oxford University Press, 1991); Shane White, *Somewhat More Independent: The End of Slavery in New York City, 1770–1810* (Athens: University of Georgia Press, 1991), 24–55; David N. Gellman, *Emancipating New York: The Politics of Slavery and Freedom, 1777–1827* (Baton Rouge: Louisiana State University Press, 2006); Leslie M. Harris, *In the Shadow of Slavery: African Americans in New York City, 1626–1863* (Chicago: University of Chicago Press, 2003); Graham Russell Hodges, *Root and Branch: African Americans in New York and East Jersey, 1613–1863* (Chapel Hill: University of North Carolina Press, 1999); Arthur Zilversmit, *The First Emancipation: The Abolition of Slavery in the North* (Chicago: University of Chicago Press, 1967).

19. The United Provinces of the Río de la Plata consisted of present-day Argentina, Uruguay, and Paraguay. Gran Colombia consists of present-day Venezuela, Colombia, and Ecuador. Recent works on this act in these areas include Magdalena Candioti, "Abolición gradual y libertades vigiladas en el Río de la Plata: La política de control de libertos de 1813," *Corpus* 6, no. 1 (January/June 2016); Yesenia Barragán, "To the Mine I Will Not Go: Freedom and Emancipation on the Colombian Pacific, 1821–1852" (PhD diss., Columbia University, 2016).

20. Andrews, *The Afro-Argentines of Buenos Aires, 1800–1900*; Geler, *Andares negros, caminos blancos*; Lewis, *Afro-Argentine Discourse*; Norberto Pablo Cirio, *Tinta negra en el gris del ayer: Los afroporteños a través de sus periódicos entre 1873 y 1882* (Buenos Aires: Teseo, 2009); Tomás Platero, *Piedra libre para nuestros negros: La broma y otros periódicos de la comunidad afroargentina (1873–1882)* (Buenos Aires: Instituto Histórico de la Ciudad de Buenos Aires, 2004); Donald Castro, *The Afro-Argentine in Argentine Culture: El negro del acordeón* (Lewiston, NY: Edwin Mellen, 2001); Daniel Schávelzon, *Buenos Aires negra: Arqueología histórica de una ciudad silenciada* (Buenos Aires: Emecé, 2003); Lea Geler, "Afrodescendientes y esfera pública en el Buenos Aires de fines del siglo XIX," in *La ruta del esclavo en el Río de la Plata: Aportes para el diálogo intercultural*, ed. Marisa Pineau (Buenos

Aires: Editorial de la Universidad Nacional de Tres de Febrero, 2011), 303–20; Mónica Minuet Cejas and Mirta Pieroni, "Mujeres en las naciones afroargentinas de Buenos Aires," *América Negra* 8 (1994): 133–45; Alicia Martín, "El carnaval y la cuestión interétnica en el Buenos Aires de fin de siglo XIX," in *La herencia cultural africana en las américas* (tomo I), ed. B. Santos Arrascaeta (Montevideo: Ediciones Populares para América Latina, 1998), 131–41.

21. For other examples of whitening throughout Latin America and the Caribbean, see George Reid Andrews, *Afro-Latin America 1800–2000* (Oxford: Oxford University Press, 2004).

22. Domingo Sarmiento, *Obras de D. F. Sarmiento: Viajes por Europa, África i América, 1845–1847*, vol. 5 (Buenos Aires: Publicadas bajo los auspicios del gobierno arjentino, 1886), 70.

23. By the turn of the twentieth century, it seemed that the modernization project had achieved success. In 1905, an article in the magazine *Caras y Caretas* stated, "The [black] race is losing . . . its primitive color. It becomes gray. It dissolves. It lightens. An African tree is producing white flowers." Juan José Soiza Reilly, "Gente de Color," *Caras y Caretas*, November 25, 1905. Another quote attributed to Sarmiento declared: "If you want to see a black person, you must go to Brazil." Nearly one hundred years later, ex-president of Argentina Carlos Menem would also draw parallels between the two countries, stating, "We [Argentina] do not have blacks in our country, that is a Brazilian problem," during a visit to Howard University in Washington, DC. Jorge Fortes and Diego Ceballos, *Afroargentinos* (Latin American Video Archives, 2002).

24. Marta Goldberg, "Mujer negra rioplatense (1750–1840)," in *La mitad del país: La mujer en la sociedad Argentina*, eds. Lidia Knecher and Marta Panaia (Buenos Aires: Centro Editor de América Latina, 1994), 67–81; Silvia Mallo, "La libertad en el discurso del estado, de amos y esclavos, 1780–1830," *Revista de historia américa* 112 (July 1991); Miguel Rosal, *Africanos y afrodescendientes en el Río de la Plata: Siglos XVIII–XIX* (Buenos Aires: Dunken, 2009); Mónica Ghirardi and Nora Siegrist, *Mestizaje, sangre y matrimonio en territorios de la actual Argentina y Uruguay: Siglos XVII–XX* (Buenos Aires: Dunken, 2008).

25. My examination of concubines joins a well-established field of gender and racial studies. Florencia Guzmán, *Los claroscuros del mestizaje: Negros, indios y castas en la Catamarca colonial* (Córdoba, Argentina: Encuentro Grupo Editor, 2010); Verena Martínez-Alier, *Marriage, Class and Colour in Nineteenth-Century Cuba: A Study of Racial Attitudes and Sexual Values in a Slave Society* (Cambridge: Cambridge University Press, 1974); Junia Ferreira Furtado, *Chica da Silva: A Brazilian Slave of the 18th Century* (Cambridge: Cambridge University Press, 2009); Michelle A. McKinley, *Fractional Freedoms: Slavery, Intimacy, and Legal Mobilization in Colonial Lima, 1600–1700* (Cambridge: Cambridge University Press, 2016); María Eugenia Chaves, "Slave Women's Strategies for Freedom and the Late Spanish Colonial State," in *Hidden Histories of Gender and the State in Latin America*, eds. Elizabeth Dore and Maxine Molyneux (Durham, NC: Duke University Press, 2000), 108–26; Gema Guevara, "Inexacting Whiteness: Blan-

queamiento as a Gender-Specific Trope in the Nineteenth Century," *Cuban Studies* 36 (2005): 105–28; Jennifer Morgan, *Laboring Women: Reproduction and Gender in New World Slavery* (Philadelphia: University of Pennsylvania Press, 2004); Muriel Nazzari, "Concubinage in Colonial Brazil: The Inequalities of Race, Class, and Gender," *Journal of Family History* 21 (1996): 107–23; Ann Twinam, *Public Lives, Private Secrets: Gender, Honor, Sexuality, and Illegitimacy in Colonial Spanish America* (Stanford, CA: Stanford University Press, 1999); Karen Y. Morrison, *Cuba's Racial Crucible: The Sexual Economy of Social Identities, 1750–2000* (Bloomington: Indiana University Press, 2015); Emily Clark, *The Strange History of the American Quadroon: Free Women of Color in the Revolutionary Atlantic World* (Chapel Hill: University of North Carolina Press, 2013); María Emma Mannarelli, *Private Passions and Public Sins: Men and Women in Seventeenth-Century Lima* (Albuquerque: University of New Mexico Press, 2007); Lisa Ze Winters, *The Mulatta Concubine: Terror, Intimacy, Freedom, and Desire in the Black Transatlantic* (Athens: University of Georgia Press, 2016).

26. See the following for more discussion on slavery and the household: Mannarelli, *Private Passions and Public Sins*; Frank "Trey" Proctor III, *Damned Notions of Liberty: Slavery, Culture, and Power in Colonial Mexico, 1640–1769* (Albuquerque: University of New Mexico Press, 2010); McKinley, *Fractional Freedoms*; Guzmán, *Los claroscuros del mestizaje*.

27. AAC Juicios Criminales (1789–1794) Leg. 37, Tomo III, Exp. 11.

28. Studies abound about marriage during the colonial period and how the Royal Pragmatic of 1776 attempted to prevent unequal marriages. See Patricia Seed, *To Love, Honor, and Obey in Colonial Mexico: Conflicts over Marriage Choice, 1574–1821* (Stanford, CA: Stanford University Press, 1988); Silvia Arrom, *The Women of Mexico City, 1790–1857* (Stanford, CA: Stanford University Press, 1985); Nicolas Robins, *Of Love and Loathing: Martial Life, Strife, and Intimacy in the Colonial Andes, 1750–1825* (Lincoln: University of Nebraska Press, 2015); Susan Socolow, "Acceptable Marriage Partners: Marriage Choice in Colonial Argentina, 1778–1810," in *Sexuality and Marriage in Colonial Latin America*, ed. Asunción Lavrin (Lincoln: University of Nebraska Press, 1989); Steinar Saether, "Bourbon Absolutism and Marriage Reform in Late Colonial Spanish America," *Américas* 59, no. 4 (April 2003): 473–509; Mónica Ghirardi, *Matrimonios y familias en Córdoba, 1700–1850* (Córdoba, Argentina: Centro de Estudios Avanzados, UNC, 2004); Jeffery M. Shumway, *The Case of the Ugly Suitor: And Other Histories of Love, Gender, and Nation in Buenos Aires, 1776–1870* (Lincoln: University of Nebraska Press, 2005); Antonio Fuentes-Barragán, "Entre acuerdos y discordias: La pragmática sanción para evitar el abuso de contraer matrimonios desiguales en la provincia de Buenos Aires," *Historia y Memoria*, June 2016; Quinteros O. Guillermo, "Ser, sentir, actuar, pensar e imaginar en torno al matrimonio y la familia: Buenos Aires, 1776–1860" (PhD diss., Universidad Nacional de la Plata, 2010).

29. The Royal Pragmatic of 1776 did not define what constituted an unequal marriage. But in 1778, racial undertones appeared. Indians were included in the law, while African descendants were excluded. Steiner Saether, "Bourbon Abso-

lutism and Marriage Reform in Late Colonial Spanish America," *Americas* 59, no. 4 (April 2003): 473–509.

30. These legal differences stem from the Royal Provision of 1542, which did not subject Indians to slavery like it did African descendants. Matthew Restall has described the difference between the legal identity of Indians and the legal identity of African descendants as a "hostility-harmony dialectic." The "hostility-harmony dialect" details comparisons between African-descendant and Indian legal identities, the formation of their communities, and cultural exchanges in the colonial and republican periods. This methodology continues to dominate the scholarship. See Mathew Restall, *Beyond Black and Red: African-Native Relations in Colonial Latin America* (Albuquerque: University of New Mexico Press, 2005), 4–5; O'Toole, *Bound Lives*; Bryant, O'Toole, and Vinson III, eds., *Africans to Spanish America*; Helg, *Liberty and Equality in Caribbean Colombia, 1770–1835*; Rappaport, *The Disappearing Mestizo*; Lasso, *Myths of Harmony*; Nicolas Cushner, *Jesuit Ranches and the Agrarian Development of Colonial Argentina, 1650–1767* (Albany: State University of New York Press, 1983); Gabriela Peña, "La evange-lización de indios, negros y gente de castas en Córdoba del Tucumán durante la dominación española" (PhD diss., Universidad Católica Córdoba, 1997); Samuel Amaral and Juan Carlos Garavagila, "Rural Production and Labor in the Late Colonial Buenos Aires," *Journal of Latin American Studies* 19, no. 2 (November 1987): 235–78; Jorge Gelman, "Sobre esclavos, peones, gauchos y campesinos: El trabajo y los trabajadores en una estancia colonial Rioplatense," in *Estructuras sociales y mentalidades en América Latina: Siglos XVII y XVIII*, ed. Torcuato Di Tella (Buenos Aires: Fundación Simón Rodríguez, 1990), 241–79; Carlos Mayo, *Las haciendas jesuíticas en Córdoba y en el noreste Argentino* (Buenos Aires: Centro Editor de América Latina, 1994); Oscar Albores, Carlos Mayo, and Judith Sweeny, "Esclavos y conchabados en la estancia de Santá Catalina, Córdoba," *Revista América* 5 (1977): 5–20; Marcela Echeverri, *Indian and Slave Royalists in the Age of Revolution: Reform, Revolution, and Royalism in the Northern Andes, 1780–1825* (Cambridge: Cambridge University Press, 2016).

31. "R.C. declarando la forma en que se ha de guardar y cumplir en las indias la pragmática sanción de 23 de marzo de 1776 sobre contraer matrimonios," in *Colección de documentos para la historia de la formación social de hispanoamérica 1493–1810*, ed. Richard Konetzke, vol. 3 (Madrid: Consejo Superior de Investiga-ciones Científicas, 1962), 438–42.

32. Camillia Cowling and María Helena Pereira Toledo Machado, "Mothering Slaves: Comparative Perspectives on Motherhood, Childlessness, and the Care of Children in Atlantic Slave Societies," *Slavery & Abolition* 38, no. 2 (2017): 224.

33. For discussions of education in colonial Latin America, see Bianca Premo, "'El modo de mi educación': Discursos sobre educación y los derechos de la madre en Lima, a finales del virreinato," in *Mujeres, familia, y sociedad en la histo-ria de América Latina, siglos XVIII–XXI*, eds. Scarlett O'Phelan Godoy and Mar-garita Zegarra Flórez (Lima: Pontificia Universidad Católica del Perú, 2006), 593–609; Mark Szuchman, "Childhood Education and Politics in Nineteenth-Century

Argentina: Case of Buenos Aires," *Hispanic American Historical Review* 70, no. 1 (February 1990): 109–38; Liliana de Denaro, *Primicias de educación femenina: Historia de la real casa de huérfanas nobles y la congregación de hermanas carmelitas de Santa Teresa de Jesús* (Córdoba, Argentina: Corintios, 2004); Matt Childs, "'Sewing' Civilization: Cuban Female Education in the Context of Africanization, 1800–1860," *Americas* 54, no. 1 (July 1997): 83–107; María Loreto Egana Baraona, *La educación primaria popular en el siglo XIX en Chile: Una práctica de política estatal* (Santiago, Chile: Dirección de Bibliotecas, Muesos, y Archivos, 2000); Claudio Kuffer, Mónica Ghirardi, and Sonia Colantonio, "Educación elemental en la ciudad de Córdoba, Argentina, en el primer tercio del siglo XIX, sus variaciones y su relación con las demás ocupaciones infantiles," *Revista iberoamericana de educación* 56, no. 1 (July 2011): 1–12; Julia Varela Fernández, "La educación ilustrada como fabricar sujetos dóciles y útiles," *Revista de educación*, no. extraordinario (1988): 245–74; René Amaro Peñaflores, "La educación en Zacatecas durante el siglo XIX," *Fuentes: Estudios humanísticos y sociales* 1 (2001): 119–42; Dorothy Tanck de Estrada, *La educación ilustrada, 1786–1836: Educación primaria en la ciudad de México* (Mexico City, Mexico: El Colegio de México, 1977); Pilar Gonzalbo Aizpuru, *Las mujeres en la nueva España: Educación y vida cotidiana* (Mexico City, Mexico: El Colegio de México, 1987); Silvia Mallo, "La mujer en el periodo colonial: Justicia, educación, y trabajo," in *CLIO, Revista del comité argentino de ciencias históricos* 2 (La Rioja, Argentina: Editorial Canguro, 1994), 15–25; Francisco García González, *Historia de la educación en Zacatecas: Su enseñanza y escritura* (Zacatecas, Mexico: UPN Unidad Zacatecas, 2001); Lucia Lionetti, "'Instruir a las niñas para salvarlas de la indigencia que aflige su cuerpo y la ignorancia que llena su espíritu': La experiencia de la casa de niñas huérfanas nobles Córdoba en el siglo XVIII," *Historia de la educación* 15, no. 1 (June 2014): http://ppct.caicyt. gov.ar/index.php/anuario/article/view/2852.

34. Linda Kerber, "The Republican Mother: Women and the Enlightenment; An American Perspective," *American Quarterly* 28, no. 2 (Summer 1976): 187–205.

35. Beginning in 1810, Argentina called upon African-descended men, both free and enslaved, to risk and often sacrifice their lives in the name of the *patria* (homeland) during the wars of independence (1810–1819). Thus, from the beginning of the war, slave emancipation was tied to an anticolonial struggle. Peter Blanchard, *Under the Flags of Freedom: Slave Soldiers and the Wars of Independence in Spanish America* (Pittsburgh, PA: University of Pittsburgh Press, 2008); Seth Meisel, "'The Fruit of Freedom': Slaves and Citizens in Early Republican Argentina," in *Slaves, Subjects, and Subversives: Blacks in Colonial Latin America*, eds. Jane Landers and Barry Robinson (Albuquerque: University of New Mexico Press, 2006), 273–306; Borucki, *From Shipmates to Soldiers*; Silvia C. Mallo, ed., *Negros de la patria* (Buenos Aires: Editorial Sb, 2010); Marisa Pineau, ed., *La ruta del esclavo en el Río de la Plata: Aportes para el diálogo intercultural* (Buenos Aires: Editorial de la Universidad Nacional de Tres de Febrero, 2011).

36. Pamela Scully and Diana Paton, eds., "Introduction: Gender and Slave

Emancipation in Comparative Perspective," in *Gender and Slave Emancipation in the Atlantic World* (Durham, NC: Duke University Press, 2005), 11.

37. Sarah Chambers, *From Subjects to Citizens: Honor, Gender, and Politics in Arequipa, Peru, 1780–1854* (University Park: Pennsylvania State University Press, 1999); Sarah Chambers, *Families in War and Peace: Chile from Colony to Nation* (Durham, NC: Duke University Press, 2015); M. Carolina Zumaglini, "Cosmopolitan Imperialism: Mann, Sarmiento, and the Origins of Universal Education in Nineteenth-Century Boston and Buenos Aires" (Miami: Florida International University, 2014); Rebecca Earle, "Rape and the Anxious Republic: Revolutionary Colombia, 1810–1830," in *Hidden Histories of Gender and the State in Latin America*, eds. Elizabeth Dore and Maxine Molyneux (Durham, NC: Duke University Press, 2000), 127–46; Scully and Paton, "Introduction."

38. Erika Edwards, "Slavery in Argentina," ed. Ben Vinson III, *Oxford Bibliographies in Latin American Studies*, June 2017.

39. For more information about late-eighteenth-century Buenos Aires, see Johnson, *Workshop of Revolution*.

40. For more discussion about sources and judicial proceedings, see Andrews, *Afro-Latin America: Black Lives, 1600–2000* (Cambridge, MA: Harvard University Press, 2016), 21; Undurraga Schuler, "Españoles oscuros y mulatos blancos," 346.

Chapter 1

1. The AHPC has since moved to another location.

2. Darío Dominino Crespo, *Escándalos y delitos de la gente plebe: Córdoba a fines del siglo XVIII* (Córdoba, Argentina: Universidad de Córdoba, 2007), 180.

3. Carlos A. Luque Colombres, *Orígenes históricos de la propiedad urbana de Córdoba: Siglos XVI y XVII* (Córdoba, Argentina: Universidad Nacional de Córdoba, Facultad de Filosofía y Humanidades, Instituto de Estudios Americanistas "Doctor Enrique Martínez Paz," Dirección General de Publicaciones, 1980), 19.

4. According to María del Carmen Ferreyra, the Santa Catalina alleyway was a unique feature that separated the cabildo and the church and did not exist in most Argentine cities. María del Carmen Ferreyra, "La ciudad de Córdoba y su gente en 1813," in *Población y sociedad en tiempos de lucha por la emancipación: Córdoba, Argentina, en 1813*, ed. Sonia Colantonio (Córdoba, Argentina: Centro de Investigaciones y Estudios sobre Cultura y Sociedad (CONICET-UNC), 2013), 87.

5. In 1623, the cabildo agreed to close the street that cut through the Jesuit estate, which included a church and a school, and increased the Jesuit estate's size to two blocks. See Luque Colombres, *Orígenes históricos de la propiedad urbana de Córdoba*, 30, 50, 51, 113.

6. Despite his assignments, the city dwellers did not construct their homes in the assigned plots. Some did not like the location, and others (such as Francisco Blázquez) for personal reasons exchanged plots; Blázquez built his home in the plot assigned to Hernando de Cespedes. See Luque Colombres, *Orígenes históricos de la propiedad urbana de Córdoba*, 26, 28.

7. Héctor Lobos, *Historia de Córdoba: Raíces y fundamentos*, vol. 1 (Córdoba, Argentina: Ediciones del Copista, 2009), 409.

8. Sonia Colantonio and Mónica Ghirardi, "Introduction," in *Población y sociedad en tiempos de lucha por emancipación: Córdoba, Argentina, en 1813,* ed. Sonia Colantonio (Córdoba, Argentina: CONICET, 2013), 16.

9. For more cases of mestiza and Indian women involved in an urban economy, see Jane E. Mangan, *Trading Roles: Gender, Ethnicity, and the Urban Economy in Colonial Potosí* (Durham, NC: Duke University Press, 2005); Lobos, *Historia de Córdoba,* 1:413–14.

10. Lobos, *Historia de Córdoba,* 1:81.

11. Lobos, *Historia de Córdoba,* 1:54.

12. Lobos, *Historia de Córdoba,* 1:55.

13. Robert Turkovic, "Race Relations in the Province of Córdoba, Argentina 1800–1853" (PhD diss., University of Florida, 1981), 277.

14. Turkovic, "Race Relations in the Province of Córdoba, Argentina 1800–1853," 16.

15. Clara Daniela Gutiérrez, "La justicia en los pueblos de indios de Córdoba a fines al siglo XVIII" (Master's thesis, Universidad Nacional de Córdoba, 2011), 27. For more information about the evangelization process in Córdoba, see Peña, "La evangelización de indios, negros y gente de castas en Córdoba del Tucumán durante la dominación española."

16. Sonia Tell and Isabel Castro Olañeta, "El registro y la historia de los pueblos de indios de Córdoba entre los siglos XVI y XIX," *Revista de Mueso de Antropología* 4 (2011): 239.

17. Ana Inés Punta, *Córdoba borbónica: Persistencias coloniales en tiempo de reformas (1750–1800)* (Córdoba, Argentina: Universidad Nacional de Córdoba, 1997), 149.

18. Punta, *Córdoba borbónica,* 150; Of the nine pueblos de indios tributaries, seven—Quilino, Soto, Pichana, San Jacinto, Cosquín, La Toma, and San Antonio de Nonsacate—had converted to Indian communities by the end of the nineteenth century. Sonia Tell and Isabel Castro Olañeta, "El registro y la historia de los pueblos de indios de Córdoba entre los siglos XVI y XIX," 239–43.

19. Punta, *Córdoba borbónica,* 150.

20. Punta, *Córdoba borbónica,* 153.

21. Punta, *Córdoba borbónica,* 158–59.

22. In 1585, after obtaining the license to import slaves, Francisco de Vitoria, the Bishop of Tucumán, "armed a frigate with 30,000 pesos worth of silver," sailed for Brazil, and returned to Buenos Aires with the first registered slaves, who would later be resold to Alto Peru. Ten years later, Pedro Gomes Reynel, a Portuguese trader, received an *asiento* to import six hundred Africans annually to Buenos Aires, marking the beginning of a continuous legal slave trade that would last for the next 217 years in the Río de la Plata. See Kara D. Schultz, "'The Kingdom of Angola Is Not Very Far from Here': The South Atlantic Slave Port of Buenos Aires, 1585–1640," *Slavery & Abolition* 36, no. 3 (July 3, 2015): 428–29; Héctor Lobos, "Acera del negocio y los comerciantes de esclavos en Córdoba," *Revista de la junta provincial de historia de Córdoba* 23 (2006): 228.

23. Schultz, "'The Kingdom of Angola Is Not Very Far from Here,'" 429.

24. Schultz, "'The Kingdom of Angola Is Not Very Far from Here,'" 429–30.

25. Borucki, *From Shipmates to Soldiers*, 6.

26. Borucki, *From Shipmates to Soldiers*, 6–7.

27. Slave traders did not note the sex of fifty slaves. Carlos Assadourian, *El tráfico de esclavos en Córdoba, 1588–1610: Según actas de protocolos del archivo histórico de Córdoba* (Córdoba, Argentina: Direccíon General de Publicaciones, 1965), resumen de las ventas.

28. Although most slaves came from Africa or Brazil, one slave named Francisco was described in the notarial records as "a slave of the casta de *xapones* (Japanese), of the provinces of *Xapon* (Japan), who has the name Francisco *Xapon*." Diego López of Lisbon sold him to Miguel Geronimo de Porras, a priest and visitor in Córdoba, for 800 pesos. Assadourian, *El tráfico de esclavos en Córdoba, 1588–1610*, 14.

29. In 1609, Juan de Castilla bought a negra named María from Mexico City who had previously lived in Potosí from Pedro Garcia Redondo and his wife, María de Garay. Assadourian, *El tráfico de esclavos en Córdoba, 1588–1610*, 33.

30. Assadourian, *El tráfico de esclavos en Córdoba, 1588–1610*, 33.

31. Sonia Colantonio and Claudio Kuffer, "Marriage in Córdoba City (Argentina) in the Late-Colonial and Early Independent Periods: Homogamy and Surnames as Emerging Features," *Journal of Family History* 39 (2014): 31.

32. Archivo Histórico de la Provincia de Córdoba (AHPC) Censo de la ciudad de Córdoba (1778); Dora Celton, *Ciudad y campaña en la Córdoba colonial* (Córdoba, Argentina: Junta Provincial de Historia de Córdoba, 1996), 80.

33. Celton, *Ciudad y campaña en la Córdoba colonial*, 20.

34. The Indian population most likely includes mestizos. Censo de la ciudad de Córdoba (1778).

35. Censo de la ciudad de Córdoba (1778).

36. These totals do not include 172 married slaves or 555 children, because sex was not specified in these categories. Censo de la ciudad de Córdoba (1778).

37. Some scholars have argued that slaveholders favored female slaves because of their reproductive ability. However, women (and not only female slaves) generally outnumbered men in virtually all the cities of colonial Latin America as opposed to the rural areas. The sex ratio difference reflected the gendered nature of labor rather than reproduction. See Susan Migden Socolow, *The Women of Colonial Latin America* (New York: Cambridge University Press, 2015), 142; Dora Celton, "La venta de esclavos en Córdoba, entre 1750–1850," in *Cuadernos de historia* (Córdoba, Argentina: Universidad de Córdoba, 2000), 5–20; Celton, *Ciudad y campaña en la Córdoba colonial*; Sonia Colantonio, Dora Celton, and Claudio Kuffer, "Las mujeres de color en la Córdoba colonial y postcolonial," in *Familias históricas: Interpelaciones desde perspectivas iberoamericanas a través de los casos de Argentina, Brasil, Costa Rica, España, Paraguay y Uruguay*, eds. Mónica Ghirardi and Ana Silvia Volpi Scott (São Leopoldo, Brazil: Okios, 2015), 276–96.

38. AHPC Censo de la ciudad de Córdoba (1813).

39. Censo de la ciudad de Córdoba (1813).

40. In 1767, the Spanish Crown joined other monarchies, such as the Portuguese, in their decision to expel the Jesuits as part of a series of policies known as the Bourbon Reforms. These reforms sought to increase revenue by centralizing and secularizing power, strengthening the military, and enacting free trade policy. In general, the Spanish Crown distrusted the Jesuit organization because it had become a powerful and self-sustaining institution within the Spanish Indies. The expulsion of the Jesuits from the Spanish Indies in 1767 greatly affected Córdoba's economy because it gave civil authorities access to the Jesuits' property, which included land and slaves. Efraín U. Bischoff, *Historia de Córdoba: Cuatro siglos* (Viamonte: Editorial Plus Ultra, 1979), 89.

41. Jorge Troisi Melean, *El oro de los jesuitas: La compañía de Jesús y sus esclavos en la Argentina colonial* (Madrid: Acadèmica Española, 2012), 43.

42. Guzmán, *Los claroscuros del mestizaje*, 19.

43. Beatriz Bixio, "Mestizos, testamentos, y configuraciones sociales en Córdoba colonial," in *Mestizaje y configuración social: Córdoba (siglos XVI y XVII)*, eds. Beatriz Bixio and Constanza González Navarro (Córdoba, Argentina: Brujas, 2013), 60.

44. Bixio, "Mestizos, testamentos, y configuraciones sociales en Córdoba colonial," 46.

45. Bixio, "Mestizos, testamentos, y configuraciones sociales en Córdoba colonial," 40.

46. Bixio, "Mestizos, testamentos, y configuraciones sociales en Córdoba colonial," 46.

47. Bixio, "Mestizos, testamentos, y configuraciones sociales en Córdoba colonial," 45.

48. Bixio, "Mestizos, testamentos, y configuraciones sociales en Córdoba colonial," 37.

49. Bixio, "Mestizos, testamentos, y configuraciones sociales en Córdoba colonial," 40–41.

50. Bixio, "Mestizos, testamentos, y configuraciones sociales en Córdoba colonial," 46.

51. Lobos, *Historia de Córdoba*, 1:506–7.

52. Bixio, "Mestizos, testamentos, y configuraciones sociales en Córdoba colonial," 45–46.

53. María del Carmen Ferreyra, "Matrimonios de españoles con esclavas durante el siglo XVIII en Córdoba," in *Cuestiones de familia a través de las fuentes*, ed. Mónica Ghirardi (Córdoba, Argentina: Universidad Nacional de Córdoba, 2005), 94.

54. Ferreyra, "Matrimonios de españoles con esclavas durante el siglo XVIII en Córdoba," 104–5.

55. Even in acts of insolence the Jesuits chose to sell the slave along with his or her family. It was worth the economic loss because they did not want the slave's bad behavior to influence others. Troisi Melean, *El oro de los jesuitas*, 147.

56. For a discussion of fictive notions of family, see Proctor III, *Damned Notions of Liberty*, 39; Sherwin Bryant, *Rivers of Gold, Lives of Bondage: Governing through Slavery in Colonial Quito* (Chapel Hill: University of North Carolina Press, 2013).

57. This is based on my observation of casta baptisms in the Archbishopric Archive in Córdoba, Argentina.

58. Jovita Novillo, "La población negra en Tucumán (1800–1820): Con especial referencia a los cuarteles urbanos y a los cuartos de los Juárez y Río Chico" (PhD diss., Universidad Nacional de Tucumán, 2006), 86–87.

59. AAC Expediente Matrimoniales 1816, Leg. 95, Exp. 7.

60. Borucki, *From Shipmates to Soldiers*, chapter 2.

61. AAC Expediente Matrimoniales 1816, Leg. 95, Exp. 7.

62. Herman L. Bennett, *Africans in Colonial Mexico: Absolutism, Christianity, and Afro-Creole Consciousness, 1570–1640* (Bloomington: Indiana University Press, 2003).

63. Samuel Parsons Scott and Robert Burns, *Las Sietes Partidas: Family, Commerce, and the Sea; The Worlds of Women and Merchants (Partidas IV and V)*, vol. 4 (Philadelphia: University of Pennsylvania Press, 2012), Law II, 902.

64. Other details in the case indicate that doña Eugenia was willing to sell her slave for 600 pesos to don José Matías. AAC Juicios Espanoles (1812–1880) Leg. 193, Tomo VIII, Exp. 12.

65. AHPC, Esc 2, Leg. 103, Exp. 12 (1802); Carolina González Undurraga, "Carta de libertad: Aproximaciones sobre la movilidad social de la población esclava en Santiago de Chile, 1700–1810" (PhD diss., Universidad de Chile, 2007), 1.

66. Ferreyra, "Matrimonios de españoles con esclavas durante el siglo XVIII en Córdoba," 130.

67. AHPC, Prot. Reg. 1, 1784, 132v–134v.

68. AHPC, Prot. Reg. 1, 1786, 267v–270v.

69. Based on slave registers, such as the Colegio de Monserrat's inventory in 1775, civil authorities gave each family a number, which suggests that the familial unit would ideally remain together if sold. For example, family number 74 comprised Pedro Pasqual, aged forty-five, his wife, Juana, aged forty-five, and their daughters, María Josepha, aged fourteen, María de los Santos, aged twelve, and Encarnación, aged nine. For a listing of temporalidades (former Jesuit holdings), see AHPC, Esc 2, Leg. 50, Exp. 4 (1775).

70. A third party is defined as an additional person other than the slave or the owner who paid for the slave's manumission. From 1776 to 1830, there was a total of 164 paid manumissions (self-manumissions: 51, or 31 percent; third-party manumissions: 94, or 57 percent; and unknown paid manumissions: 19, or 12 percent). This information came from the AAC Juicios criminals and eclesiásticos and the AHPC escribanías 1–4.

71. AHPC, Prot. Reg. 1, 1778, 253v–254v; AHPC, Prot. Reg. 1, 1784, 240v–241v; AHPC, Prot. Reg. 1, 1785, 150r–151r; AHPC, Prot. Reg. 1, 1793, 142r–143r.

72. AHPC, Prot. Reg. 1, 1778, 253v–254v.

73. AHPC, Prot. Reg. 1, 1791, 233v–235v.

74. Fathers also freed their children, but in only one recorded instance did a father attempt to free his unborn children. This was mainly because the family unit was well-established. The Portuguese slave Gregorio Ferreyra freed his unborn children, first in 1781 and again in 1787. His wife, Antonia, however, remained a slave. AHPC, Prot. Reg. 1, 1781, 134v–135v; AHPC, Prot. Reg. 3, 1787, 8r–9r.

75. The 1778 census lists Juan Nuñez de Olivera as a member of don Josef Nuñez's household. Censo de la ciudad de Córdoba (1778); AHPC, Prot. Reg. 1, 1782, 75v–77r.

76. AHPC, Prot. Reg. 1, 1782, 148v–150r.

77. AHPC, Prot. Reg. 4, 1802, 60r–61v.

78. While it is true that a few people of African descent did participate in the buying and selling of slaves, these cases were very much exceptions. Most free African descendants would not achieve this level of wealth and continued to labor alongside other free people in the city.

79. Ferreyra, "La ciudad de Córdoba y su gente en 1813," 247.

80. AHPC, Prot. Reg. 4, 1803, 416v–418r.

81. AHPC, Prot. Reg. 1, 1806, 189r–190v.

82. AHPC, Prot. Reg. 4, 1810, 674r–675v; AHPC, Prot. Reg. 1, 1813, 355v–357r.

83. Of the 310 commerciantes (merchants), the census listed 17 free pardos and 1 slave in that profession in 1813. Censo de la ciudad de Córdoba (1778); Ferreyra, "La ciudad de Córdoba y su gente en 1813," 247.

84. AHPC, Prot. Reg. 2, 1801, 298r–303v; Hugo Moyano, *La organización de los gremios en Córdoba sociedad artesanal y producción artesanal* (Córdoba, Argentina: Centro de Estudios Historicos, 1986), 186.

85. Clarisa Eugenia Pedrotti, "La música religiosa en Córdoba del Tucumán durante la época colonial (1699–1840)" (PhD diss., Universidad Nacional de Córdoba, 2013), 100.

86. AHPC, Prot. Reg. 2, 1798, 296r–297r.

87. Comparisons of slave prices come from my analysis of notarial records. AHPC, Prot. Regs. 1–4, 1776–1830.

88. Pedrotti, "La música religiosa en Córdoba del Tucumán durante la época colonial (1699–1840)," 100–101.

89. AAC Juicios Eclesiásticos, Leg. 35, Tomo IV, Exp. 13 (1790–1799).

90. AAC Juicios Eclesiásticos, Leg. 35, Tomo IV, Exp. 13 (1790–1799).

91. Punta, *Córdoba borbónica*, 163.

92. Gutiérrez, "La justicia en los pueblos de indios de Córdoba a fines al siglo XVIII" (Master's thesis, Universidad Nacional de Córdoba, 2011), 36.

93. Andrews, "Calidad, Genealogy, and Disputed Free-Colored Tributary Status in New Spain."

94. AHPC, Esc 1, Leg. 439, Exp. 12 (1811).

Chapter 2

1. Censo de la ciudad de Córdoba (1778).

2. Socolow, "Acceptable Marriage Partners," 215.

3. Tau Anzoátegui, *Los bandos de buen gobierno del Río de La Plata, Tucumán, y Cuyo*.

4. Rafael Garzón, *Sobremonte: Córdoba y las invasiones Inglesas* (Córdoba, Argentina: Corredor Austral, 2000), 18–19.

5. Tau Anzoátegui, *Los bandos de buen gobierno del Río de la Plata, Tucumán, y Cuyo*, 379.

6. Tau Anzoátegui, *Los bandos de buen gobierno del Río de la Plata, Tucumán, y Cuyo*, 380.

7. Tau Anzoátegui, *Los bandos de buen gobierno del Río de la Plata, Tucumán, y Cuyo*, 381.

8. Tau Anzoátegui, *Los bandos de buen gobierno del Río de la Plata, Tucumán, y Cuyo*, 373.

9. Tau Anzoátegui, *Los bandos de buen gobierno del Río de la Plata, Tucumán, y Cuyo*, 374.

10. Tau Anzoátegui, *Los bandos de buen gobierno del Río de la Plata, Tucumán, y Cuyo*, 400.

11. Tau Anzoátegui, *Los bandos de buen gobierno del Río de la Plata, Tucumán, y Cuyo*, 402.

12. In 1804, Governor Intendant don José González Gomez de Ribera revised various edicts. His revisions qualified the calidad in the edicts. For example, all mulatos, negros, or jornaleros caught without their papel de conchabado would be sentenced to serve in the royal militia and suffer twenty-five lashes. This is a bit different from Sobremonte, who did not mention the calidad of the person but clearly targeted castas and nonelites. Tau Anzoátegui, *Los bandos de buen gobierno del Río de la Plata, Tucumán, y Cuyo*, 467.

13. Abel Cháneton, *La Instrucción primaria en la época colonial* (Buenos Aires: Biblioteca de la Sociedad de historia Argentina XII, 1942), 267.

14. Abel Cháneton, *Un precursor de Sarmiento y otros ensayos históricos* (Buenos Aires: M. Gleizer, 1934), 39.

15. Cháneton, *La instrucción primaria en la época colonial*, 71.

16. Dr. Fray Joseph Antonio San Alberto, *Colección de instrucciones pastorales, que en diferentes ocasiones, y con varios motivos público para edificación de los fieles, arreglo y dirección de sus diócesis el ilustrísimo y reverendísimo señor D. Fr. Joseph Antonio de S. Alberto, Obispo Antes de Córdoba del Tucumán, y al presente Arzobispo de la Ciudad de La Plata en America*, vol. 1 (Madrid: Imprenta Real, 1786), 242.

17. Gaspar Melchor Jovellanos, "Memoria sobre educación pública," in *La reforma ilustrada: Propuestas democráticas en la España borbónica; Gaspar Melchor de Jovellanos*, ed. Franco Cerutti, 1st ed. (San José, Costa Rica: Libro Libre, 1987), 84.

18. Jovellanos, "Memoria sobre educación pública," 90.

19. Jovellanos, "Memoria sobre educación pública," 88–89.

20. Jovellanos, "Memoria sobre educación pública," 90.

21. Domingo Sarmiento, *Facundo: Civilization and Barbarism*, trans. Kathleen Ross (Berkeley: University of California Press, 2003).

22. Recent discussions of Sarmiento's book, however, have revealed that many

of his ideas from the 1840s may have come from Córdoba's civilizing efforts in the 1830s under the rule of José María Paz. By examining the newspaper *La Aurora Nacional* from Córdoba, the scholar Ariel de la Fuente compared the lines from Facundo and found very similar writings. This suggests that although Sarmiento looked to Europe as his model, his inspiration to create a more civilized society came from the interior, and not because it was a place full of barbarism and despair but because the city of Córdoba under Unitarian rule from 1830 to 1831 was an example to follow. See Ariel de la Fuente, "'Civilización y barbarie': Fuentes para una nueva explicación del Facundo," *Boletin del Instituto de historia Argentina y Americana Dr. Emilio Ravignani*, no. 44 (2016): 135–79.

23. Sixty years before Sarmiento proposed the first classic formulation of the effects of the sparseness of population on the River Plate way of life, San Alberto reached conclusions that foreshadowed those of Facundo: the low population density was leading to a breakdown of social bonds, the consequences of which alarmed him, especially in their political and religious aspects. Tulio Halperín-Donghi, *Politics, Economics, and Society in Argentina in the Revolutionary Period* (Cambridge: Cambridge University Press, 1975), 57.

24. Colegio de Huerfanas de San Miguel, a girl's school in Buenos Aires with a similar mission, also opened in 1755. It existed until 1823, when it was dissolved and the mission to educate girls transferred to the Sociedad de Beneficencia in Buenos Aires. Unlike the Colegio de Huerfanas de San Miguel, Colegio de Niñas Educandas continues to function today and remains dedicated to educating both girls and boys in the city of Córdoba. Comparsions about the two institutions are in Mónica Ghirardi, Dora Celton, and Sonia Colantonio, "Niñez, iglesia y 'política social': La fundación del colegio de huérfanas por el obispo San Alberto en Córdoba, Argentina, a fines del siglo XVIII," *Revista de Demografía Histórica* 26, no. 1 (2008).

25. San Alberto, *Colección de instrucciones pastorales . . .*, 243.

26. San Alberto, *Colección de instrucciones pastorales . . .*, 306.

27. For a comparison of the education of mulatas and other castas in the Colegio Huerfanas de San Miguel, see María Teresa Fuster, "La casa de niñas huerfanas de San Miguel. Beneficencia, prestigio y poder. Las dispustas por su control (1755–1810)" (Master's thesis, Universidad de Buenos Aires, 2009).

28. San Alberto, *Colección de instrucciones pastorales . . .*, 327–29.

29. de Denaro, *Primicias de educación femenina*, 11.

30. Cháneton, *La Instrucción primaria en la época colonial*, 268.

31. Cháneton, *La Instrucción primaria en la época colonial*, 267.

32. Rock, David, *Argentina, 1516–1982: From Spanish Colonization to the Falklands War* (Berkeley: University of California Press, 1985), 76.

33. Rock, *Argentina, 1516–1982*, 89.

34. Rock, *Argentina, 1516–1982*, 81.

35. AHPC Gobierno, 1813, Tomo 36, F 405–8.

36. Turkovic, "Race Relations in the Province of Córdoba, Argentina, 1800–1853," 260.

37. Turkovic, "Race Relations in the Province of Córdoba, Argentina, 1800–1853," 239–40.

38. Turkovic, "Race Relations in the Province of Córdoba, Argentina, 1800–1853," 242.

39. Turkovic, "Race Relations in the Province of Córdoba, Argentina, 1800–1853," 243.

40. Seth Meisel, "War, Economy, and Society, Post-Independence Córdoba, Argentina" (PhD diss., Stanford University, 1999), 70.

41. Hugo Moyano, "Los Artesanos esclavos en Córdoba (1810–1820)," *Investigaciones y Ensayos* 33 (1982): 448.

42. Moyano, "Los Artesanos esclavos en Córdoba (1810–1820)," 448–49.

43. Moyano, "Los Artesanos esclavos en Córdoba (1810–1820)," 449.

44. The new law stated that any slave who entered the United Provinces of the Río de la Plata would automatically be granted freedom. The law pertained both to those who had been brought into Argentina by a slave trader and to those who had entered the country of their own free will. But the law was hard to enforce, and in 1814 it was weakened when the United Provinces declared that any slave who entered Argentina from Brazil would be returned. Instituto Estudios Americanistas, 1813, 7255; Andrews, *The Afro-Argentines of Buenos Aires, 1800–1900*, 54.

45. Camillia Cowling, *Conceiving Freedom: Women of Color, Gender and the Abolition of Slavery in Havana and Rio de Janeiro* (Chapel Hill: University of North Carolina Press, 2013), 60.

46. Instituto Estudios Americanistas, 1813, 7302–3.

47. Instituto Estudios Americanistas, 1813, 11831.

48. AHPC, Prot. Reg. 3, 1837, 5v–7r.

49. Instituto Estudios Americanistas, 1813, 11831.

50. Instituto Estudios Americanistas, 1813, 11831.

51. AHPC Gobierno, "Junta Protectora de Escuelas," 1823, Caja 83, F 491.

52. AHPC, Esc 4, Leg. 78, Exp. 10 (1836).

53. The original abolishment of Indian tribute came from the Buenos Aires Junta in September 1811, following a decree from the Crown that abolished Indian tribute in March 1811. Turkovic, "Race Relations in the Province of Córdoba, Argentina 1800–1853," 300.

54. Lazaro Flury, *Legislación indigentista de Argentina* (Mexico City, Mexico: Insituto Indigenista Interamericano, 1957), 14, 17–18.

55. Flury, *Legislación indigentista de Argentina*, 18.

56. The commissaries served the same role in the countryside and Indian pueblos as alcaldes did in the city. Gutiérrez, "La justicia en los pueblos de indios de Córdoba a fines al siglo XVIII," 58–60.

57. AAC Juicios Criminales, Leg. 37, Tomo V, Exp. 13 (1808–1815).

58. Instituto Estudios Americanistas, 1814, 10148.

59. Instituto Estudios Americanistas, 1814, 10148.

60. Censo de la ciudad de Córdoba (1813).

61. AHPC Censo de la ciudad de Córdoba (1822).

62. AHPC Censo de la ciudad de Córdoba (1832).

63. Censo de la ciudad de Córdoba (1778); Censo de la ciudad de Córdoba (1832).

64. Over the course of the eighteenth century, 402 slaves gained their freedom, and 192 are reflected in the 1813 census. Ferreyra, "La ciudad de Córdoba y su gente en 1813," 94.

65. Ferreyra, "La ciudad de Córdoba y su gente en 1813," 279.

66. Ferreyra, "La ciudad de Córdoba y su gente en 1813," 97.

67. Censo de la ciudad de Córdoba (1822).

68. Mónica Ghirardi, "Experiencias de desigualdad: El régimen matrimonial homogámico y sus tensiones en Córdoba en la transición del orden monárquico al republicano," in *Mestizaje, sangre y matrimonio en territorios de la actual Argentina y Uruguay: Siglos XVII–XX* (Buenos Aires: Dunken, 2008), 60; *Constituciones de la provincia de Córdoba desde 1821 hasta 1900: Publicación oficial* (Córdoba, Argentina: Córdoba, 1901), 10.

69. For more discussions about calidad in the nineteenth century, see González Undurraga, "De la casta a la raza"; Rebecca Earle, "'Two Pairs of Pink Satin Shoes!': Clothing, Race and Identity in the Americas (17th–19th Centuries)," *History Workshop Journal* 52 (2001): 175–95.

70. Scholars have argued that in Córdoba pardo does not just refer to African descendants but can also refer to a racial drift. Colantonio and Ghirardi suggest that mestizos became pardos in the nineteenth century, whereas Endrek argues that this category represented a growing indiscriminate group. Borucki also argues that the term "pardo" described a mixed ancestry in the Río de la Plata. Faberman's observation of pardo in Los Llanos along with my own observation of pardo in Córdoba's censuses, from the late eighteenth through the nineteenth centuries, suggest that over time pardo described those formerly labeled as "castas." These regional practices differ from those in Buenos Aires, where, according to Andrews, pardo always referred to African descendants. See Colantonio and Ghirardi, "Introduction," 21; Emiliano Endrek, *El mestizaje en Córdoba: Siglo XVIII y principios del XIX* (Córdoba, Argentina: Universidad de Córdoba, 1966), 27; Borucki, *From Shipmates to Soldiers*, 18; Farberman, "Imaginarios sociales en la colonia tardía," 48; Andrews, *The Afro-Argentines of Buenos Aires, 1800–1900*, 84; Erika Edwards, "Mestizaje, Córdoba's Patria Chica: Beyond the Myth of Black Disappearance in Argentina," *African and Black Diaspora: An International Journal* 7, no. 2 (July 3, 2014): 89–104.

71. *Constituciones de la provincia de Córdoba desde 1821 hasta 1900: Publicación oficial*, 9.

72. *Constituciones de la provincia de Córdoba desde 1821 hasta 1900: Publicación oficial*, 10.

Chapter 3

1. AHPC, Prot. Reg. 1, 1780, 188r–189v.

2. AAC Juicios Criminales (1789–1794) Leg. 37 Tomo III, Exp. 11.

3. Archivo General de la Nación, 1800, Leg. 4, Administración, Exp. 124.

4. In colonial Latin America, baptism, marriage, and death records were recorded in separate books. One book recorded Spaniards, which included anyone associated with pureza de sangre (purity of blood). The other book recorded castas or naturales, which included nonelite, nonwhite, and sometimes illegitimate children. María Gregoria's father is not listed. "Argentina, Córdoba, Registros Parroquiales, 1557–1974," Database with images, FamilySearch (https://familysearch.org/Ark:/61903/1:1:XF5P-685: January 21, 2015), María Gregoria, March 11, 1772; citing Baptism, Nuestra Señora de la Asunción, Córdoba Capital, Córdoba, Argentina, parroquias Católicas (Catholic Church Parishes, Córdoba); FHL Microfilm 772,078.

5. Censo de la ciudad de Córdoba (1778).

6. AHPC, Prot. Reg. 1, 1780, 188r–189v.

7. AAC Juicios Criminales (1789–1794) Leg. 37, Tomo III, Exp. 11.

8. Furtado, *Chica da Silva*, 116.

9. Mannarelli, *Private Passions and Public Sins*, 120.

10. Socolow, *The Women of Colonial Latin America*, 144.

11. McKinley, *Fractional Freedoms*, 13.

12. Scully and Paton, "Introduction," 7.

13. Censo de la ciudad de Córdoba (1813); Censo de la ciudad de Córdoba (1832).

14. Christine Hunefeldt, *Paying the Price of Freedom: Family and Labor among Lima's Slaves, 1800–1854* (Berkeley: University of California Press, 1994), 167.

15. Over the course of the eighteenth century, only twenty-five marriages between slave women and Spanish men took place. Ferreyra, "Matrimonios de españoles con esclavas durante el siglo XVIII en Córdoba"; Eugenia Soledad Ambroggio, *Violencia, genéro y honor en la Córdoba borbónica: Justicia y mecanismos informales de control social* (Córdoba, Argentina: Ferreyra, 2013), 214–15.

16. A common punishment for women caught cohabitating was to place them in a casa de depósito or other places of corrective behavior. Ambroggio, *Violencia, genéro y honor en la Córdoba borbónica*, 215.

17. AHPC Crimen, Leg. 73, Exp. 3 (1796).

18. Crespo, *Escándolos y delitos de la gente plebe*, 40.

19. AHPC Crimen, Leg. 85, Exp. 17 (1799).

20. AHPC Crimen, Leg. 85, Exp. 17 (1799).

21. AAC Juicios Criminales (1789–1794) Leg. 37, Tomo III, Exp. 11.

22. AAC Juicios Criminales (1789–1794) Leg. 37, Tomo III, Exp. 11.

23. AAC Juicios Criminales (1789–1794) Leg. 37, Tomo III, Exp. 11.

24. AAC Juicios Criminales (1789–1794) Leg. 37, Tomo III, Exp. 11.

25. AAC Juicios Criminales (1789–1794) Leg. 37, Tomo III, Exp. 11.

26. Priests who solicited sex are also documented in sixteenth- and seventeenth-century Peru. See Mannarelli, *Private Passions and Public Sins*, 42.

27. Jaqueline Vassallo, "Algunas notas sobre sacerdotes solicitantes y amancebados en Córdoba del Tucumán durante el siglo XVIII," *Tiempos Modernos* 19, no. 2 (2002): 2.

28. Jaqueline Vassallo, "Esclavas peligrosas en la Córdoba tardo colonial," *Dos Puntas* 4, no. 6 (2012): 214.

29. Vassallo, "Algunas notas sobre sacerdotes solicitantes y amancebados en Córdoba del Tucumán durante el siglo XVIII," 10, 16.

30. Ultimately don José Lino de León's actions could not be stopped, and the Church eventually excommunicated him.

31. Archivo General de la Nación, 1800, Leg. 4, Administración, Exp. 124.

32. Archivo General de la Nación, 1800, Leg. 4, Administración, Exp. 124.

33. Tau Anzoátegui, *Los bandos de buen gobierno del Río de la Plata, Tucumán, y Cuyo.*

34. Mannarelli, *Private Passions and Public Sins,* 40.

35. Tau Anzoátegui, *Los bandos de buen gobierno del Río de la Plata, Tucumán, y Cuyo,* 374.

36. The doors were to be open during the day and closed at night. Doors opened during the day revealed there was nothing to hide, while doors closed at night blocked out the dangers of the outside world. Sonya Lipsett-Rivera, *Gender and the Negotiation of Daily Life in Mexico, 1750–1856* (Lincoln: University of Nebraska Press, 2012), 70; AHPC Crimen, Leg. 105, Exp. 24 (1806).

37. For an examination of the household and the street, see Sandra Lauderdale Graham, *House and Street: The Domestic World of Servants and Masters in Nineteenth-Century Rio de Janerio* (Cambridge: Cambridge University Press, 1988); Twinam, *Public Lives, Private Secrets.*

38. AHPC Crimen, Leg. 105, Exp. 24 (1806).

39. AAC Juicios Criminales (1789–1794) Leg. 37, Tomo III, Exp. 11.

40. Mannarelli, *Private Passions and Public Sins,* 44; Ambroggio, *Violencia, genéro y honor en la Córdoba borbónica,* 219.

41. Chambers, *From Subjects to Citizens,* 164–65.

42. Spain, *limpieza de sangre* (cleansing of blood) referred to religion. Only Catholics were considered to have pure blood; Jews and Muslims had *mala sangre.* Even those who converted, *nuevos conservos* (converted Jews) and *moriscos* (converted Muslims), did not have pure blood. See María Elena Martínez, *Genealogical Fictions: Limpieza de Sangre, Religion, and Gender in Colonial Mexico* (Stanford, CA: Stanford University Press, 2008).

43. Farberman, "Imaginarios sociales en la colonia tardía," 29.

44. Guzmán, "Performatividad social de las (sub)categorías coloniales," 59; AAC Juicios Criminales (1789–1794) Leg. 37, Tomo III, Exp. 11.

45. Lyman Johnson, "Introduction," in *The Faces of Honor: Sex, Shame, and Violence in Colonial Latin America,* eds. Lyman Johnson and Sonya Lipsett-Rivera (Albuquerque: University of New Mexico Press, 1998).

46. Twinam, *Public Lives, Private Secrets.*

47. AAC Juicios Criminales (1789–1794) Leg. 37, Tomo III, Exp. 11.

48. Earle, "'Two Pairs of Pink Satin Shoes!'" 187.

49. von Germeten, *Violent Delights, Violent Ends,* 165.

50. Cecilia Moreyra, "Entre lo íntimo y lo público: La vestimenta en la ciudad

de Córdoba a fines del siglo XVIII," *Fronteras de la historia* 15, no. 2 (2010): 390.

51. Alan Hunt, *Governance of the Consuming Passions: A History of Sumptuary Law* (New York: Palgrave Macmillan, 1996), 216.

52. AAC Juicios Criminales (1789–1794) Leg. 37, Tomo III, Exp. 11.

53. AAC Juicios Criminales (1789–1794) Leg. 37, Tomo III, Exp. 11.

54. For more about material culture in colonial Peru, see Tamara J. Walker, *Exquisite Slaves: Race, Clothing, and Status in Colonial Lima* (New York: Cambridge University Press, 2017).

55. von Germeten, *Violent Delights, Violent Ends*, 152.

56. Moreyra, "Entre lo íntimo y lo público," 398–99.

57. Moreyra, "Entre lo íntimo y lo público," 397.

58. von Germeten, *Violent Delights, Violent Ends*, 137.

59. Moreyra, "Entre lo íntimo y lo público," 398.

60. Moreyra, "Entre lo íntimo y lo público," 399.

61. Moreyra, "Entre lo íntimo y lo público," 389.

62. Concolorcorvo, *El Lazarillo: A Guide for Inexperienced Travelers between Buenos Aires and Lima, 1771–1773* (Bloomington: Indiana University Press, 1965), 80.

63. AAC Juicios Criminales (1789–1794) Leg. 37, Tomo III, Exp. 11.

64. von Germeten, *Violent Delights, Violent Ends*, 147.

65. Earle, "'Two Pairs of Pink Satin Shoes!'" 187.

66. Tau Anzoátegui, *Los bandos de buen gobierno del Río de La Plata, Tucumán, y Cuyo*, 402.

67. Pedrotti, "La música religiosa en Córdoba del Tucumán durante la época colonial (1699–1840)," 32–33.

68. Hunt, *Governance of the Consuming Passions*, 105.

69. AAC Juicios Criminales (1789–1794) Leg. 37, Tomo III, Exp. 11.

70. AAC Juicios Criminales (1789–1794) Leg. 37, Tomo III, Exp. 11.

71. For more on clothing, status, and slavery in eighteenth- and nineteenth-century Lima, Peru, see Walker, *Exquisite Slaves*, 64.

72. Furtado, *Chica da Silva*, 147.

73. The case references this phrase when the prosecutor accused don José Lino de Leon of having another affair with doña Francisca Bejarano, whom the prosecutor described as a woman of "equal class." Archivo General de la Nación, 1800, Leg. 4, Administración, Exp. 124.

Chapter 4

1. AHPC, Esc 4. Leg. 98, Exp. 22 (1799).

2. I examined seventy-eight marriage dissent cases involving African descendants. Thirty of the seventy-eight cases centered on the woman's mala sangre as the main reason to prevent the marriage.

3. Between 1810 and 1839, there were seventeen marriages of free and enslaved women and white men recorded in ecclesiastical records of Spanish marriages. Dora Celton, "Selección matrimonial y mestizaje en Córdoba," in *III Jornadas de historia de Córdoba, junta provincial de historia de Córdoba*, 327–44 (Córdoba,

Argentina: Junta Provincial, 1997), 338; Ferreyra, "Matrimonios de españoles con esclavas durante el siglo XVIII en Córdoba," 92–93.

4. Ferreyra, "Matrimonios de españoles con esclavas durante el siglo XVIII en Córdoba," 140.

5. Censo de la ciudad de Córdoba (1778).

6. Ferreyra, "Matrimonios de españoles con esclavas durante el siglo XVIII en Córdoba," 121–22.

7. Ferreyra, "Matrimonios de españoles con esclavas durante el siglo XVIII en Córdoba," 118.

8. Cecilia Moreyra, "Mestizaje, vida cotidiana y cultura material: Una mirada sociocultural a dos matrimonios interétnicos en la ciudad de Córdoba, siglo XVIII," *Dialogos: Revista electrónica de historia* 13, no. 2 (February 2012): 101.

9. Moreyra, "Mestizaje, vida cotidiana y cultura material," 103.

10. Moreyra, "Mestizaje, vida cotidiana y cultura material," 105.

11. Ferreyra, "Matrimonios de españoles con esclavas durante el siglo XVIII en Córdoba," 119; Moreyra, "Mestizaje, vida cotidiana y cultura material," 106.

12. María del Carmen Ferreyra, "El matrimonio de las castas en Córdoba, 1700–1799," *Jornadas Argentinas de estudios de población, junta provincial de historia de Córdoba* 3 (1997): 307.

13. "Real provisión: Las leyes nuevas," in *Colección de documentos para la historia de la formación social de hispanoamérica, 1493–1810*, ed. Richard Konetzke, vol. 1 (Madrid: Consejo Superior de Investigaciones Científicas, 1953), 216–20.

14. Daisy Rípodas Ardanaz, *El matrimonio en Indias: Realidad social y regulación jurídica* (Buenos Aires: Fundación para la Educación, la Ciencia y la Cultura, 1977), 15–16.

15. Ferreyra, "El Matrimonio de las castas en Córdoba, 1700–1799," 307.

16. Ferreyra, "El Matrimonio de las castas en Córdoba, 1700–1799," 300.

17. Troisi Melean, *El oro de los jesuitas*, 115. For more information about the Jesuit Missions in Paraguay, see Julia Sarreal, *The Guaraní and Their Missions: A Socioeconomic History* (Stanford, CA: Stanford University Press, 2014).

18. The Pragmatic of 1776 was of personal interest to King Charles III, as he found his own family in a precarious position after the marriage of his brother, Luis Antonio de Borbón, to María Teresa de Vallabriga. The marriage threatened the bloodline and status of the royal family because María was not of equal status to him. To counteract Luis's decision and protect the royal family's interests, the marriage was eventually allowed but with strict conditions. His wife and her descendants would not have rights to "honors, heritages, or properties of the Bourbon dynasty." Saether, "Bourbon Absolutism and Marriage Reform in Late Colonial Spanish America," 478.

19. The Royal Pragmatic does not define "unequal."

20. "Pragmática sanción para evitar los abusos de contraer matrimonios desiguales," in *Colección de documentos para la historia de la formación social de hispanoamérica, 1493–1810*, ed. Richard Konetzke, vol. 3 (Madrid: Consejo Superior de Investigaciones Cientificias, 1962), 406.

21. "Pragmática sanción para evitar los abusos de contraer matrimonios desiguales," 408.

22. "Pragmática sanción para evitar los abusos de contraer matrimonios desiguales," 407.

23. "Pragmática sanción para evitar los abusos de contraer matrimonios desiguales," 409.

24. "Pragmática sanción para evitar los abusos de contraer matrimonios desiguales," 407.

25. "Pragmática sanción para evitar los abusos de contraer matrimonios desiguales," 409.

26. "Real cédula declarando la forma en que se ha de guardar y cumplir en las indias la pragmática sanción de 23 de Marzo de 1776 sobre contraer matrimonios," 438–41; "Pragmática sanción para evitar los abusos de contraer matrimonios desiguales."

27. AHPC, Esc 2, Leg. 97, Exp. 9 (1798); AHPC, Esc 3, Leg. 20, Exp. 6 (1821); AHPC, Esc 4, Leg. 64, Exp. 17 (1825).

28. "Pragmática sanción para evitar los abusos de contraer matrimonios desiguales," 407–8.

29. Saether, "Bourbon Absolutism and Marriage Reform in Late Colonial Spanish America," 491.

30. "Real cédula la forma en que se ha de guardar y cumplir en las indias la pragmática sanción de 23 de marzo de 1776 sobre contraer matrimonios," 440.

31. Bixio, "Mestizos, testamentos, y configuraciones sociales en Córdoba colonial," 27.

32. Mangan notes that in 1514 the Crown allowed marriages between Spanish men and Indian women. This was done to solidify military alliances with native chieftains and to "quiet church voices" that spoke against cohabitation. Jane E. Mangan, *Transatlantic Obligations: Creating the Bonds of Family in Conquest-Era Peru and Spain* (Oxford: Oxford University Press, 2015), 37–38.

33. "Real cédula la forma en que se ha de guardar y cumplir en las indias la pragmática sanción de 23 de marzo de 1776 sobre contraer matrimonios," 439.

34. "Real cédula la forma en que se ha de guardar y cumplir en las indias la pragmática sanción de 23 de marzo de 1776 sobre contraer matrimonios," 439.

35. AAC Real cédula de 27 de Mayo de 1805, Leg. 15 (1701–1820)."

36. Punta, *Córdoba borbónica*, 114.

37. Ferreyra, "Matrimonios de españoles con esclavas durante el siglo XVIII en Córdoba," 131–32.

38. Socolow, "Acceptable Marriage Partners," 215.

39. AHPC, Esc 4, Leg. 64, Exp. 17 (1825).

40. AHPC, Esc 4, Leg. 64, Exp. 17 (1825).

41. AHPC, Esc 4, Leg. 64, Exp. 17 (1825).

42. AHPC, Esc 4, Tomo II, Leg. 46, Exp. 31 (1813).

43. AHPC, Esc 4, Tomo II, Leg. 46, Exp. 31 (1813).

44. AHPC, Esc 4, Tomo II, Leg. 46, Exp. 31 (1813).

45. AHPC, Esc 4, Leg. 8, Exp. 10 (1797).

46. AHPC, Esc 4, Leg. 8, Exp. 10 (1797).

47. AHPC, Esc 4, Leg. 8, Exp. 10 (1797).

48. AHPC, Esc 1, Leg. 402, Exp. 4 (1784–1785).

49. Dora Celton, "Abandono de niños e ilegitimidad: Córdoba, Argentina, siglos XVIII–XIX," in *Familias iberoamericanas ayer y hoy: Una mirada interdisciplinaria*, ed. Mónica Ghirardi (Rio de Janeiro, Brazil: Asociación Latinamericana de Población, 2008), 231–50.

50. AHPC, Esc 1, Leg. 410, Exp. 6 (1790).

51. AHPC, Esc 1, Leg. 410, Exp. 6 (1790).

52. AHPC, Esc 1, Leg. 410, Exp. 6 (1790).

53. AHPC, Esc 2, Leg. 97, Exp. 9 (1798).

54. AHPC, Esc 2, Leg. 97, Exp. 9 (1798).

55. AHPC, Esc 4, Leg. 21, Exp. 17 (1803).

56. AHPC, Esc 4, Leg. 21, Exp. 17 (1803).

57. AHPC, Esc 4, Leg. 21, Exp. 17 (1803).

58. AHPC, Esc 4, Leg. 21, Exp. 17 (1803).

59. AHPC, Esc 4, Leg. 21, Exp. 17 (1803).

60. McKinley, *Fractional Freedoms*, 116.

Chapter 5

1. AHPC, Esc 4, Leg. 50, Exp. 11 (1817).

2. AHPC, Prot. Reg. 2, 1803, 201v–202r.

3. AHPC, Prot. Reg. 2, 1802, 129r–130r.

4. AHPC, Censo de la ciudad de Córdoba (1813).

5. Ferreyra, "La ciudad de Córdoba y su gente en 1813," 258.

6. AHPC, Prot. Reg. 1, 1781, 364r–365v; AHPC, Prot. Reg. 4, 1791, 200r–203r.

7. AHPC, Prot. Reg. 2, 1797, 114r–115r.

8. AHPC, Prot. Reg. 1, 1785, 86r–88r.

9. AHPC, Prot. Reg. 1, 1788, 431r–433r.

10. A total of 393 manumissions occurred between 1776 and 1830. Most (229 [58 percent]) were gratuitous manumissions (or slaveholders who liberated their slaves); followed by third-party manumissions, 94 (24 percent); self-manumissions, 51 (13 percent); and unknown paid manumissions, 19 (5 percent). This information comes from the AAC Juicios criminals and eclesiásticos and the AHPC Escribanías 1–4.

11. McKinley, *Fractional Freedoms*, 111. The household and gendered relationships described by McKinley have also been argued by Frank "Trey" Proctor III for seventeenth- and eighteenth-century Mexico. He argues that scholarship should move beyond the amorous relationship between enslaved women and white male slaveholders. He found more instances of manumission between slaveholders and slaves of the same sex than between slaveholders and slaves of the opposite sex. Frank "Trey" Proctor III, "Gender and Manumission of Slaves in New Spain," *Hispanic American Historical Review* 86, no. 2 (2006): 311–35.

12. McKinley, *Fractional Freedoms*, 110; Proctor III, "Gender and Manumission of Slaves in New Spain," 315. Proctor also found a similar pattern in New Spain during the seventeenth and eighteenth centuries. He found "contact between adult slaves and masters of the same sex within gendered social spaces—particularly the domestic sphere for women, had more influence on manumission patterns than did contact between masters and slaves of the opposite sex, especially male masters and female slaves."

13. AHPC, Prot. Reg. 1, 1781, 90r–91v.

14. AHPC, Prot. Reg. 3, 1810, 44r–44v.

15. AHPC, Prot. Reg. 2, 1796, 158v–160r.

16. AHPC, Prot. Reg. 3, 1804, 10v–13r.

17. I cannot determine whether it was the same mother in both cases. More than likely the women were sisters. AHPC, Prot. Reg. 1, 1781, 142r–143r; AHPC, Prot. Reg. 1, 1785, 150r–151r.

18. AHPC, Prot. Reg. 1, 1783, 86v–88v.

19. The protections of "liberty, equality, security and property," introduced by leaders of the independence movement such as Manuel Belgrano in Buenos Aires, were newfound liberal freedoms that weakened "elements of colonial rule." Blanchard, *Under the Flags of Freedom*, 45.

20. The rest of the Indian population that lived outside these jurisdictions, the city and the pueblos, were considered barbarous and uncivilized. Turkovic, "Race Relations in the Province of Córdoba, Argentina, 1800–1853," 280.

21. AHPC, Esc 4, Leg. 50, Exp. 11 (1817).

22. AHPC, Esc 1, Leg. 454, Exp. 13 (1821).

23. Ferreyra, "El matrimonio de las castas en Córdoba, 1700–1799," 309.

24. AHPC Censo de la ciudad de Córdoba (1813).

25. AHPC, Esc 4, Leg. 39, Exp. 27 (1810).

26. AHPC, Esc 4, Leg. 50, Exp. 11 (1817).

27. "R.C. alcarando dudas sobre el cumplimiento," in *Colección de documentos para la historia de la formación social de Hispanoamérica, 1493–1810*, ed. Richard Konetzke, vol. 1 (Madrid: Consejo Superior de Investigaciones Científicas, 1953), 527–29.

28. "Real provisión: Las leyes nuevas," 217; "Real provisión que no se pueda cautivar, ni hacer esclavo a ningún indio," in *Colección de documentos para la historia de la formación social de Hispanoamérica, 1493–1810*, ed. Richard Konetzke, vol. 1 (Madrid: Consejo Superior de Investigaciones Científicas, 1953), 134.

29. AHPC, Esc 3, Leg. 79, Exp. 7 (1825).

30. AHPC, Esc 3, Leg. 79, Exp. 7 (1825).

31. These cases were for sexual abuse, disputes about the set manumission price, and debts owed to the slaveholder.

32. AAC Juicios Criminales, 1811 Exp. 8.

33. AAC Juicios Criminales, 1811 Exp. 8.

34. AAC Juicios Criminales, 1811 Exp. 8.

35. AAC Juicios Criminales, 1811 Exp. 8.

Chapter 6

1. AHPC, Prot. Reg. 4, 1816, 430r–431v.

2. AHPC, Prot. Reg. 4, 1816, 430r–431v.

3. Szuchman, "Childhood Education and Politics in Nineteenth-Century Argentina."

4. Earle, "'Two Pairs of Pink Satin Shoes!'"; González Undurraga, "De la casta a la raza."

5. Carlos Newland, *Buenos Aires no es pampa: La educación elemental porteña, 1820–1860* (Buenos Aires: Grupo Editor Latinoamericano, 1992), 39.

6. "Memoria sobre que conviene limitar la infamia anexá a varias castas de gentes que hay en nuestra América," *Telégrafo mercantil: Rural político económico e historiógrafo de la Río de la Plata,* June 27, 1801, 205, UNCC Special Collections.

7. "Memoria sobre que conviene limitar la infamia anexá á varias castas de gentes que hay en muestra América," 207.

8. "Educación: Reflexiones sobre la educación de las mugeres; Traducida del celebre leveo, por una señora porteña," *Telégrafo mercantil: Rural político económico e historiógrafo de la Río de la Plata,* March 4, 1802, vol. 3, 204, UNCC Special Collections.

9. Leslie Walker, *A Mother's Love: Crafting Feminine Virtue in Enlightenment France* (Lewisburg, PA: Bucknell University Press, 2008), 23.

10. "Educación," March 4, 1802, 204, UNCC Special Collections.

11. "Educación: Reflexiones sobre la educación de las mugeres; Traducida del celebre leveo, por una señora porteña," *Telégrafo mercantil: Rural político económico e historiógrafo de la Río de la Plata,* July 28, 1802, vol. 3, 190, UNCC Special Collections.

12. "Educación," March 4, 1802, 204, UNCC Special Collections.

13. "Educación," March 4, 1802, 205, UNCC Special Collections.

14. Ceferino Garzón Maceda, "La revolución de mayo y la Universidad de Córdoba," *Revista de laUniversidad Nacional de Córdoba* 2, nos. 1–2 (June 1961): 13–14.

15. de Denaro, *Primicias de educación femenina,* 15.

16. Endrek, *El mestizaje en Córdoba,* 52.

17. William G. Acree Jr., "Divisas and Deberes: Women and the Symbolic Economy of War Rhetoric in the Río de la Plata, 1810–1910," *Journal of Latin American Cultural Studies* 22, no. 2 (June 1, 2013): 213–37.

18. Manuel Belgrano, "La educación de las mujeres," *Correo de comercio de Buenos-Ayres,* July 21, 1810, 21st and 22nd eds.

19. Belgrano, "La educación de las mujeres."

20. Candioti, "Abolición gradual y libertades vigiladas en el Río de la Plata."

21. San Alberto, *Colección de instrucciones pastorales . . .,* 334–35.

22. San Alberto, *Colección de instrucciones pastorales . . .,* 336.

23. Mónica Ghirardi, Dora Celton, and Sonia Colantonio, "Niñez, iglesia y 'política social': La fundación del colegio de huérfanas por el obispo San Alberto en Córdoba, Argentina, a fines del siglo XVIII," *Revista de Demografía Histórica*

26, no. 1 (2008): 140.

24. IEA, 1825, 9900, 9901, de Denaro, *Primicias de educación femenina*, 16.

25. Turkovic, "Race Relations in the Province of Córdoba, Argentina, 1800–1853," 366–67.

26. Arrom, *The Women of Mexico City, 1790–1857*, 17.

27. Censo de la ciudad de Córdoba (1822).

28. Censo de la ciudad de Córdoba (1778).

29. Censo de la ciudad de Córdoba (1813).

30. The census also listed two pardos, Estanislao Pajon and Gregorio Nis, who labored as servants in the household. See Censo de la ciudad de Córdoba (1813).

31. This further suggests that over time "pardos" grew to encompass all formerly labeled as "castas" in Córdoba: negro, mulato, zambo, indio, and mestizo during the republican period. Moreover, the 1822 census also shows that some formerly labeled "indios" in the 1813 census were labeled "libre" sans the Indian qualifier in the 1822 census.

32. Ghirardi, Celton, and Colantonio, "Niñez, iglesia y 'política social,'" 160.

33. *Constituciones de la provincia de Córdoba desde 1821 hasta 1900: Publicación oficial* (Córdoba, Argentina: Córdoba, 1901), 72.

34. *Constituciones de la provincia de Córdoba desde 1821 hasta 1900*, 7–8, 26.

35. Emiliano Endrek, *Escuela, sociedad y finanzas en una autonomía provincial: Córdoba, 1820–1829* (Córdoba, Argentina: Junta Provincial de Historia de Córdoba, 1994), 31.

36. Hernán Ramírez, *Socialización y reproducción de la elite en el periodo colonial y principios del independiente* (Córdoba, Argentina: Ferreyra, 2002), 70–71.

37. AHPC Gobierno "Junta Protectora de Escuelas," 1823, 358–59.

38. Endrek, *Escuela, sociedad y finanzas en una autonomía provincial*, 32, 274.

39. *Constituciones de la provincia de Córdoba desde 1821 hasta 1900*, 68.

40. Endrek, *El mestizaje en Córdoba*, 53.

41. Endrek, *El mestizaje en Córdoba*, 53.

42. Endrek, *El mestizaje en Córdoba*, 53.

43. Szuchman, "Childhood Education and Politics in Nineteenth-Century Argentina," 120.

44. Turkovic, "Race Relations in the Province of Córdoba, Argentina, 1800–1853," 267.

45. Olsen Ghirardi, *Vicente Fidel López en Córdoba* (Córdoba, Academia Nacional de Derecho y Ciencias Sociales de Córdoba, 2005), 31.

46. Meisel, "War, Economy, and Society, Post-Independence Córdoba, Argentina," 201, 206.

47. AHPC Censo de la ciudad de Cordoba (1813); AHPC Censo de la ciudad de Cordoba (1832).

48. Newland, *Buenos Aires no es pampa*, 32.

49. Censo de la ciudad de Córdoba (1813).

50. Censo de la ciudad de Córdoba (1832).

51. La Toma's proximity to the city was attractive to many Indians who had

been displaced from smaller pueblos tribuatrios. They relocated to La Toma and sought employment, which most likely suggests that census takers included them in the city census. See Turkovic, "Race Relations in the Province of Córdoba, Argentina, 1800–1853," 315; Sonia Tell and Isabel Castro Olañeta," El registro y la historia de los pueblos de indios de Córdoba entre los siglos XVI y XIX," 242.

52. Censo de la ciudad de Córdoba (1832).

53. de Denaro, *Primicias de educación femenina,* 200, 207.

Conclusion

1. Alberto and Elena's *Rethinking Race in Modern Argentina* similarly suggests a rethinking of identity that complicates Argentina's notion of whiteness.

Bibliography

Archives

Archivo Arzobispado de la Catedral (AAC)
Archivo General de la Nación (AGN)
Archivo Histórcio de la Provincia de Córdoba (AHPC)
Instituto Estudios Americanistas (IEA)

Primary Printed Sources

"Argentina, Córdoba, Registros Parroquiales, 1557–1974," database with images, FamilySearch (https://Familysearch.org/Ark:/61903/1:1:XF5P-685: January 21, 2015), María Gregoria, March 11, 1772; citing Baptism, Nuestra Señora de la Asunción, Córdoba Capital, Córdoba, Argentina, parroquias Católicas (Catholic Church Parishes, Córdoba); FHL Microfilm 772,078.

Belgrano, Manuel. "La educación de las mujeres." Correo de Comercio de Buenos-Ayres. July 21, 1810, 21st and 22nd ed.

Constituciones de la provincia de Córdoba desde 1821 hasta 1900: Publicación oficial. Córdoba, Argentina: Córdoba, 1901.

"Educación: Reflexiones sobre la educación de las mugeres. Traducida del Celebre Leveo, por una señora porteña." *Telégrafo mercantil: Rural político económico e historiógrafo de la Río de la Plata*, March 4, 1802, vol. 3. University of North Carolina at Charlotte, Special Collections.

"Educación: Reflexiones sobre la educación de las mugeres: Traducida del Celebre Leveo, por una señora porteña." *Telégrafo mercantil: Rural político económico e historiógrafo de la Río de la Plata.* July 28, 1802, vol. 3. University of North Carolina at Charlotte, Special Collections.

"Memoria sobre que conviene limitar la infamia anexá a varias castas de gentes que hay en nuestra América." In *Telégrafo mercantil: Rural político económico e historiógrafo de la Río de la Plata.* June 27, 1801, University of North Carolina at Charlotte.

San Alberto, Dr. Fray Joseph Antonio. *Colección de instrucciones pastorales, que en diferentes ocasiones, y con varios motivos publico para edificación de los fieles, arreglo y dirección de sus diócesis el ilustrísimo y reverendísimo señor D.Fr. Joseph Antonio de S. Alberto, Obispo Antes de Córdoba del Tucumán, y al presente arzobispo de la ciudad de La Plata en América.* Vol. 1. Madrid: Imprenta Real, 1786. http://bdh-rd.bne.es/viewer. vm?id=0000015076&page=1.

Secondary Sources

Acree, William G., Jr. "Divisas and Deberes: Women and the Symbolic Economy of War Rhetoric in the Río de la Plata, 1810–1910." *Journal of Latin American Cultural Studies* 22, no. 2 (June 1, 2013): 213–37.

Alberto, Paulina, and Eduardo Elena, eds. *Rethinking Race in Modern Argentina.* New York: Cambridge University Press, 2016.

Albores, Oscar, Carlos Mayo, and Judith Sweeny. "Esclavos y conchabados en la estancia de Santá Catalina, Córdoba." *Revista América* 5 (1977): 5–20.

Amaral, Samuel, and Juan Carlos Garavagila. "Rural Production and Labor in the Late Colonial Buenos Aires." *Journal of Latin American Studies* 19, no. 2 (November 1987): 235–78.

Ambroggio, Eugenia Soledad. *Violencia, género y honor en la Córdoba borbónica: Justicia y mecanismos informales de control social.* Córdoba, Argentina: Ferreyra, 2013.

Andrews, George Reid. *Afro-Latin America, 1800–2000.* Oxford: Oxford University Press, 2004.

———. *Afro-Latin America: Black Lives, 1600–2000.* Cambridge, MA: Harvard University Press, 2016.

———. *The Afro-Argentines of Buenos Aires, 1800–1900.* Madison: University of Wisconsin Press, 1980.

Andrews, Norah. "Calidad, Genealogy, and Disputed Free-Colored Tributary Status in New Spain." *Americas* 73, no. 2 (April 2016): 139–70.

Araya Espinoza, Alejandra. "Registrar a la plebe o el color de las castas: 'Calidad' 'clase' y 'casta' en la matrícula de Alday (Chile, siglo XVIII)." In *América colonial: Denominaciones, clasificaciones e identidades,* edited by Alejandra Araya Espinoza and Jaime Valenzuela, 331–61. Santiago, Chile: Universidad de Chile/Pontificia Universidad Católica de Chile, 2010.

Ardanaz, Daisy Rípodas. *El matrimonio en indias: Realidad social y regulación jurídica.* Buenos Aires: Fundación para la Educación, la Ciencia y la Cultura, 1977.

Arrom, Silvia. *The Women of Mexico City, 1790–1857.* Stanford, CA: Stanford University Press, 1985.

Assadourian, Carlos. *El tráfico de esclavos en Córdoba, 1588–1610: Según actas de protocolos del archivo histórico de Córdoba.* Córdoba, Argentina: Direccíon General de Publicaciones, 1965.

Barragán, Yesenia. "To the Mine I Will Not Go: Freedom and Emancipation on the Colombian Pacific, 1821–1852." PhD diss., Columbia University, 2016.

Bennett, Herman L. *Africans in Colonial Mexico: Absolutism, Christianity, and Afro-Creole Consciousness, 1570–1640.* Bloomington: Indiana University Press, 2003.

Bernand, Carmen. "El color de los criollos: De las naciones a las castas, a las castas a la nación." In *Huellas a África en América: Perspectivas para Chile,* edited by Celia Cussen, 13–34. Santiago, Chile: Editorial Universitaria/Universidad de Chile, 2008.

Bischoff, Efraín U. *Historia de Córdoba: Cuatro siglos.* Viamonte, Argentina: Editorial Plus Ultra, 1979.

Bixio, Beatriz. "Mestizos, testamentos, y configuraciones sociales en Córdoba colonial." In *Mestizaje y configuración social: Córdoba (siglos XVI y XVII)*, edited by Beatriz Bixio and Constanza González Navarro, 19–82. Córdoba, Argentina: Brujas, 2013.

Black, Chad. *Limits of Gender Domination: Women, the Law, and Political Crisis in Quito, 1765–1830.* Albuquerque: University of New Mexico Press, 2010.

Blanchard, Peter. *Under the Flags of Freedom: Slave Soldiers and the Wars of Independence in Spanish America.* Pittsburgh, PA: University of Pittsburgh Press, 2008.

Borucki, Alex. *From Shipmates to Soldiers: Emerging Black Identities in the Río de La Plata.* Albuquerque: University of New Mexico Press, 2015.

———. "The Slave Trade to the Río de La Plata, 1777–1812: Trans-Imperial Networks and Atlantic Warfare." *Colonial Latin American Review* 20, no. 1 (April 2011): 81–107.

Bryant, Sherwin. *Rivers of Gold, Lives of Bondage: Governing through Slavery in Colonial Quito.* Chapel Hill: University of North Carolina Press, 2013.

Bryant, Sherwin, Rachel Sarah O'Toole, and Ben Vinson III, eds. *Africans to Spanish America: Expanding the Diaspora.* Urbana: University of Illinois Press, 2012.

Candioti, Magdalena. "Abolición gradual y libertades vigiladas en el Río de la Plata: La política de control de libertos de 1813." *Corpus* 6, no. 1 (January/June 2016).

Cañizares-Esguerra, Jorge, Matt Childs, and James Sidbury, eds. *The Black Urban Atlantic in the Age of the Slave Trade.* Philadelphia: University of Pennsylvania Press, 2013.

Castro, Donald. *The Afro-Argentine in Argentine Culture: El negro del acordeón.* Lewiston, NY: Edwin Mellen, 2001.

Celton, Dora. "Abandono de niños e ilegitimidad: Córdoba, Argentina, siglos XVIII–XIX." In *Familias iberoamericanas ayer y hoy: Una mirada interdisciplinaria*, edited by Mónica Ghirardi, 231–50. Rio de Janeiro: Asociación Latinamericana de Población, 2008.

———. *Ciudad y campaña en la Córdoba colonial.* Córdoba, Argentina: Junta Provincial de Historia de Córdoba, 1996.

———. "La venta de esclavos en Córdoba, entre 1750–1850." In *Cuadernos de historia*, 5–20. Córdoba, Argentina: Universidad de Córdoba, 2000.

———. "Selección matrimonial y mestizaje en Córdoba." In *III Jornadas de historia de Córdoba, junta provincial de historia de Córdoba*, 327–44. Córdoba: Junta Provincial, 1997.

Chambers, Sarah. *Families in War and Peace: Chile from Colony to Nation.* Durham, NC: Duke University Press, 2015.

———. *From Subjects to Citizens: Honor, Gender, and Politics in Arequipa, Peru, 1780–1854.* University Park: Pennsylvania State University Press, 1999.

Cháneton, Abel. *La instrucción primaria en la época colonial*. Buenos Aires: Biblioteca de la Sociedad de historia Argentina XII, 1942.

———. *Un precursor de Sarmiento y otros ensayos históricos*. Buenos Aires: M. Gleizer, 1934.

Chaves, María Eugenia. "Slave Women's Strategies for Freedom and the Late Spanish Colonial State." In *Hidden Histories of Gender and the State in Latin America*, edited by Elizabeth Dore and Maxine Molyneux, 108–26. Durham, NC: Duke University Press, 2000.

Childs, Matt. "'Sewing' Civilization: Cuban Female Education in the Context of Africanization, 1800–1860." *Americas* 54, no. 1 (July 1997): 83–107.

Cirio, Norberto Pablo. *Tinta negra en el gris del ayer: Los afroporteños a través de sus periódicos entre 1873 y 1882*. Buenos Aires: Teseo, 2009.

Clark, Emily. *The Strange History of the American Quadroon: Free Women of Color in the Revolutionary Atlantic World*. Chapel Hill: University of North Carolina Press, 2013.

Colantonio, Sonia, Dora Celton, and Claudio Kuffer. "Las mujeres de color en la Córdoba colonial y postcolonial." In *Familias históricas: Interpelaciones desde perspectivas iberoamericanas a través de los casos de Argentina, Brasil, Costa Rica, España, Paraguay y Uruguay*, edited by Mónica Ghirardi and Ana Silvia Volpi Scott, 276–96. São Leopoldo, Brazil: Okios, 2015.

Colantonio, Sonia, and Claudio Kuffer. "Marriage in Córdoba City (Argentina) in the Late-Colonial and Early Independent Periods: Homogamy and Surnames as Emerging Features." *Journal of Family History* 39 (2014): 22–39.

Colantonio, Sonia, and Mónica Ghirardi. "Introduction." In *Población y sociedad en tiempos de lucha por emancipación: Córdoba, Argentina, 1813*, edited by Sonia Colantonio, 15–28. Córdoba, Argentina: Centro de Investigaciones y Estudios sobre Cultura y Sociedad (CONICET-UNC), 2013.

Concolorcorvo. *El Lazarillo: A Guide for Inexperienced Travelers between Buenos Aires and Lima, 1771–1773*. Bloomington: Indiana University Press, 1965.

Conrad, Sebastian. "Enlightenment in Global History: A Historiographical Critique." *American Historical Review* 117 (October 2012): 998–1,027.

Cowling, Camillia. *Conceiving Freedom: Women of Color, Gender and the Abolition of Slavery in Havana and Rio de Janeiro*. Chapel Hill: University of North Carolina Press, 2013.

Cowling, Camillia, and María Helena Pereira Toledo Machado. "Mothering Slaves: Comparative Perspectives on Motherhood, Childlessness, and the Care of Children in Atlantic Slave Societies." *Slavery & Abolition* 38, no. 2 (2017): 223–31.

Crespo, Darío Dominino. *Escándalos y delitos de la gente plebe: Córdoba a fines del siglo XVIII*. Córdoba, Argentina: Universidad de Córdoba, 2007.

Cushner, Nicolas. *Jesuit Ranches and the Agrarian Development of Colonial Argentina, 1650–1767*. Albany: State University of New York Press, 1983.

de Denaro, Liliana. *Primicias de educación femenina: Historia de la real casa de huérfanas nobles y la congregación de hermanas carmelitas de Santa Teresa de Jesús*. Córdoba, Argentina: Corintios, 2004.

Dellaferrera, Nelson C. *Procesos canónicos catálogo, 1688–1888*. Buenos Aires: Pontificia Universidad Católica Argentina, 2007.

Earle, Rebecca. "Rape and the Anxious Republic: Revolutionary Colombia, 1810–1830." In *Hidden Histories of Gender and the State in Latin America*, edited by Elizabeth Dore and Maxine Molyneux, 127–46. Durham, NC: Duke University Press, 2000.

———. "'Two Pairs of Pink Satin Shoes!' Clothing, Race and Identity in the Americas (17th–19th Centuries)." *History Workshop Journal* 52 (2001): 175–95.

Echeverri, Marcela. *Indian and Slave Royalists in the Age of Revolution: Reform, Revolution, and Royalism in the Northern Andes, 1780–1825*. New York: Cambridge University Press, 2016.

Edwards, Erika Denise. "The Making of a White Nation: The Disappearance of the Black Population in Argentina." *History Compass*. Accessed June 2018: https://onlinelibrary.wiley.com/doi/abs/10.1111/hic3.12456.

———. "Mestizaje, Córdoba's Patria Chica: Beyond the Myth of Black Disappearance in Argentina." *African and Black Diaspora: An International Journal* 7, no. 2 (July 3, 2014): 89–104.

———. "Slavery in Argentina." Edited by Ben Vinson III. *Oxford Bibliographies in Latin American Studies*. Accessed June 2017: http://www.oxfordbibliographies.com/view/document/obo-9780199766581/obo-9780199766581-0157.xml.

Egaña Baraona, María Loreto. *La educación primaria popular en el siglo XIX en Chile: Una práctica de política estatal*. Santiago, Chile: Dirección de Bibliotecas, Muesos y Archivos, 2000.

Endrek, Emiliano. *El mestizaje en Córdoba: Siglo XVIII y principios del XIX*. Córdoba, Argentina: Universidad de Córdoba, 1966.

———. *Escuela, sociedad y finanzas en una autonomía provincial: Córdoba, 1820–1829*. Córdoba, Argentina: Junta Provincial de Historia de Córdoba, 1994.

Estrada, Dorothy Tanck. *La educación ilustrada 1786–1836: Educación primaria en la ciudad de México*. Mexico City: El Colegio de México, 1977.

Farberman, Judith. "Imaginarios sociales en la colonia tardía: Clasificaciones y jerarquías del color en Los Llanos de La Rioja, siglo XVIII y XIX." In *Cartografías afrolatinoamericanas: Perspectivas situadas desde la Argentina*, edited by Florencia Guzmán, Lea Geler, and Alejandro Frigerio, 25–50. Buenos Aires: Biblos, 2016.

Fernández, Raúl. *Historia de La Educación Primaria de Córdoba*. Córdoba, Argentina: Universidad Nacional de Córdoba, 1965.

Ferreyra, Ana Inés. *Un intento de organización desde el interior del País: José María Paz en Córdoba, 1829–1831*. Córdoba, Argentina: Centro de Estudios Históricos, 2005.

Ferreyra, María del Carmen. "El matrimonio de las castas en Córdoba, 1700–1799." *Jornadas Argentinas de estudios de población, junta provincial de historia de Córdoba* 3 (1997): 285–327.

———. "La ciudad de Córdoba y su gente en 1813." In *Población y sociedad en tiempos de lucha por la emancipación: Córdoba, Argentina, en 1813*, edited by Sonia Colantonio, 83–313. Córdoba, Argentina: Centro de Investigaciones y Estudios sobre Cultura y Sociedad (CONICET-UNC), 2013.

———. "Matrimonios de españoles con esclavas durante el siglo XVIII en Córdoba." In *Cuestiones de familia a través de las fuentes*, edited by Mónica Ghirardi, 91–140. Córdoba, Argentina: Universidad Nacional de Córdoba, 2005.

Flury, Lázaro, ed. *Legislación indigenista de Argentina*. Mexico City: Instituto Indigenista Interamericano, 1957.

Fortes, Jorge, and Diego Ceballos. *Afroargentinos*. Latin American Video Archives, 2002.

Frigerio, Alejandro. "Los afroargentinos: Formas de comunalización, creación de identidades colectivas y resistencia cultural y política." In *Afrodescendientes y Africanos en Argentina*, edited by Rubén Mercado and Gabriela Catterberg, 1–51. Buenos Aires: Programa de las Naciones Unidas para Desarrollo (PNUD), 2011.

———. "'Negros' y 'blancos' en Buenos Aires: Repensando nuestras categorías raciales." *Temas de Patrimonio Cultural* 16 (2006): 77–98.

Fuente, Ariel de la. "'Civilización y barbarie': Fuentes para una nueva explicación del facundo." *Boletín del Instituto de historia Argentina y Americana Dr. Emilio Ravignani* 44 (2016): 135–79.

Fuentes-Barragán, Antonio. "Entre acuerdos y discordias: La pragmática sanción para evitar el abuso de contraer matrimonios desiguales en la provincia de Buenos Aires." *Historia y memoria*, June 2016.

Furtado, Junia Ferreira. *Chica da Silva: A Brazilian Slave of the 18th Century*. New York: Cambridge University Press, 2009.

Fuster, María Teresa. "La casa de niñas huerfanas de San Miguel: Beneficencia, prestigio y poder; Las disputas por su control (1755–1810)." Master's thesis, Universidad de Buenos Aires, 2009.

García González, Francisco. *Historia de la educación en Zacatecas: Su enseñanza y escritura*. Zacatecas, Mexico: UPN Unidad Zacatecas, 2001.

Garzón Maceda, Ceferino. "La revolución de mayo y la Universidad de Córdoba." *Revista de la Universidad Nacional de Córdoba* 2, no. 1–2 (June 1961): 7–33.

Garzón, Rafael. *Sobremonte: Córdoba y las invasiones inglesas*. Córdoba, Argentina: Corredor Austral, 2000.

Geler, Lea. "Afrodescendientes y esfera pública en el Buenos Aires de fines del siglo XIX." In *La ruta del esclavo en el Río de la Plata: Aportes para el diálogo intercultural*, edited by Marisa Pineau, 303–20. Buenos Aires: Editorial de la Universidad Nacional de Tres de Febrero, 2011.

———. *Andares negros, caminos blancos: Afroporteños, estado y nación Argentina a fines del siglo XIX*. Rosario, Argentina: Prohistoria, 2010.

Geler, Lea, Florencia Guzmán, and Alejandro Frigerio, eds. *Cartografías afrolatino-americanas: Perspectivas situadas desde Argentina*. Buenos Aires: Biblos, 2016.

Gellman, David N. *Emancipating New York: The Politics of Slavery and Freedom, 1777–1827*. Baton Rouge: Louisiana State University Press, 2006.

Gelman, Jorge. "Sobre esclavos, peones, gauchos y campesinos: El trabajo y los trabajadores en una estancia colonial rioplatense." In *Estructuras sociales y mentalidades en América Latina: Siglos XVII y XVIII*, edited by Torcuato Di Tella, 241–79. Buenos Aires: Fundación Simón Rodríguez, 1990.

Ghirardi, Mónica. *Matrimonios y familias en Córdoba, 1700–1850*. Córdoba, Argentina: Centro de Estudios Avanzados, Universidad Nacional de Córdoba, 2004.

Ghirardi, Mónica, Dora Celton, and Sonia Colantonio. "Niñez, iglesia y 'política social': La fundación del colegio de huérfanas por el obispo San Alberto en Córdoba, Argentina, a fines del siglo XVIII." *Revista de Demografía Histórica* 26, no. 1 (2008): 125–71.

Ghirardi, Mónica, and Nora Siegrist. *Mestizaje, sangre y matrimonio en territorios de la actual Argentina y Uruguay: Siglos XVII–XX*. Buenos Aires: Dunken, 2008.

Ghirardi, Olsen. *Vicente Fidel López en Córdoba*. Córdoba, Argentina: Academia Nacional de Derecho y Ciencias Sociales de Córdoba, 2005.

Goldberg, Marta. "Las afroargentinas (1750–1880)." In *Historia de las mujeres en la Argentina*, edited by Fernanda Gil Lozano, Valeria Silvina Pita, and María Gabriela Ini, 67–85. Buenos Aires: Tarus, 2000.

———. "Mujer negra rioplatense (1750–1840)." In *La mitad del Pais: La mujer en la sociedad Argentina*, edited by Lidia Knecher and Marta Panaia, 67–81. Buenos Aires: Centro Editor de América Latina, 1994.

Gonzalbo Aizpuru, Pilar. *Las mujeres en la nueva España: Educación y vida cotidiana*. Mexico City: El Colegio de México, 1987.

González Undurraga, Carolina. "Carta de libertad: Aproximaciones sobre la movilidad social de la población esclava en Santiago de Chile, 1700–1810." PhD diss., Universidad de Chile, 2007.

———. "De la casta a la raza: El concepto de raza; Un singular colectivo de la modernidad, México, 1750–1850." *Historia Mexicana* 60 (January 2011): 1,491–1,525.

Graham, Sandra Lauderdale. *House and Street: The Domestic World of Servants and Masters in Nineteenth-Century Rio de Janeiro*. Cambridge: Cambridge University Press, 1988.

Greene, Jack P., and Philip D. Morgan, eds. *Atlantic History: A Critical Appraisal*. 1st ed. Oxford: Oxford University Press, 2008.

Gudmundson, Lowell, and Justin Wolfe, eds. *Blacks and Blackness in Central America: Between Race and Place*. Durham, NC: Duke University Press, 2010.

Guevara, Gema. "Inexacting Whiteness: Blanqueamiento as a Gender-Specific Trope in the Nineteenth Century." *Cuban Studies* 36 (2005): 105–28.

Guillermo, Quinteros O. "Ser, sentir, actuar, pensar e imaginar en torno al matrimonio y la familia: Buenos Aires, 1776–1860." PhD diss., Universidad Nacional de la Plata, 2010.

Gutiérrez, Clara Daniela. "La justicia en los pueblos de indios de Córdoba a fines al siglo XVIII." Master's thesis, Universidad Nacional de Córdoba, 2011.

Guzmán, Florencia. "Bandas de música de libertos en el ejército de San Martín: Una exploración sobre la participación de los esclavizados y sus descendientes durante las guerras de independencia." *Anuario de la escuela de historia virtual*, no. 7 (October 17, 2015): 18–36.

———. *Los claroscuros del mestizaje: Negros, indios y castas en la Catamarca colonial*. Córdoba, Argentina: Encuentro Grupo, 2010.

———. "Performatividad social de las (sub)categorías coloniales: Mulatos, pardos, mestizos y criollos en tiempos de cambios, guerra y política, en el interior de la Argentina." In *Cartografías afrolatinoamericanas: Perspectivas situadas para análisis transfronterizos*, edited by Florencia Guzmán and Lea Geler, 57–86. Buenos Aires: Biblos, 2013.

Halperín-Donghi, Tulio. *Politics, Economics, and Society in Argentina in the Revolutionary Period*. Cambridge: Cambridge University Press, 1975.

Harris, Leslie M. *In the Shadow of Slavery: African Americans in New York City, 1626–1863*. Chicago: University of Chicago Press, 2003.

Helg, Aline. *Liberty and Equality in Caribbean Colombia, 1770–1835*. Chapel Hill: University of North Carolina Press, 2004.

Hodges, Graham Russell. *Root and Branch: African Americans in New York and East Jersey, 1613–1863*. Chapel Hill: University of North Carolina Press, 1999.

Hunefeldt, Christine. *Paying the Price of Freedom: Family and Labor among Lima's Slaves, 1800–1854*. Berkeley: University of California Press, 1994.

Hunt, Alan. *Governance of the Consuming Passions: A History of Sumptuary Law*. New York: Palgrave Macmillan, 1996.

Johnson, Lyman. "A Lack of Legitimate Obedience and Respect: Slaves and Their Masters in the Courts of Late Colonial Buenos Aires." *Hispanic American Historical Review* 87, no. 4 (2007): 631–57.

———. "Introduction." In *The Faces of Honor: Sex, Shame, and Violence in Colonial Latin America*, edited by Lyman Johnson and Sonya Lipsett-Rivera, 1–17. Albuquerque: University of New Mexico Press, 1998.

———. *Workshop of Revolution: Plebeian Buenos Aires and the Atlantic World, 1776–1810*. Durham, NC: Duke University Press, 2011.

Jovellanos, Gaspar Melchor. "Memoria sobre educación pública." In *La reforma ilustrada: Propuestas democráticas en la España borbónica; Gaspar Melchor de Jovellanos*, edited by Franco Cerutti. San José, Costa Rica: Libro Libre, 1987.

Kerber, Linda. "The Republican Mother: Women and the Enlightenment; An American Perspective." *American Quarterly* 28, no. 2 (Summer 1976): 187–205.

Konetzke, Richard, ed. *Colección de documentos para la historia de la formación social de hispanoamérica, 1493–1810*. Vol. 3. Madrid: Consejo Superior de Investigacoiones Científicas, 1962.

———. *Colección de documentos para la historia de la formación social de hispanoamérica, 1493–1810*. Vol. 1. Madrid: Consejo Superior de Investigacoiones Científicas, 1953.

Kuethe, Allan J., and Kenneth J. Andrien. *The Spanish Atlantic World in the Eighteenth Century: War and the Bourbon Reforms, 1713–1796*. New York: Cambridge University Press, 2014.

Kuffer, Claudio, Mónica Ghirardi, and Sonia Colantonio. "Educación elemental en la ciudad de Córdoba, Argentina, en el primer tercio del siglo XIX, sus variaciones y su relación con las demás ocupaciones infantiles." *Revista iberoamericana de educación* 56, no. 1 (July 2011): 1–12.

Lasso, Marixa. *Myths of Harmony: Race and Republicanism during the Age of Revolution, Colombia, 1795–1831.* Pittsburgh, PA: University of Pittsburgh Press, 2007.

Lewis, Marvin. *Afro-Argentine Discourse: Another Dimension of the Black Diaspora.* Columbia: University of Missouri Press, 1996.

Linton, Marisa. *The Politics of Virtue in Enlightenment France.* New York: Palgrave, 2001.

Lionetti, Lucia. "'Instruir a las niñas para salvarlas de la indigencia que aflige su cuerpo y la ignorancia que llena su espíritu': La experiencia de la casa de niñas huérfanas nobles Córdoba en el siglo XVIII." *Historia de la educación* 15, no. 1 (June 2014): http://ppct.caicyt.gov.ar/index.php/anuario/article/view/2852.

Lipsett-Rivera, Sonya. *Gender and the Negotiation of Daily Life in Mexico, 1750–1856.* Lincoln: University of Nebraska Press, 2012.

Lobos, Héctor. "Acera del negocio y los comerciantes de esclavos en Córdoba." *Revista de la junta provincial de historia de Córdoba* 23 (2006): 223–54.

———. *Historia de Córdoba: Raíces y fundamentos.* Vol. 1. Córdoba, Argentina: Ediciones del Copista, 2009.

Luque Colombres, Carlos A. *Orígenes históricos de la propiedad urbana de Córdoba: Siglos XVI y XVII.* Córdoba, Argentina: Universidad Nacional de Córdoba, 1980.

Mallo, Silvia C. "La libertad en el discurso del estado, de amos y esclavos, 1780–1830." *Revista de historia América* 112 (July 1991).

———. "La mujer en el periodo colonial: Justicia, educación, y trabajo." In *CLIO, Revista del comité argentino de ciencias históricos* 2:15–25. La Rioja, Argentina: Editorial Canguro, 1994.

———, ed. *Negros de la patria.* Buenos Aires: Editorial Sb, 2010.

Mangan, Jane E. *Trading Roles: Gender, Ethnicity, and the Urban Economy in Colonial Potosí.* Durham, NC: Duke University Press, 2005.

———. *Transatlantic Obligations: Creating the Bonds of Family in Conquest-Era Peru and Spain.* Oxford: Oxford University Press, 2015.

Mannarelli, María Emma. *Private Passions and Public Sins: Men and Women in Seventeenth-Century Lima.* Albuquerque: University of New Mexico Press, 2007.

Martín, Alicia. "El carnaval y la cuestión interétnica en el Buenos Aires de fin de siglo XIX." In *La herencia cultural africana en las américas* (tomo I), edited by B. Santos Arrascaeta, 131–41. Montevideo, Uruguay: Ediciones Populares para América Latina, 1998.

Martínez, María Elena. *Genealogical Fictions: Limpieza de Sangre, Religion, and Gender in Colonial Mexico.* Stanford, CA: Stanford University Press, 2008.

Martínez-Alier, Verena. *Marriage, Class and Colour in Nineteenth-Century Cuba:*

A Study of Racial Attitudes and Sexual Values in a Slave Society. Cambridge, UK: Cambridge University Press, 1974.

Mayo, Carlos. *Las haciendas jesuíticas en Córdoba y en el noreste Argentino.* Buenos Aires: Centro Editor de América Latina, 1994.

McKinley, Michelle A. *Fractional Freedoms: Slavery, Intimacy, and Legal Mobilization in Colonial Lima, 1600–1700.* Cambridge, UK: Cambridge University Press, 2016.

Meisel, Seth. "'The Fruit of Freedom' Slaves and Citizens in Early Republican Argentina." In *Slaves, Subjects, and Subversives: Blacks in Colonial Latin America,* edited by Jane Landers and Barry Robinson, 273–306. Albuquerque: University of New Mexico Press, 2006.

———. "War, Economy, and Society, Post-Independence Córdoba, Argentina." PhD diss., Stanford University, 1999.

Melish, Joanne Pope. *Disowning Slavery: Gradual Emancipation and "Race" in New England, 1790–1860.* Ithaca, NY: Cornell University Press, 1998.

Minuet Cejas, Mónica, and Mirta Pieroni. "Mujeres en las naciones afroargentinas de Buenos Aires." *América negra* 8 (1994): 133–45.

Moreyra, Cecilia. "Entre lo íntimo y lo público: La vestimenta en la ciudad de Córdoba a fines del siglo XVIII." *Fronteras de la historia* 15, no. 2 (2010): 388–413.

———. "Mestizaje, vida cotidiana y cultura material: Una mirada sociocultural a dos matrimonios interétnicos en la ciudad de Córdoba, siglo XVIII." *Dialogos: Revista electronica de historia* 13, no. 2 (February 2012): 92–111.

Morgan, Jennifer. *Laboring Women: Reproduction and Gender in New World Slavery.* Philadelphia: University of Pennsylvania Press, 2004.

Morrison, Karen Y. *Cuba's Racial Crucible: The Sexual Economy of Social Identities, 1750–2000.* Bloomington: Indiana University Press, 2015.

Moyano, Hugo. *La organización de los gremios en Córdoba sociedad artesanal y producción artesanal.* Córdoba, Argentina: Centro de Estudios Historicos, 1986.

Nash, Gary B., and Jean R. Soderlund. *Freedom by Degrees: Emancipation in Pennsylvania and Its Aftermath.* Oxford: Oxford University Press, 1991.

Nazzari, Muriel. "Concubinage in Colonial Brazil: The Inequalities of Race, Class, and Gender." *Journal of Family History* 21 (1996): 107–23.

Nesbitt, Nick. *Universal Emancipation: The Haitian Revolution and the Radical Enlightenment.* Charlottesville: University of Virginia Press, 2008.

Newland, Carlos. *Buenos Aires no es pampa: La educación elemental porteña, 1820–1860.* Buenos Aires: Grupo Editor Latinoamericano, 1992.

Novillo, Jovita. "La población negra en Tucumán (1800–1820): Con especial referencia a los cuarteles urbanos y a los cuartos de Los Juárez y Río Chico." PhD diss., Universidad Nacional de Tucumán, 2006.

O'Toole, Rachel. *Bound Lives: Africans, Indians, and the Making of Race in Colonial Peru.* Pittsburgh, PA: University of Pittsburgh Press, 2012.

Patterson, Orlando. *Slavery and Social Death: A Comparative Study.* Cambridge, MA: Harvard University Press, 1982.

Pearce, Adrian J. *The Origins of Bourbon Reform in Spanish South America, 1700–1763*. New York: Palgrave Macmillan, 2014.

Pedrotti, Clarisa Eugenia. "La música religiosa en Córdoba del Tucumán durante la época colonial (1699–1840)." PhD diss., Universidad Nacional de Córdoba, 2013.

Peña, Gabriela. "La evangelización de indios, negros y gente de castas en Córdoba del Tucumán durante la dominación española." PhD diss., Universidad Católica Córdoba, 1997.

Peñaflores, René Amaro. "La educación en Zacatecas durante el siglo XIX." *Fuentes: Estudios humanísticos y sociales* 1 (2001): 119–42.

Picconi, María Lina. "El 'negro cordobés': Formación de alteridad en la ciudad de Córdoba a comienzos del siglo XXI." In *Estudios afrolatinoamericanos 3: Actas de Las Quintas Jornadas de GEALA*, edited by Eva Lamborghini, María Cecilia Martino, and Juan Francisco Martínez Peria, 284–94. Buenos Aires: Ediciones del Centro Cultural de la Cooperación Floreal Gorini, 2017.

Pineau, Marisa, ed. *La ruta del esclavo en el Río de la Plata: Aportes para el diálogo intercultural*. Buenos Aires: Editorial de la Universidad Nacional de Tres de Febrero, 2011.

Platero, Tomás. *Piedra libre para nuestros negros: La broma y otros periódicos de la comunidad afroargentina (1873–1882)*. Buenos Aires: Instituto Histórico de la Ciudad de Buenos Aires, 2004.

Premo, Bianca. *The Enlightenment on Trial: Ordinary Litigants and Colonialism in the Spanish Empire*. Oxford: Oxford University Press, 2017.

———. "'El modo de mi educación': Discursos sobre educación y los derechos de la madre en Lima, a finales del virreinato." In *Mujeres, familia, y sociedad en la historia de américa latina, siglos XVIII–XXI*, edited by Scarlett O'Phelan Godoy and Margarita Zegarra Flórez, 593–609. Lima, Peru: Pontificia Universidad Católica del Perú, 2006.

———. *Children of the Father King: Youth, Authority and Legal Minority in Colonial Lima*. Chapel Hill: University of North Carolina Press, 2005.

Proctor, Frank "Trey," III. *Damned Notions of Liberty: Slavery, Culture, and Power in Colonial Mexico, 1640–1769*. Albuquerque: University of New Mexico Press, 2010.

———. "Gender and Manumission of Slaves in New Spain." *Hispanic American Historical Review* 86, no. 2 (2006): 309–36.

Punta, Ana Inés. *Córdoba borbónica: Persistencias coloniales en tiempo de reformas (1750–1800)*. Córdoba, Argentina: Universidad Nacional de Córdoba, 1997.

Ramírez, Hernán. *La Universidad de Córdoba: Socialización y reproducción de la elite en el periodo colonial y principios del independiente*. Córdoba, Argentina: Ferreyra, 2002.

Rappaport, Joanne. *The Disappearing Mestizo: Configuring Difference in the Colonial New Kingdom of Granada*. Durham, NC: Duke University Press, 2014.

Restall, Matthew. *Beyond Black and Red: African-Native Relations in Colonial Latin America*. Albuquerque: University of New Mexico Press, 2005.

————. *The Black Middle: Africans, Mayans, and Spaniards in Colonial Yucatan.* Stanford, CA: Stanford University Press, 2009.

Robins, Nicholas A. *Of Love and Loathing: Martial Life, Strife, and Intimacy in the Colonial Andes, 1750–1825.* Lincoln: University of Nebraska Press, 2015.

Rosal, Miguel. *Africanos y afrodescendientes en el Río de la Plata: Siglos XVIII–XIX.* Buenos Aires: Dunken, 2009.

Saether, Steinar. "Bourbon Absolutism and Marriage Reform in Late Colonial Spanish America." *Americas* 59, no. 4 (April 2003): 473–509.

San Martín Aedo, William. "Colores oscuros y estatus confusos: El problema de la definición de categorías étnicas y del estatus de 'esclavo' y 'libre' en litigios de negros, mulatos, y pardos (Santiago a Fines Del Siglo XVIII)." In *América Colonial: Denominaciones, Clasificaciones e Identidades,* edited by Alejandra Araya Espinoza and Jaime Valenzuela Márquez, 257–84. Santiago: Universidad de Chile/Pontificia Universidad Católica de Chile, 2010.

Sarmiento, Domingo. *Facundo: Civilization and Barbarism.* Translated by Kathleen Ross. Berkeley: University of California Press, 2003.

————. *Obras de D. F. Sarmiento: Viajes por Europa, África i América, 1845–1847.* Vol. 5. Buenos Aires: Publicadas bajo los auspicios del gobierno arjentino, 1886.

Schávelzon, Daniel. *Buenos Aires negra: Arqueología histórica de una ciudad silenciada.* Buenos Aires: Emecé, 2003.

Schultz, Kara D. "'The Kingdom of Angola Is Not Very Far from Here': The South Atlantic Slave Port of Buenos Aires, 1585–1640." *Slavery & Abolition* 36, no. 3 (July 3, 2015): 424–44.

Schwaller, Robert C. *Géneros de Gente in Early Colonial Mexico: Defining Racial Difference.* Norman: University of Oklahoma Press, 2016.

Scott, Samuel Parsons, and Robert Burns. *Las Sietes Partidas: Family, Commerce, and the Sea; The Worlds of Women and Merchants (Partidas IV and V).* Vol. 4. Philadelphia: University of Pennsylvania Press, 2012.

Scully, Pamela, and Diana Paton, eds. "Introduction: Gender and Slave Emancipation in Comparative Perspective." In *Gender and Slave Emancipation in the Atlantic World,* 1–17. Durham, NC: Duke University Press, 2005.

Seed, Patricia. *To Love, Honor, and Obey in Colonial Mexico: Conflicts over Marriage Choice, 1574–1821.* Stanford, CA: Stanford University Press, 1988.

Shumway, Jeffery M. *The Case of the Ugly Suitor: And Other Histories of Love, Gender, and Nation in Buenos Aires, 1776–1870.* Lincoln: University of Nebraska Press, 2005.

Silveira, Alina. "Educating a City's Children: British Immigrants and Primary Education in Buenos Aires (1820–1880)." *Americas* 70, no. 1 (2013): 33–62.

Socolow, Susan. "Acceptable Marriage Partners: Marriage Choice in Colonial Argentina, 1778–1810." In *Sexuality and Marriage in Colonial Latin America,* edited by Asunción Lavrin, 209–51. Lincoln: University of Nebraska Press, 1989.

————. *The Women of Colonial Latin America.* New York: Cambridge University Press, 2015.

Szuchman, Mark. "Childhood Education and Politics in Nineteenth-Century Argentina: Case of Buenos Aires." *Hispanic American Historical Review* 70, no. 1 (February 1990): 109–38.

Tau Anzoátegui, Víctor. *Los bandos de buen gobierno del Río de la Plata, Tucumán, y Cuyo.* Buenos Aires: Instituto de Investigación de Historia del Derecho, 2004.

Tell, Sonia, and Isabel Castro Olañeta. "El registro y la historia de los pueblos de indios de Córdoba entre los siglos XVI y XIX." *Revista de Mueso de Antropología* 4 (2011): 235–48.

Troisi Melean, Jorge. *El oro de los jesuitas: La compañía de Jesús y sus esclavos en la Argentina colonial.* Madrid: Editorial Académica Española, 2012.

Turkovic, Robert. "Race Relations in the Province of Córdoba, Argentina, 1800–1853." PhD diss., University of Florida, 1981.

Twinam, Ann. *Public Lives, Private Secrets: Gender, Honor, Sexuality, and Illegitimacy in Colonial Spanish America.* Stanford, CA: Stanford University Press, 1999.

———. *Purchasing Whiteness: Pardos, Mulattos, and the Quest for Social Mobility in the Spanish Indies.* Stanford, CA: Stanford University Press, 2015.

Undurraga Schuler, Verónica. "Españoles oscuros y mulatos blancos: Identidades múltiples y disfraces del color en el ocaso de la colonia Chilena, 1778–1820." In *Historias de racismo y discriminación en Chile,* edited by Rafael Gaune and Martín Lara, 341–68. Santiago, Chile: Uqbar, 2009.

Varela Fernández, Julia. "La educación ilustrada como fabricar sujetos dóciles y útiles." *Revista de educación,* no. extraordinario (1988): 245–74.

Vassallo, Jaqueline. "Algunas notas sobre sacerdotes solicitantes y amancebados en Córdoba del Tucumán durante el siglo XVIII." *Tiempos modernos* 19, no. 2 (2002): 1–24.

———. "Esclavas peligrosas en la Córdoba tardo colonial." *Dos puntas* 4, no. 6 (2012): 199–217.

Vedoya, Juan Carlos. *Historia de la instrucción primaria en la república Argentina.* Tandil, Argentina: Universidad Nacional Centro de la Provincia de Buenos Aires, 1984.

Vinson, Ben, III. *Bearing Arms for His Majesty: The Free-Colored Militia in Colonial Mexico.* Stanford, CA: Stanford University Press, 2001.

———. *Before Mestizaje: The Frontiers of Race and Caste in Colonial Mexico.* New York: Cambridge University Press, 2017.

Vinson, Ben, III, and Matthew Restall, eds. *Black Mexico: Race and Society from Colonial to Modern Times.* Albuquerque: University of New Mexico Press, 2009.

von Germeten, Nicole. *Black Blood Brothers: Confraternities and Social Mobility for Afro-Mexicans.* 1st ed. Gainesville: University Press of Florida, 2006.

———. *Violent Delights, Violent Ends: Sex, Race, and Honor in Colonial Cartagena de Indias.* Albuquerque: University of New Mexico Press, 2013.

Walker, Leslie. *A Mother's Love: Crafting Feminine Virtue in Enlightenment France.* Lewisburg, PA: Bucknell University Press, 2008.

Walker, Tamara J. *Exquisite Slaves: Race, Clothing, and Status in Colonial Lima.* Cambridge, UK: Cambridge University Press, 2017.

Weber, David J. *Bárbaros: Spaniards and Their Savages in the Age of Enlightenment.* 1st ed. New Haven, CT: Yale University Press, 2006.

White, Shane. *Somewhat More Independent: The End of Slavery in New York City, 1770–1810.* Athens: University of Georgia Press, 1991.

Winters, Lisa Ze. *The Mulatta Concubine: Terror, Intimacy, Freedom, and Desire in the Black Transatlantic.* Athens: University of Georgia Press, 2016.

Zilversmit, Arthur. *The First Emancipation: The Abolition of Slavery in the North.* Chicago: University of Chicago Press, 1967.

Zumaglini, M. Carolina. "Cosmopolitan Imperialism: Mann, Sarmiento, and the Origins of Universal Education in Nineteenth-Century Boston and Buenos Aires." PhD diss., Florida International University, 2014.

Index

Page numbers in italics indicate figures or tables.